Purnell's
Pictorial Encyclopedia of
DOGS
Michael Geary

Purnell's
Pictorial Encyclopedia of
DOGS
Michael Geary

Above: The Great Dane had its origins in the large hounds and mastiffs of Europe.

Right: No one knows how the Newfoundland, a relative of the St. Bernard, came to be in Canada centuries ago.

Below: Boston Terriers are probably the smartest of all the dogs originally bred in America.

Published in 1978 by Purnell Books,
Berkshire House, Queen Street, Maidenhead, Berkshire.
Designed and produced for Purnell Books by
Intercontinental Book Productions.
Copyright © 1978 Intercontinental Book Productions.
Devised and created by Berkeley Publishers,
9 Warwick Court, London WC1R 5DJ

SBN 361 04231 0

Printed by Purnell & Sons Ltd., Paulton, Bristol.

Contents

Top to bottom:
Afghan Hound,
Rhodesian
Ridgeback, Cavalier
King Charles
Spaniel, Pyrenean
Mountain Dog.

Foreword

If I had read this book without any knowledge of Michael Geary I would have thought that the author was a man who had spent a whole lifetime concerned almost entirely with dogs. But he is, in fact, a gifted young Veterinary Surgeon whose experience and knowledge are beyond his years. In the relatively short time that his name has been on the Veterinary Register, he has already achieved his Fellowship of the Royal College, a considerable feat in its own right.

In this Pictorial Encyclopedia Michael Geary sets out clearly and readably the history of dogs from the beginning of time. He shows how man has used dogs and why dogs have proved themselves so useful to man. His discussion of the special scenting powers and how the different breeds employ them is first-rate.

His sensible advice on selecting the right sort of dog for the individual's circumstances, his accurate account of the diseases which man can acquire from his closest pet, and his insistence that dog owning is not only a fulfilling pleasure but a demanding responsibility, will go a long way towards putting into a balanced perspective the proper place of the dog in our society. The research which has gone into this book must have been enormous and the result is truly encyclopedic.

Encyclopedias, as we know, are usually reference tomes, full of worthy facts, but this book is both informative and entertaining. I can wholeheartedly recommend that all those people who are interested in dogs should read it.

Michael Stockman M.R.C.V.S.

Origins of the Dog

When we consider the great variations in dog breeds – Great Danes, Papillons, Bulldogs and Maltese Terriers, to name just a few – it is perhaps difficult to believe that they are all examples of the one species, the domestic dog, *Canis familiaris*. In fact, the shape and conformation of some dogs give them the appearance of being more closely related to other animals altogether – Fox Terriers to foxes or German Shepherd Dogs (Alsatians) to wolves, for example – although we know this is not so. Few other branches of the animal world display such tremendous variations in size, shape, coat type and behaviour as the different breeds of dogs. Shetland ponies are very different from Shire horses but no one would ever class either as anything but a horse. Some varieties of mice look quite dissimilar to other varieties but never so unalike as Old English Sheepdogs and Whippets! Nearly all of this great variation in form of dogs is a result of man's influence, for no other animal has such a long and close history of domestication as the dog. The history of the dog began long before the history of man itself.

Below: The bond between man and dog has existed since earliest times and dogs have often featured in primitive art, as this Ninevehan carving shows.

Pre-history

To investigate the origin of the dog it is necessary to consider the evolution of its close neighbours, too, because it is with them that much of the mystery concerning the dog's past lies. Mammals, the warm-blooded, fur-covered class of animals which suckle their young, are a fairly recent development in the evolution of animals. Their early stages of development occurred during the Cretaceous period, which started about 140 million years ago. At that time, mammals co-existed with dinosaurs. The Creodonts were a group of early mammals and these tiny flesh-eating creatures gave rise to the carnivorous polecat-like animal called Miacis. This was the primitive ancestor of bears, cats, civets and the other carnivores, including dogs. Miacis lived about forty million years ago (at which time monkeys had only just begun to develop) and it was not at all like our present-day dogs; it had five toes, was flat-footed, could climb trees and had retractile claws like a cat.

About nineteen million years ago, another fossil ancestor developed from Miacis. This animal, known as Cynodictis, had lost the fifth toe, which had become a rudimentary dew claw. From Cynodictis descended the true primitive forerunners of the dog, Cynodesmus and another fossil canid which was the ancestor of

Above left: The ancient Egyptians actually worshipped the dog in the form of Anubis.

Above right: Egyptian frescos and carvings commonly showed dogs which are virtually identical to Greyhounds and Salukis.

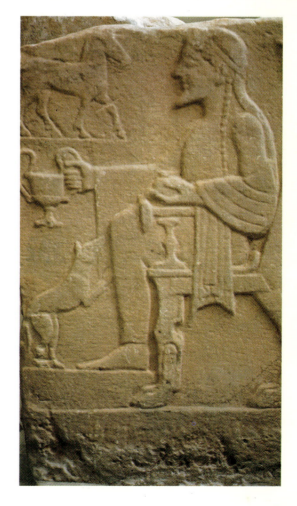

Right: This primitive bas-relief sums up the centuries-old bond of companionship between man and dog.

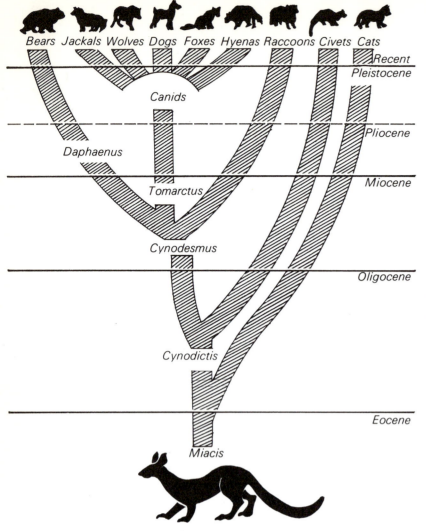

Bears Jackals Wolves Dogs Foxes Hyenas Raccoons Civets Cats

Recent

Pleistocene

Canids

Pliocene

Daphaenus

Miocene

Tomarctus

Cynodesmus

Oligocene

Cynodictis

Eocene

Miacis

Above: The evolution of the dog family and other mammals from the pre-historic Miacis.

Below: Wolves, foxes and dogs are close cousins, and share many behaviour traits.

examples of the *canidae* – the wolves, jackals, foxes, hyenas and dogs. All these show similar bone formations and are fast predators, with good sight and hearing, a keen sense of smell and excellent stamina.

The story is relatively simple so far, giving us 140 million years of traceable development and yet, within the last few thousand years, the history of the dog is clouded. There appears to be some sort of missing link which would enable us to determine the direct ancestor of the dog beyond any doubt. Possibly that ancestor was Tomarctus himself, and perhaps jackals and wolves are the dog's developmental cousins; or perhaps the wolf was that ancestor.

Before considering the wolf descent theory, it is important to look at the evidence that eliminates other *canidae* from the dog's ancestry. The fox, although it is not a pack hunter or social canine, does have similarities of form with some breeds of dog. However, dog/fox crosses would be infertile (in the extremely unlikely event of a dog mating with a fox) as their chromosomes are dissimilar. The gestation period of a fox is about fifty days, which is thirteen days shorter than the dog, at sixty-three days. Other variations, such as the eye pupil shape and foot structure, further imply that foxes cannot be close progenitors of dogs. Hyenas can also be ruled out of the dog's immediate family, as their pups are born with open eyes and are more mobile and active than dog or wolf puppies.

Jackals and coyotes are really very close to dogs and crosses with them and dogs are fertile. (This is generally an indication that animals are extremely closely related.) However, there are some skeletal differences between jackals and coyotes and dogs, which suggest that they are related, rather than one and the same species. The Dingo, however, is sufficiently close to be classified as the same species as the dog. In Australia, the Dingo's natural home, it is becoming increasingly difficult, in fact, almost impossible to find Dingos which do not have domesticated dog blood in their ancestry.

Most authorities now agree that the nearest 'wild' canid is the wolf and there is much evidence to suggest that modern dogs are descended directly from wolves. The tooth formation of wolves shows very little difference from that of dogs, and, like jackals and coyotes, they can mate with dogs and produce fertile offspring. A marked difference in the reproduction of dogs and wolves, however, is that female wolves only come on heat annually while dogs usually are on heat twice a year, although this may have been caused by man's selectivity. Wolves hunt in packs, are very sociable within the pack and, most important, respond favourably to domestication.

These comparisons between the closer re-

the so-called 'false dogs' – dogs such as the African Cape hunting dog, the Indian wild dog or Dhole, and the South African bush dog.

Cynodesmus was a much taller mammal than its predecessors. It was followed by Tomarctus, which was very much like a dog in appearance and, indeed, its skeletal remains are virtually indistinguishable from modern-day wolves or wild dogs. Between Tomarctus and the advent of man (only two million years ago), fossil remains suggest that many dog-like creatures evolved, although these are probably not important in relation to our present dogs. It is sufficient to say that Tomarctus gave rise to all the existing

Above: This Assyrian bas-relief from Asshur-bandipal shows that hunting was one of the earliest ways in which civilized man used Mastiffs.

lations of the domestic dogs, valid though they are, do not provide us with the answer to our original question – what is the direct descent of the dog? Two possible answers exist. Firstly, that the dog is a 'modified wolf' and that successive domesticated generations have resulted in our present-day dogs. If this is the case, then there have been changes over the generations, which have resulted in dogs with variations in size and shape. Some show giantism, like the Deerhound, and others, such as the Pekinese, show miniaturization. Other changes have resulted in modification of head shape, relatively smaller teeth or jaws, and variations in tail and ear carriage. Man must also have selected for early maturity (most dogs can breed by six months old, whereas wolves are not sexually mature until they are two years old at the earliest) and also high fertility.

The other possibility is that there was a wolf cum dog-like mutant canid which was the direct ancestor of dogs. There is a theory that this early dog evolved in northern Asia before man himself came on the scene, although to date there is no fossil evidence to prove this theory. Equally, there is none to disprove it, as that area of the world has not been extensively explored archaeologically.

Some authorities have even gone so far as to suggest that the small Asiatic wolf, *Canis lupus pallipes*, is that living ancestor, and that prehistoric tribes in northern Asia first domesticated it. Whatever the answer to our question, we can say that the greatest influence on the development of the dog's ancestor was man, because without man's selective breeding and influence, the dog of today would not exist. In essence, man created dog in the form which he wanted; it is the precise original biological substance of that creation which still eludes us.

Domestication

Whether the first encounter between man and *canidae* was with a wolf or an early dog, one thing is certain – that there was no sudden appearance of a quiet, human-loving, obedient dog. Domestication is a long, slow process, whereby an animal is progressively and selectively bred for its capacity to socialize with humans. Domestication is quite different from tameness. One can train a lion (or any other ferocious wild animal) not to kill humans, to perform tricks and to come to command, but such behaviour remains solely characteristic of that animal alone. Tameness is not passed through successive generations; lion cubs born to tame parents are not themselves tame unless they are subjected to the same training routine as their parents. Released in the jungle, they will act as any other wild lion, and, if released, the parents would also soon revert to the wild state.

Domestication is achieved by continuously selecting the most tractable and humanly socialized animals and breeding from them until the end result is an animal which is not only tolerant of humans, but actively seeks socialization with man. At six weeks of age, hyena pups born in captivity will show marked aggression to humans by biting at them and doing all they can to avoid contact. In marked contrast, domestic pet puppies will run towards humans, inviting them to play. Domestic puppies are obviously happy in human company. The desire to socialize with man is clearly inherent, for no one could have taught these pups to associate with a human. It has taken thousands of years for dogs to arrive at this state and the degree of this domestication is without parallel.

Man's domestication of the dog, however, is more than just an association; it is a complex

9

process which has resulted in the selected behaviours of guarding, hunting, herding and haulage. These traits have gone very much hand-in-hand with the dog's innate desire to socialize with humans, for there would be no sense in having a superb hunting dog which was aggressive and anti-social to its owner.

There are several physical and behavioural characteristics of the dog which make it more suited to domesticity than other animals. Firstly, it is of a convenient size to live with man in his home. Secondly, as a predatory pack hunter, it is of value to man. Thirdly, it breeds comparatively soon in its adulthood, has a short gestation period and produces a large number of young – so one man in his lifetime could not only breed many successive generations of dogs, but would also have a very large number of pups from which to select those with desirable traits. Compare this to the horse, which has slow sexual development, a long gestation and usually only a single offspring.

The most important factor of all, though, is that the dog species has a great range of physical and behavioural characteristics which it is able to inherit. The potential physical range of a pig's size, for example, seems very small – from the South American mini-pigs up to large white boars of twice their size. The horse's physical range is between Shetland pony (or the even smaller Falabella, of Argentina) and Shire. That of a dog, though, is between Chihuahua and St. Bernard, giving nearly an eighty-fold weight difference! The range of behavioural characteristics is even more amazing if one considers the variations between the breeds with respect to sight, scenting ability, herding capacity or physical stamina. In short, the dog shows

tremendous plasticity of genetic range.

Finally, variations within these ranges are generally quite stable and 'throwbacks' are not too common. A sociable bitch mated to a sociable dog usually has pups that show greater friendliness than either parent, and even more important, this friendliness is usually displayed by all the pups in the litter; a 'wild' one would be uncommon. Obviously, similar genetic stabilities are seen with complex behaviours such as sheep herding or hunting. Were this not so, man would never have been able to develop the specialist breeds.

By constantly picking the best example for breeding, man eventually produced dogs showing all the traits he wanted, together with a submissive attitude to him and an acceptance of his restraints and desires.

The origins of domestication

Reasons for domestication of the dog, the date when it first took place and who was responsible, can only be speculative, based on a few sketchy facts. We know the dog was domesticated fairly early in man's history, but we are unable to say exactly how or when, as it occurred before man had started recording his own story. As we have said, dogs would not have suddenly become associated with man; the process of domestication would have been gradual. Possibly, they were first attracted to man's camps by the bones and scraps of rotten meat cast on one side. Perhaps a gang of dogs became associated with a tribe of nomads and moved with them as they hunted for food. The dogs may have proved of value as guards to man by barking when some intruder – a man or animal – came close to the camp.

Probably successive generations of these scavengers became less and less timid. Tribesmen may have begun to recognize them by their coat markings and started to throw odd scraps of food to them. (A modern equivalent would be that of primitive tribes in New Guinea, who have dogs in association with their villages. The dogs eat up rubbish and so help to keep the environs of the camp clean.) It seems likely that gradually such dogs would be absorbed into 'camp life' and, assuming that the tribesmen did not frighten them away, would begin to recognize man as a friend and food provider – an important incentive to domestication.

The hunting of food could have been another vital link in the dog/man association. Possibly packs of dogs went with man when he hunted away from the camp and helped him to chase and kill prey. Man may have chosen the quieter type of dogs for this purpose; loud-barking dogs would have prematurely frightened and scattered the herds of deer or oxen. Possibly, early

Below:
Archaeological evidence suggests that the Dingo was introduced into Australia via the Australasian land bridge at least 50,000 years ago.

Right: Greyhounds were popular hunting dogs with the Romans. When they conquered northern Europe, the dogs went with them and were thus introduced in to Britain.

Below: German Shepherd Dogs (Alsatians) are the result of inter-breeding of three ancient strains of European shepherds' dogs.

man recognized these better hunters and bred from them, although this is likely to have followed much later. We know that Palaeolithic man drove herds of wild horses into pits and then slaughtered them; probably, dogs were used to help in this and then shared in the excess of food after the kill.

Different hunting situations would eventually have resulted in a need for dogs of different characteristics. For the pursuit of timid game, man would have required silent hunters that barked furiously only when they got close to cornering the prey, thus alerting the human hunter for the final part of the attack. Strong, fierce hunting dogs would have been needed for large animals such as oxen and wild boar; fast, good-sighted dogs for hares or rabbits; and good scenting dogs for capturing the first odour of a distant herd of game. Such requirements would have varied depending on the food available in the area. Certainly, the greatest bond between man and dog would have been that both were predators and both were capable of co-operating with one another in the chase.

There is also a possibility that the dog may have proved useful as a haulage animal. Remains of 6,000-year-old sledges, found in northern Europe, reinforce this theory, although sledge-drawing would have come sometime after the dog had been accepted into the community. Although man's penetration into the Arctic is a comparatively recent event (nomadic Thule Eskimos first reached the Arctic about A.D. 900), it could not have occurred without the use of sledge dogs. The Eskimos' use of dogs for haulage can be considered an ethnological development quite separate from western culture.

The use of dogs by primitive man as a source of food is unlikely to have been a major part of domestication, although the dog would certainly have had a value in times of food scarcity. In primitive pagan festivals, the dog may have been sacrificed to invoke the aid of the hunting gods and then eaten by man in an attempt to acquire an enhanced hunting ability by ingestion of the dog's body.

As man realized the value of the dog to his life, he may have regarded it in the light of a god, in the same way as other static and living objects are still worshipped by primitive cultures. Dogs, unlike other feared or wild animals, would have seemed less of a mystery to primitive man because he could understand and, to some extent, even dictate the dog's behaviour. There is evidence, too, that man had put dog on a religious pedestal even before the Egyptians began to deify their jackal-like dog god, Anubis.

Early civilizations and their dogs

Just as it is difficult exactly to date and to typify civilizations, so it is not easy to investigate the importance of dogs to those civilizations. Civilization, as such, may be measured in chronological time and also in terms of man's social development. The latter aspect has occurred at differing rates in different parts of the world. Thus, the Chinese civilization was well developed 3,000 years ago, in terms of social evolution and culture; while, today, there are primitive tribes living on islands in the Pacific Ocean who have cultures, which can only be described as Neolithic Stone Age.

Presuming that dogs follow these separate civilizations, their domestication will vary accordingly. To see how they arrived in their various states of domestication, therefore, we must follow their path with their masters. The complex 'bio-mix' of dogs now found all over the world resulted from man's widespread use of the dog. Much of this movement is comparatively recent – the influx of European breeds into the New World and Australasia is an example. More recent still is the movement of long-established indigenous breeds, such as the African Basenji, Tibetan Spaniel and Shih Tzu. These breeds have begun to infiltrate the western civilizations, which are hungry for the appeal of such 'newly-discovered breeds'.

But how did the Shih Tzu get to Tibet originally, or the Basenji to the Congo? Did they develop there, or were they taken there by nomadic tribesmen, or early settlers, from a single original dog source? It seems probable that the centre of dog domestication was northern Asia, which fits in with theories about the Asiatic wolf. The time for more advanced domestication of the dog has been set, rather arbitrarily, at 15–13,000 years ago. However, 50,000-year-old Spanish cave-paintings depict man hunting with dogs. The Dingo also provides a chronological fly in the ointment, for it is a true dog. Dingo fossils dating back 50,000 years have been found in Australia, and the only way that the Dingo

Above: This Chalcidian vase (dating from 550–530 B.C.) shows how popular dogs were as a motif on the ceramics of ancient Rome.

could have entered this continent was with man, as a semi-domesticated animal, when the Australasian land mass was joined to Asia. The bridge between the continents disappeared when the sea bed rose as a result of ice melting during the Mesolithic period. Only marsupials are truly indigenous to Australia and certainly the development of mammals, such as dogs, did not occur in this continent. These two pieces of somewhat tentative evidence suggest, therefore, that dogs were pretty closely associated with man at least 50,000 years ago.

Indisputable evidence of domestication, however, did not come to light until the skeletons of domesticated dogs were found in excavations in Frankfurt-am-Main. These remains were found in association with the bones of an extinct ox and have been dated as 9000 B.C. Eight-thousand-year-old fossilized dog bones have been found in the kitchens of excavated dwellings belonging to primitive man in Denmark and Sweden. They are found in the kitchen middens – the forerunners of the modern-day rubbish tips – which suggests either that dogs were eaten or, more probably, that these were the remains of scavenging dogs.

Studies of fragments of skeletons, and early paintings and carvings, lead us to suppose that there may have been four main types of dogs which evolved fairly rapidly from the basic stock animal. Firstly, there was the Northern Spitz group which, being hardy and strong, was ideal for use as a hunting and haulage dog. As man's way of life developed to embrace agriculture as well as hunting, man not only grew crops but systematically grazed captive beasts. This dog then doubled as a cattle and sheep herder, as well as a guard dog for the flocks. In this capacity, it was soon found as far south as the Rhinelands.

The second group was the Dingo, which seems to have been exploited rapidly by peoples in warmer climates as a guard and scavenger. It tends to be rather an outcast of domesticity and has not been greatly developed by man for highly specialized capacities. It will be discussed in greater detail later.

The third mainstream group was the Mastiff. It has been suggested that the Mastiff's forerunner was the Tibetan wolf. The spread of the Mastiff was mainly east and west from central Asia and its size and heavy bones made it a useful guard and war dog. The Mastiff group was thus the origin of large flock guards, such as the Pyrenean Mountain Dogs, and other giant breeds, such as the Great Dane. Its good sense of smell makes it probable that there is a Mastiff origin to the large scenting hounds, such as the Bloodhound. Representatives of the group were probably crossed with the Spitz group to combine strength and herding ability in one animal.

The final important original group was the Greyhound-type, gazehounds (dogs which hunt by sight). Whether these dogs actually originated in the North African desert regions or travelled with man into these areas, where they were further developed, is uncertain. The latter seems more likely. Although they had an Asiatic birthplace, it was the 'cradle of Egypt' which gave them a home and developed their full potential as silent and fast hunters.

The great cultural centre of Mesopotamia has provided us with the first detailed knowledge about the state of dog development. Bronzes, frescoes, carvings and other art forms have shown Egyptian man with dogs virtually identical to modern-day Greyhounds and Salukis. They even show these dogs in action, sight-hunting for game, and it is obvious that by 2000 B.C. the science of dog breeding was sufficiently developed to be capable of producing highly specialized types of dogs for specific purposes. Heavier, Mastiff-type dogs were shown in portrayals of battles, where the dogs were either used for war in association with horses, or were being pitted in packs against them. Pre-dynastic Egypt had developed toy breeds which were very similar to Maltese Terriers. These show that this advanced culture had the time and opportunity not only to find socializing with dogs useful, but also pleasant.

Greyhounds also appear to have formed the main breed for the Greeks and the Celtic cultures. These dogs had apparently been transported from their desert 'origins' in North Africa up into the Mediterranean and northern Europe. Possibly, as we have already mentioned, this journey northwards was a retracing of their original steps.

Movement of dogs with man from Asia also occurred when the American Indian colonized the American continent, by migration across the land bridge which once replaced the Bering Strait. By this stage in its domestication, the dog had probably become too far removed from wolves to breed with any indigenous wolves in America. Most probably these new dogs remained quite distinct and separate. Furthermore, it is unlikely that the nomads would choose to try to cross their prize domestic dogs with any local wolves. Definitely, many of the new American imports were the Spitz-type Eskimo dogs with heavy shoulders, broad muzzles and tails curled over their backs. It would appear that this type of dog was well suited to the climate of northern Asia and Europe and so survived in North America.

It is hard to say whether trading, sailing and conquest had much early influence on the development of breeds in the continents and, if so, when and what changes came about. Dogs would have been an important object of barter and commerce; visitors to foreign shores would have seen dogs which had been developed for special local tasks and they would have been eager to procure them to improve their own dogs' capacities. Exchange of dogs would have occurred and new blood would have arisen from unplanned matings, when ships put in at ports.

Below: Sculptors, as well as potters and artists, often used dogs as subjects for representations.

13

Development of the Breeds

If northern Asia was the birthplace of the dog, then Egypt was its cradle and Europe was ultimately its playground. Although it would be wrong to suggest that Europe was the only centre of breed development, there is no doubt that this part of the world did more than anywhere else to exploit fully the genetic potential of the dog and was certainly mainly responsible for the great diversity of fixed breeds we see today.

As we have already mentioned, dog followed man wherever he went and as great civilizations and cultural centres evolved, so they developed their own dog breeds. The European cultures of the seventeenth, eighteenth and nineteenth centuries did most to develop the diversity of dog breeds. There were three reasons for this. Firstly, they were the most specialized cultures the world had known, both culturally and scientifically, and so had a greater opportunity to develop 'canine cults'. Secondly, Europeans are great dog lovers – a characteristic most prevalent in the British, who carry this devotion to its highest pitch. Americans, too, have now caught the fever, with the result that the United States has exerted great influence recently on thinking and fashion in the dog world. Thirdly, the Europeans had the facilities and opportunities for travel and communication, which meant that the breeds they developed could be spread, not merely within Europe, but also around the rest of the world.

The story is very different in naturally insular countries, such as China or Tibet. The Pekinese – a breed known to be in existence in China as early as A.D. 565 – was virtually unknown to the rest of the world and it was not until the sacking of China that it was brought to the west. In 1860, five specimens were taken from the Imperial Palace and transported to Victorian England.

Principles of dog genetics

Just as the domestication of the dog did not take place overnight, so no breed 'suddenly' appeared. It is not always easy to realize that the Yorkshire Terrier we see today did not exist as such in 1850, and may well not be around in the same form in 2050. By selective breeding of dogs, man has and will continue to alter the breeds we take for granted as 'standard'.

Each fertile animal is capable of passing on its own genetic make-up. All newborn animals are a fifty-fifty genetic compound of their parents. Although they may look or behave much more like one or other of the parents, this does *not* alter the fundamental genetic rule.

Every single cell in every dog carries thirty-nine identical pairs of chromosomes – tiny structures in the nucleus of the cell which carry the genetic messages of the dog. The exception to this is the sex cells, both sperms and eggs, which only have either the male or the female half of the thirty-nine pairs. When the egg is fertilized by the sperm, the full thirty-nine paired complement of chromosomes is restored in the cells which develop into the young dog. Each chromosome carries many genes, which are the biochemical mini-messengers of heredity. They each control one simple chemical reaction in the body. It is the incredibly complex inter-relationships of these reactions which give both form and function to the whole of the dog.

New genes are produced by chance chemical changes, called mutations. Mutations are very rare but, if the changes in the genes express

Below: The small dog in Van Eyck's *The Marriage of Arnolfini* bears a close resemblance to a modern Cairn Terrier.

themselves, then we see variations in the new dog offspring. If the genes are stable and the dog is fertile, then the genes will continue to be passed on and, if these mutants are 'dominant', they will be continually apparent.

Although new genes can only arise by mutation, variations are seen in all dogs as a result of a much more subtle and common system. A gene has two components to it – that is, it is paired. Mendel, an Austrian monk, first discovered that inheritance is dependent on this pairing. A gene may be *dominant* or *recessive*. If it is dominant, it is *expressed*, which means it is noticeable. Dominant genes over-ride the recessive genes, which are subordinate and are not 'seen'. The exception is when two recessive genes are found in the same pair. Then there is no dominant gene present to over-ride them and

they *must* be seen. This can be demonstrated by a simple example, taking the coat colour of Labrador Retrievers.

Labradors can either be yellow or black (leaving aside liver-coloured Labradors for the moment). Black is dominant to yellow. If the dominant black gene is indicated by B, and the recessive yellow gene by b – the coat colours could be shown as:

BB – Black dog   Bb – Black dog
bB – Black dog   bb – Yellow dog
BB, Bb and bB are all black, and all indistinguishable from one another at a cursory

The Pomeranian has been selectively bred to produce a small dog. The modern Pom (above left) has an apple-shaped head and a smaller body than the dogs that Thomas Gainsborough painted (above right). The breed is of the Spitz group, all of which carry their tails curled tightly over their backs.
Below: Sporting dogs were often included in eighteenth century portraits.

Left: Porcelain models of Chinese dogs were popular long before the breeds reached Europe.

glance. However, if these dogs are mated, it becomes possible to distinguish between them and to work out their gene make-up. A law of heredity is that gene pairs distribute independently of each other in the offspring. So, a mating of BB and BB will produce all BB pups – that is, all black. A mating of BB and Bb will produce some BB pups and some Bb but they will still all be black as B is dominant. However, if Bb and Bb are mated, they will produce some BB pups (black), some Bb pups (black), and some bb pups (yellow). Mutation of genes has nothing to do with the appearance of yellow pups. Instead, two recessive genes have doubled up to give a 'new' colour.

The word 'dominance' is also used in breeding as a general genetic term implying that a form or behavioural trait tends to 'over-ride' other recessive characteristics. A well-known example is the body form of the Labrador. The Labrador is a dominant breed genetically in that, when crossed with other breeds, the offspring often look more like the Labrador parent than the other parent breed.

There is, however, a third behavioural connotation to the word 'dominant'. We speak of a member of a group of dogs being dominant – i.e. it is the leader. We even speak of a breed of dogs being dominant; Staffordshire Bull Terriers, for example. The behaviour concept of the word has no connection with the breeding concept, and a dog that is dominant in behaviour will not necessarily (or even probably) be dominant genetically.

Although the principles underlying genetics were not known to man in the early Middle Ages, he clearly was able to produce the type of dogs he wanted. Quite simply, the early dog breeder worked on the principle of breeding from the dogs with the traits he wanted and eliminating those dogs he did not want. In fact, this is very similar to natural selection. All animals are born with slightly different characteristics and behaviour. Depending on the situation, some will have a better chance of survival than others. 'Survival of the fittest' – Charles Darwin's concept of natural selection – means that those creatures which survive are those best suited to their situation. For instance, long-haired, thick-coated animals survive better in cold climates than do thin-coated ones, and so have more chance to breed and perpetuate their type.

Man, in protecting his dogs from the rigours of natural selection, was able to impose his own *unnatural* selection. If he wanted to develop a short-legged dog capable of tunnelling underground easily he selected shorter-legged specimens and bred from them. It did not matter if that dog could not catch hares – man provided food for it. This, for example, is how the Dachshund was developed. Similarly, when man decided he wanted a miniature Spaniel-type of dog, he constantly bred from the smaller specimens of Spaniels until he produced the desired result – in this case, the Cavalier King Charles Spaniel. No matter if the dog could be killed by a single kick from a horse or could not catch even the most sluggish pheasant; he would always be fed household titbits and could spend his life on his mistress's lap.

Above: Boar hunting was one of the earliest and strongest bonds between man and dog as shown in this early Italian vase.

Above: Despite their forbidding appearance, modern day Mastiffs are very amenable to man.

Below: Modern Mastiffs can vary in colour. Apricot, silver fawn and dark fawn are the most common.

Man soon learned that the most reliable method of producing a dog with a heightened characteristic was by breeding between closely related dogs. This 'inbreeding' involves crossing dogs from the same immediate family, where both dogs show the desired characteristic. The offspring of this mating receives a 'double dose' of the genes. Inbreeding may be practised with dogs which are very closely related, such as brother to sister or son to mother, but this is to be deprecated in nearly all cases as the results are rarely successful, even in the short term. Such close inbreeding can cause problems for two reasons. Firstly, incestuous relationships tend to result in offspring which are lacking in vigour, stamina and size and which have rather poor mental abilities. Secondly, although a double dose of genes can result in a heightening of the desired characteristics, equally it can increase undesirable traits.

Much safer, although less rapid and dramatic, is 'line breeding'. This is still a form of inbreeding, in that the parents are related, but not by a close family link in the final generation. The common ancestry will be, for example, in the great-grandparents. By this method of breeding, vigour is maintained in the offspring while at the same time the desired characteristics are enhanced.

An obvious method of introducing a desired characteristic to a line of dogs is cross-breeding, which actually refers to the act of breeding between dogs of different types. In fact, it is perhaps better called 'cross-typing' as the term 'cross-breeding' is now reserved for breeding between dogs of specific, *recognized* breeds.

There is much evidence to suggest that cross-typing occurred very early in the development of the various breeds. For example, the Asian Mastiffs were crossed with Spitz-type dogs to produce the large shepherd and guarding breeds such as the German Shepherd Dog (Alsatian) and Hungarian Komondor. The great advantages of this cross-typing are the rapid introduction of new traits (instead of the laborious process of selective close breeding) and, most important, the production of a dog which is highly vigorous (sometimes referred to as 'hybrid vigour'). One disadvantage is that often the resultant dog is not 'stable' – that is, it does not 'breed true' when mated to a dog of the same origin as itself and the resultant offspring does not resemble either parent closely in form or behaviour. Another problem is that a much-prized trait in either parent could be lost in the offspring, being overshadowed by a more dominant characteristic from the other parent.

Despite the problems of cross-typing, there have been some notable successes over the centuries. A particular example is the Airedale. This is a quite stable breed, which resulted originally from crossing Welsh Terriers and Otterhounds. Another is the Bull Mastiff – originally a conglomerate of the old-fashioned Bulldog and the Mastiff, with some Bloodhound breeding introduced into the genetic mix to enhance the scenting ability. There is even a suggestion, from writings of the seventeenth century, that Terrier types come from mating Beagles with a stocky type of Mastiff mongrel.

As the type of dogs became more standardized and true breeds developed, so cross-breeding was more likely to result in stable crosses. Many of the long list of terrier breeds were produced by

17

experimental, yet considered, cross-breeding during the eighteenth and nineteenth centuries – a period referred to as the 'Golden Age of Terriers'. Nowadays, purposeful cross-breeding between stable breeds of dogs is rare except, perhaps, to produce Lurchers, which are usually the result of Greyhound/terrier crosses. However, 'out-crossing' – the breeding between unrelated dogs of the same breed – is common and results in good vigour and a dog which combines the strong points of both parents. The accent is on breeding so that traits are 'complemented' or gently enhanced, rather than ridiculously heightened or totally obliterated.

The appearance of the breeds

Much happened in the few thousand years between the appearance of the four basic types of dog and the present day. There are now about eight hundred well-recognized and stable breeds in the world. Clearly, it would be a tremendous task to attempt to trace the development of each breed chronologically or even to select a few examples. A simpler, but nonetheless valid, exercise is to attempt to outline the history of the various group classifications of breeds. These are drawn up by the national Kennel Clubs. To consider breeds in group history is not as artificial as it may at first appear. After all, the groups are classifications of dogs by character and capacity, which are the important factors, both for selective breeding and for the development of a breed of dogs.

The Kennel Club in Great Britain classifies the breeds of dog it recognizes into six groups. These are as follows: Hounds, Gundogs, Terriers, Working Dogs, Toy Dogs and Utility Dogs. The American Kennel Club similarly incorporates all its accepted breeds into six groups – Hounds, Sporting Dogs, Terriers, Working Dogs, Toys and Non-sporting Dogs.

In general, the American Sporting Dogs correspond to the English Gundog group – both incorporating the Pointers, Retrievers, Setters, Spaniels and the Weimaraners. The Americans also include the Wire-haired Pointing Griffon in this group, which is not a breed that is recognized by the English Kennel Club. The Hounds, Terriers, Working Dogs and Toys of both Kennel Clubs generally correspond. The few variations that exist arise mainly when a breed is recognized by one organization and not by the other. The English Utility group is equivalent to the American Non-sporting Dogs group, again

Above: Hounds were bred specifically for hunting. Physical appearance was not one of the original criteria when selecting dogs and bitches for breeding.

Left: Terriers became popular during the nineteenth century and were extensively developed as a group.

Right: Even when standing quite still, the powerful build of the Greyhound is quite obvious.

with one or two variations. Shih Tzus, for example, are included in the Utility group, but are classified as a Toy by the American Kennel Club. Tibetan Spaniels and Terriers, classified as Utility breeds in Britain, are not recognized at all by the American Kennel Club.

Hounds

Most members of the large hound group can trace a very ancient lineage. This is largely because the capacity to hunt is a very basic attribute of dogs that has been exploited for centuries over almost the whole of the Northern hemisphere.

Pharaoh Hounds and Ibizan Hounds probably have a common or very close ancestry, dating to at least 4000 B.C. in Egypt. Recently, they have been 'rediscovered' by the Western world as a companion and show dog. Ibizan Hounds are natives of the Balearic Islands and probably became isolated there after their introduction by Phoenician traders. These traders may also have introduced the Pharaoh Hounds to Malta and Gozo.

Greyhounds, as we have said, spread from Mesopotamia up into Europe, the Mediterranean and western Asia. They have retained their basic characteristics virtually unaltered for at least five thousand years.

The other gazehounds – the Afghans and Salukis – travelled with man into Persia and Arabia. The Afghans became established in Afghanistan and were 'lost' to European culture until the 1890s, when they were brought to England. Salukis became the only breed favoured by the Arab tribes in Persia and the near East and did not enter Western breeding and showing societies until after the first World War had finished in 1919.

Above: Greyhounds, which were commonly used for hare coursing in the nineteenth century, have changed very little in appearance over 5000 years.

Below: Deerhounds are now a very rare breed. They hunt by sight and move very quickly.

Above: The Persian Greyhound was bred in Persia, Arabia and Afghanistan for gazelle coursing.

Above right: The Italian Greyhound has never enjoyed widespread popularity despite its elegance.

Below: This young Saluki still lacks the final points of grace of a fully matured dog.

Other hounds with very ancient origins are the Elkhound and the Finnish Spitz. Elkhounds were distributed throughout Scandinavia many thousands of years ago and were probably used for guard purposes before elk tracking and hunting became established. Ultimately, the breed was adopted for stalking and encircling elks, to enable guns to be used. The Finnish Spitz probably had a similar origin to that of the Elkhound and yet was developed for small game hunting, squirrel hunting and for putting up birds. It is still very popular in Finland.

A small but elite cadre of large hounds was developed in many Northern temperate and Arctic regions for hunting bigger game. These included Deerhounds, Borzois and Irish Wolfhounds. The origin of the Irish Wolfhound is hard to trace, since it is somewhat shrouded in the mists of the first few centuries A.D. At this time Wolfhounds were certainly used for hunting in Ireland and they probably had a link with the Deerhound in Scotland. The breed was disseminated throughout Europe in the later Middle Ages, but it became virtually extinct in Ireland about one hundred years ago. Happily, a revival of the breed occurred just in time. A similar uncertainty surrounds the origin of the Borzoi, but it was undoubtedly the popularity of wolf hunting in Imperial Russia that led to its present development. Deerhounds have been steadily developed in Scotland over the last two thousand years, although the introduction of guns in the eighteenth century reduced the demand for a dog capable of catching and killing deer.

The medium-sized breeds of hounds, kept in packs for hunting hares, foxes, wolves, stags, badgers and other animals, were developed in France, Germany and Britain. The largest – the Bloodhounds – were adapted from stag-scenting to man-scenting. Bloodhounds share their keen sense of smell with Foxhounds, which have been popular since the thirteenth century. Otterhounds are one of the rarer types of dogs and, in recent times, Foxhound blood has been introduced into the breed. Beagles and Bassets both have fairly ancient origins. Beagles were developed in England as early as the fifteenth century for small game and hare scenting and Bassets were developed in France for hunting on foot or for driving game to the guns.

An interesting aspect of genetics surrounds the development of the shortest-legged members of the hound group, the Dachshunds. These breeds (and there are six of them – the Standard Wire-, Long- and Smooth-haired Dachshunds and corresponding miniatures of each of these) all

Above: Whippets probably result from selectively breeding Greyhounds for smaller specimens.

Above right: The Cocker Spaniel.

Below: King Charles Spaniels were developed in Stuart times.

Below right: This print shows a Modern Blenheim, an old Blenheim and a King Charles Spaniel.

show chondrodystrophy (see Chapter Eight). This is a premature cessation of limb and bone growth which produces dogs that are low to the ground and are thus well-suited to 'going to earth' in search of badgers. Dachshunds were quite an early development in Germany and became popular in Europe during the nineteenth century. The literal translation of Dachshund, from German, is *badger-dog*.

Many other dogs with hunting characteristics were developed in centres of civilization all over the world. For example, Rhodesian Ridgebacks were developed for lion-worrying in South Africa, and Basenjis for small game hunting in the Sudan. During the nineteenth century, Whippets were developed and extensively used for rabbit coursing in England.

Some hounds are still used exclusively for hunting but the majority are kept as domestic pets – with varying degrees of success.

Gundogs

As the name implies, dogs of this group are used in the sport of game shooting. Pointers are used to indicate the presence of game, Spaniels and Setters to flush and drive the birds, and Retrievers to collect the shot birds. However, nearly all the gundog breeds were well in evidence centuries before the gun was invented, having been bred to point, put up and flush game into nets.

Spaniels can be considered to be the grandfathers of nearly all the gundogs and they

were spread throughout Europe in the eighteenth century. As the name implies, they originated in Spain – a country which has always had a history of bird hunting. The strong, robust, English Springer Spaniel was probably an ancestral type for most other Spaniels, including the Welsh Springer. Field Spaniels – now rather rare and numerically overshadowed by Cocker Spaniels – came to prominence during the eighteenth and nineteenth centuries. Original Spaniel stock was also the ancestor of the Clumber, a rather isolated breed from Spanish cross-breeding. Irish Water Spaniels appeared in the mid-1800s as did the Cocker Spaniel, which was to become popular both as a working dog and as a pet.

Setters (dogs which will put up game after having first pointed to it) were developed fairly early in Europe. There are eighteenth century descriptions and paintings of dogs which are definitely identifiable as early Setters. Gordon Setters, the heavier dogs with great endurance, evolved during the eighteenth century in Scotland, and the finer-boned, red-coated Irish Setter appeared a century later.

Pointers were in existence in Spain and Italy well before their eighteenth century popularity in England. The German Pointers developed about this time, too, and were especially useful in the shooting field since they were also bred for their hunting and retrieving abilities. Other 'all rounders' from this group are the Hungarian Vizsla and the Weimaraners, which both have some pointing blood in their ancestry.

The breeds which are probably regarded as being more of a gundog than any others – the Retrievers – are the most recent in development. This is not so surprising, for retrieval of shot game has clearly only been necessary since the advent of the shotgun. The Curly-coated, Flat-coated and the Golden Retriever (which had achieved tremendous popularity by the end of the last century) all have Setters and Spaniels in their ancestry. The Labrador Retriever – a late acquisition from Newfoundland in the 1820s – was introduced to the gun and adapted to bird retrieval. It soon became the most popular and adaptable of retrieving gundogs.

It should not be forgotten that other breeds, such as the Poodle, were probably used for game-bird hunting in the early stages of their development, although this is no longer a noticeable characteristic in the breeds today. Gundogs, like hounds, are now also very popular as household pets.

Terriers

When a hound had scented and chased its quarry, it would probably achieve a kill, unless the prey 'went to earth'. If this happened, the fox, badger, rabbit or otter was safe and the hound could do no more than stand around the burrow baying in vain. Clearly, there was a need for a small, short-legged, tough and fearless dog which would pursue the prey down the tunnel and would then have the courage and ability to fight the prey on its own home ground. The terrier – or to be more precise, a whole army of terrier breeds – was developed for this purpose.

The very name terrier – or *terroure* (Fr. *Terre* – earth) – is descriptive. Originally, all Terriers could dig and would go to ground, not only at a crucial point in the hunt but also to keep farms and house-surroundings free from rats and rabbits. The need for aggression and ferocity is obvious and these behaviour traits are often very prevalent in the terrier breeds. The sixteenth, seventeenth and eighteenth centuries saw much development of terriers in Europe, particularly in

Top: Sir Edward Landseer's skill as an animal painter is well demonstrated in this picture of Toy Spaniels.

Above: Newfoundlands are quite at home in water but their origins and the reasons for their development are obscure.

Above: The Cavalier King Charles should grow to weigh between ten and eighteen pounds and should have fine feathering on its legs, ears and tail.

Above right: The Cairn Terrier was originally used to forage out foxes, badgers, martens and wild-cats in the Hebrides and Western Highlands of Scotland.

Right: Dogs were a popular subject with French porcelain craftsmen of the seventeenth and eighteenth centuries.

Britain. Because of their somewhat mundane and ubiquitous work, they were not generally shipped to other places in the world – or even around their countries of origin. Very often, local breeding and districts gave their name to the dog which evolved in that area; hence Cairn, Kerry Blue, Lakeland, Scottish and even Manchester Terrier. This localization not only gave rise to each breed's uniqueness of form but also to its character. In no other group of dogs is there such variation.

Terriers were very much the 'popular dog' and carried with them little of the grandiose history of breeding that belonged to the hounds or gundogs. They were, to some extent, a 'poor man's hound' and true breeds, such as the Bull Terrier and the Staffordshire Bull Terrier, were selectively bred for their prowess in the dog-fight pits. Social fashion has done much to change the form and popularity of the terrier breeds. Some, such as the now extinct English White Terrier, fell by the wayside. It is unfortunate that some of the dignity and working ability of a few breeds of terrier has been lost in the elaborate coiffeur of the show ring, although this in no way applies only to these dogs.

Working group

This rather varied set of breeds includes those recognized as guard dogs, herding dogs, heelers, haulage dogs and trackers, from all over the world. They vary in shape and size from Welsh Corgis to St. Bernards. Many were developed for highly specialized tasks, in particular the larger working dogs of the original Spitz type or Mastiff

23

Far left: The Bulldog was bred for bull-baiting in the eighteenth century.

Left: The twentieth century Bulldog has an even more exaggerated heavy muzzle and enormous chest than its ancestors.

type. The Siberian Husky, Samoyed and Alaskan Malamute are strong Spitz dogs which were all developed for haulage. The Norwegian Buhunds (also Spitz type) are herders and watchdogs of less massive proportions. Pyrenean Mountain Dogs have Mastiff origins and were developed as flock guards, a duty also ascribed to Rottweillers, which were originally used in the tenth century for hunting boars in central Europe. In the Middle Ages, Mastiffs were used as herd and house guards, while the largest of the dogs with Mastiff type origins – the St. Bernard – was developed specifically for work as a travelling companion and rescue dog by the monks of the St. Bernard Hospice in Switzerland.

It is apparent, therefore, that crossing an ancestral Spitz type with a Mastiff type gave rise to useful guarding and herding dogs. The Alsatian, or German Shepherd Dog, as it is now officially called, is the epitome of this all-round working dog and was developed from several hardy strains. The adaptability and intelligence of these large working herders have led to their well-known use as dogs for the Services and the police. Other herders and smaller sheepdogs were developed in local pockets all over the Northern hemisphere:- Belgian Shepherd Dogs (Groenendaels), Old English Sheepdogs, Welsh Collies, Hungarian Pulis and Polish Sheedogs are a few examples.

The smaller herders and heelers probably had small Spitz type dogs (similar to Buhunds) in their distant ancestry. 'Distant' must, however, be emphasized, for Welsh Corgis are an ancient breed and so are Border Collies.

Some of the smaller guard dogs (small, that is, in comparison with Pyrenean Mountain Dogs) are of very recent development. The Boxer, for example, was produced as a stable cross, with English Bulldogs and Continental Bullenbeissers in the blood, less than eighty years ago. The Doberman is probably derived from Rottweilers and terriers. Its history spans only sixty years.

Working dogs have now gained favour as domestic pets. One problem is that they must be kept very well exercised and mentally occupied to prevent them from becoming 'undomestic'.

Toy group

In considering many of the famous toy breeds, such as the Papillons, Italian Greyhounds and King Charles Spaniels, it would be easy to conclude – erroneously – that all toy breeds are a relatively recent development. Nothing could be further from the truth. For example, the Maltese was known to the Roman and Greek empires, while the Pekinese, Japanese Chin and Chihuahua were present in the Chinese, Japanese and Mexican civilizations in very early times.

Dogs of the toy groups comprise miniature varieties of larger breeds, many examples of tiny Spitz type Asian dogs, and a large number of miniscule breeds of uncertain origin. Toy dogs show two predominant characteristics of behaviour and form. Firstly, because they were all developed as human companions, they show great affection for people. This affection is occasionally directed solely to their owners, particularly among Pekingese and Yorkshire Terriers. Besides acting as companions there is also some historical evidence to suggest that some breeds, such as the Chihuahua and King Charles Spaniel, were used as 'comforters' and were kept close to a sick person in the belief that the evil spirits would be transferred to the animal. In fact, on occasion, more than evil

Left: The Chow Chow, another Spitz breed, with curled tail, was raised and eaten as meat in China.

spirits were passed on to the dog; there are allusions in the literature of the Middle Ages to lap dogs being kept by ladies to rid them of fleas, the insect preferring dogs to a human host!

The second characteristic is that miniaturization and selective breeding for dwarf varieties has resulted in short-limbed dogs and an infantile head-shape. Thus, many toy breeds have rounded skulls, flattened noses, pop-eyes and short jaws which are the characteristics of the brachycephalic breeds (Greek – short head). The retention of puppy characteristics, both physical and behavioural, is a particular tendency of the toy breeds.

Many toy breeds emerged in Europe in the nineteenth and early twentieth centuries. Some were imported from the Far East and Asia.

Utility groups

This somewhat artificial grouping is a real conglomeration of breeds, and tends to embrace all those that will not fit into the other groups. Many of the breeds categorized here were developed for highly localized and specialized purposes, or because of a current fashion at a particular time. The purposes or fashions passed away but the dogs remained. Thus, there are no more horse-drawn coaches for Dalmatians to trot alongside; the bull baiting for which the Bulldog was bred has thankfully disappeared; and, probably, the Chinese penchant for Chow meat has faded, along with the fashion for making wool and leather from its coat and pelt. Two dogs from the Netherlands – Keeshonds and Schipperkes – were originally developed primarily as guard dogs for the canal barges; Schipperkes were also used for catching rats. Nowadays, they are more universally popular as watch dogs and general companions.

Frequently, however, we do not know the factors which encouraged the development of many of the utility breeds. Schnauzers and French Bulldogs are two breeds whose origins

Above: The form of most dogs has only changed slightly in the last 100 years. Spaniels, Greyhounds, Sheepdogs, Bloodhounds, and Bassets are easily recognizable.

remain a mystery. Others have a romantic past. The Shih Tzu, for example, which is a native of Tibet, could, according to Lamaist legend, transform itself into a lion if the need arose. In fact, there is one trait – adaptability – that stands out as being common to all the utility breeds. This characteristic is admirably demonstrated in the Poodle, which may originally have been used as a setting and water retrieving dog, but which later became a companion and, in its miniature and toy guise, an incredibly popular house pet.

The last century of breed development

Social changes have had a tremendous influence on dogs in the last century. Although many dogs are still used for work purposes, the vast majority are kept as household pets and this has done much to alter dogs' characters. The inception of a worldwide series of national Kennel Clubs, which have laid down breed standards by which dogs are judged, has proved a major step to establishing international uniformity. In a way, however, this is a somewhat artificial system; at any rate, it is a system that bases its classifications on one criterion. Golden Retrievers are Golden Retrievers because they are good at retrieving shot game birds besides being an all-round sporting dog. No amount of laying down precise weight limits, prize schedules and coat points will alter that fact, yet it explains why we now often see obvious variations between show 'types' of a breed and working types. Nevertheless, by establishing the major criterion for a champion dog as not always what it *does*, but how it *looks*, the Kennel Clubs and Breed Show Societies have done much to prevent ill-considered breeding. Had it been allowed, this would have made breed development something of a farce.

The fact that there are variations between show specimens and working dogs of the same breed verifies that breeds are always changing and will continue to do so.

Characteristics of the Dog

How is it that the dog has become involved in so many people's lives? Why have the dogs of today survived in so many different forms and why are they found all over the world? Why is the dog 'man's best friend'?

The answers probably lie in the dog's adaptability. Adaptable to temperature, climate and all external conditions, the dog is almost unique in being found both within the Polar circles and the Equator. Similarly, the dog is adaptable in its diet; it is not tied to one type of food, it can survive on virtually any type of protein, carbohydrate and fat.

But the dog, as a species, has a tremendous capacity to adapt within its genetic capabilities. Not just variations in size but differences in development of its senses and behaviour have meant that man has been able, by judicious breeding, to produce dogs capable of pulling him along, protecting him, helping him to hunt and retrieve his food, herding his animals and, ultimately, giving him pleasure and company.

The senses and behavioural characteristics which give the dog a special place in association with man deserve a closer look.

Sense of smell

Of all the dog senses, it is probably the incredible sense of smell which, to us anyway, seems the most heightened. One could imagine that

Below: An alert and curious Bearded Collie waits for a word from his master.

primitive dog identified the smell of a wounded animal in a herd and so was able to detect the easiest prey. The dog with the best sense of smell would presumably have been the one to find the prey first, to kill it and enjoy the spoils. Already, we see an example of Charles Darwin's natural law of adaptation and survival of the fittest – it seems reasonable to assume that this dog would be the most likely to survive and so be able to breed even when times were hard and food scarce.

Dogs possess, in common with other mammals, specially adapted structures and cells for the recognition and definition of odours. Scent-laden air passes into the dog's nostrils and flows backwards over specially adapted bones called turbinates. These thin bones are shaped like scrolls laid end-on to the air flow. The bones are covered in an epithelium – that is, a thin layer of tissue which contains special cells which are activated by scent. When the dog is breathing normally, slowly and deeply, the air takes a lower path in the nasal chambers before entering the back of the throat and passing down to the lungs. However, when the dog is sniffing and air is passing backwards and forwards in the nose, the shorter intakes of air are directed upwards to the higher parts of the chambers and more air passes over the sensitive ethmo-turbinates in this region. We do the same thing when we 'sniff' a tasty delicacy but of course the dog has it down to a fine art.

Once the scent cells are stimulated by an odour, they change the chemical impulse (for

Above: Tibetan Spaniels were originally bred in the monasteries of Tibet, and were kept as watchdogs and companions.

Below: Pug puppies, like other short-headed dogs, often make snuffling noises.

smells are minute particles of the chemical structure of a compound, vapourized in air) to an electrical one which then travels down the branches of the olfactory nerve.

In addition to the individual scent receptors on the turbinates of the nose, there is also a special scent organ (absent in man) which is highly developed in dogs. This is the vomeronasal organ (or Organ of Jacobson), which is buried behind the canine teeth in the tissue on the roof of the mouth. This organ is also excited by smells and sends nerve impulses to the brain.

Much can be told of what these impulses convey to a dog's brain by determining to which part of the brain they travel. Smell impulses go to an important area of the brain called the rhinencephalon. This can be described as a 'smell centre' and in dogs, as in most other animals, it is quite large. It is relatively smaller in man, which may partly explain our comparatively poor sense of smell. This smell centre is enormous in such primitive animals as dog-fish, who rely almost entirely on smell to locate their food. We know that in humans the rhinencephalon also functions as a memory centre and is also associated with emotion – one of the reasons why smells can be so poignant in humans and recall, often in a very keen way, long-forgotten episodes. Of course, we cannot tell for certain that this is so in dogs and we have no way of testing a dog's 'emotion' but there is no evidence to the contrary. The meaning and importance of smells to dogs will be discussed in greater detail later. Meanwhile we will take a further look at their incredible scenting capacity.

Some scientific investigations have suggested that a dog's scenting capacity is 100 million times greater than man's. This is an extreme, however,

and probably in most cases, dogs have a smell capacity about 100 times greater than that of man. It is known that dogs have about fifteen times as many scenting cells in their noses as man.

Sophisticated experiments have been designed to test a dog's sense of smell by training dogs to detect a particular smell and giving them a reward when they do so. This can be arranged by an automatic feeding machine which delivers a food reward when a dog pushes on a panel which is laced with a particular smell. It ignores panels which have other smells on them and do not deliver food. These experiments have shown that dogs can detect the scent of sulphuric acid even when diluted ten million fold, and also that not only can they detect odours very well but they can distinguish between them – an ability which probably has greater significance for a hunting animal. Practical experience, of course, tells us the same thing. Trained tracking dogs can follow the scent of a person for a considerable distance, even when this scent has become diluted by time and when it crosses the scent of other people. Tracking a person may not simply involve recognizing his body odour, though. Probably other 'clues', such as crushed vegetation, particles of clothing and shoes help. That the dog can discriminate between those smells which are *not* specific to the person and the smell that *is* specific, reinforces the conclusion that the discriminating capacity of a dog's scenting ability is superb.

Discriminating between odours can be a 'party trick' of some tracking dogs. A dog can be introduced to the smell of a person by allowing the dog to sniff an object like a handkerchief or even a piece of wood touched briefly by the

Below: The scenting mechanism of a dog is superbly developed although, in essence, it functions in the same way as a human's.

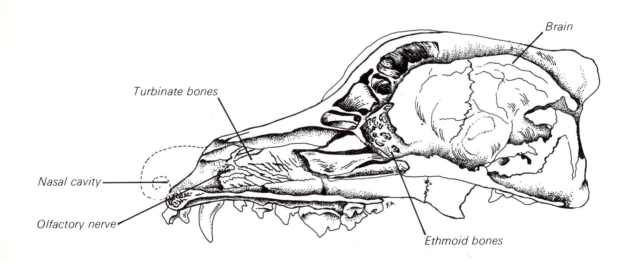

Brain

Turbinate bones

Nasal cavity

Olfactory nerve

Ethmoid bones

Above: All dogs have a good sense of smell but probably dogs with short noses, like this Boxer, do not have such good scenting capacities as those with longer muzzles.

person, who need not be the dog's handler. The object would then be placed, unseen by the dog, under one cover, while similar objects from other people are put under other similar covers. The dog is released to select the appropriate object after a search under the covers. Some dogs can even discriminate between the odours of identical twins, when the odours are presented together.

A study of tracking dogs may show us the tricks which a dog uses to discriminate odours. Dogs often do not follow a trail directly but swing from side to side across it. They may be detecting the change in strength of the odour so that they can ultimately follow it more accurately.

The same principle may be employed when Foxhounds or Beagles 'cast about' looking for a scent. They rarely run in straight lines but,

instead, weave from side-to-side or even circle to follow the path of the strongest scent.

It is interesting that the scenting ability of dogs is improved if they have been injected with amphetamine – a stimulant drug. The precise reason for this improvement is uncertain but it may be that the drug has the effect of increasing motivation in dogs; it could even provide indirect evidence that there is a link between scent, memory and emotion in dogs, as there is in man.

Development of sense of smell
It is not easy to determine whether a newborn puppy can sense odours but it is thought that it can. The first thing a puppy does after birth is to crawl towards the mother's nipple. The mammary glands are warm, so it could be argued that

the pup feels the increased heat, but this is only part of the mechanism. Bitches emit scents from their bodies called pheromones; these are particularly active from the mammary gland around birth. The smell attracts the pup, causing him to seek the nipple. Once the pup is sucking, it learns that pheromones means food! These pheromones disappear after a few weeks, when the puppy has learnt to find the nipple, is able to see and can even take other foods. More proof that newborn puppies can smell has been provided by a simple experiment. Puppies usually withdraw from the unpleasant smell of aniseed but, if aniseed is placed on the nipples of the mother, they associate the smell with food

and within a short spell of time will crawl towards the smell.

Observations show that newborn puppies are not attracted to the smell of meat, which is not surprising as their food at this stage is purely milk. However, by three to four weeks, they are excited by a meat smell and will run towards it.

As a pup grows older, its sense of smell increases and all the adult behavioural signs associated with smell gradually develop. It learns the associations of smell with food, sexual encounters, human encounters and other dogs. Much of this behaviour is discussed later in the section.

As with so many other characteristics of dogs,

Left: Scenting plays an important part in the initial encounter between dogs. At first this sniffing is exploratory and sensitive.

Below: Having initially sniffed each other, both parties are still wary and tensely anticipate the next move.

there appear to be great variations between individuals of a breed, although one can make generalizations between breeds. As a species, Pekinese are not generally considered to have an outstanding scenting ability but there is no doubt that some individuals have a quite superb sense of smell. Correspondingly, there are probably some Alsatians with relatively poor senses of smell. In general, we can say that no dog has a poor sense of smell but, in some breeds, the scenting capacity is unusually superb. Much depends on the training the dog has had, the use to which it puts its scenting and the practice it has had in this use.

The scent hunting breeds have superb scenting ability. Legendary amongst them is the Bloodhound, which was developed as a breed with this one facility in mind – the capacity to hunt the scent of man. Many people have the mistaken opinion that the Bloodhound is a vicious creature which hunts the 'blood' of man, eventually finding its quarry and killing it. In fact, quite the opposite is true; Bloodhounds are a very 'soft' breed, unlikely to harm anyone.

Other examples of man's selection of dogs for scent-hunting a quarry are Foxhounds, Beagles, Bassets (for hares), Otterhounds, and Pointers (for game birds). In each case the dog has a particular scent acuity for its specific quarry, reinforced by training, circumstances and by practice. Foxhounds will, on occasion, 'run riot' and go after the scent of badgers or other animals but the scent must be very strong for this to occur and it is generally swiftly curbed.

The single-mindedness of the Foxhound's desire to follow fresh fox scent is almost legendary. It has been known for a fox to double-back completely on its tracks and run head-on through a Foxhound pack. The Foxhounds failed to recognize the fox by sight but continued their chase in exactly the same loop.

The head-shape which seems to be common to most breeds that possess a superb scenting ability is a medium length, deep nose and domed forehead. The head length is not as extreme as is seen with gazehounds.

The breeds whose scenting ability is pre-eminent, could be said virtually to see with their noses. Obviously, the nerve pathway from the nose and eye are quite different and the messages arrive at different areas of the brain but the interpretation which the dog puts upon the message is very similar in both cases.

Vision

Whereas vision is probably the most important of man's orientational senses, it plays a very variable role in dogs, according to the breed. The basic visual mechanism is the same in all dogs but the extent to which it is developed and the use to which it is put varies greatly.

Rays of light enter the eye, pass through the transparent cornea and anterior chamber and then on, through the lens and vitreous body, ultimately to strike the retina. The comparison of the eye and a camera is very valid; the lens of the eye is directly comparable to that in a camera and the retina functions in the same way as the light-sensitive film in the back of the camera. Instead of light rays causing a chemical reaction on the film, they cause chemical changes in the retinal cells of the eye, which result in electrical impulses travelling from these cells up to the optic nerve to the brain. In the still camera the chemical changes are a 'one-off phenomenon' but, in the eye, the changing light patterns and continued response of the retinal cells result in a continuous picture – different from that of movie cameras, where the film is moving to give a series of changing pictures.

When a camera is pointed at a dull object, the diaphragm opens wide to allow more light to enter. Similarly, in the eye, the iris opens wide in

Below: Alsatians are often trained as tracking dogs, most recently in the detection of narcotics. The breed is sometimes labelled as aggressive and vicious, but if it is firmly handled and encouraged to socialize at an early age, there is no reason why an Alsatian should not make a good-tempered and kindly-natured pet.

dull light but produces a more constricted pupil when the light is intense, so that the retinal cells are not damaged or 'over-exposed' by the bright light.

In the camera, the lens is moved to focus so that a clear image results on the film. In the eye, the lens itself is variable in shape and its focal length is altered by muscles which surround it. Studies on the anatomy of the dog's eye have suggested that the point of focus of the image is just in front of the retina. Curiously, this is a similar situation to the point of focus in short-sighted people when they are viewing an object which is located a long way away. It would suggest, therefore, that the image transferred to the brain may be 'fuzzy' or slightly out of focus. Such a mistake of nature is difficult to envisage and it may be that the dog's brain can interpret the image slightly differently from man so that, to the dog, the picture is sharp. A dog certainly does not have such well-developed powers of eye-focusing as man and it may be that dogs just do not need such a 'sharp' picture. It is even possible that their sense of smell complements their fuzzy vision to produce a mentally sharp overall 'visual-olfactory image'.

The light-sensitive cells of the retina are of two types depending on their shape – rods and cones. Rods are concerned with night vision and a dog has proportionately many more rods than cones, which partly explains his excellent ability to see in the dark. A chemical action involving visual purple (a substance that contains Vitamin A)

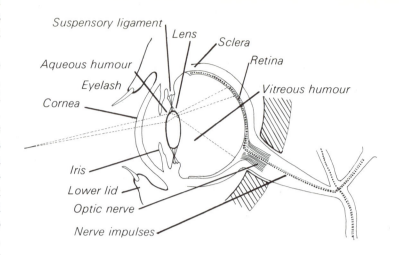

occurs when light shines on the rods and so 'night-blindness' may be an early sign of vitamin A deficiency. Rods are found around the edge of the retina and do have a function in daytime sight, that of peripheral vision. A reflecting layer of cells at the back of the retina, called the tapetum lucidum, aids the rods in their action by reflecting light back on to them and so helps night-time vision. It is this reflecting blanket which shows up when lights shine on a dog's eyes at night.

Daylight 'high intensity' vision is the function of the cones. These are mainly found in the centre

Above: A diagram of a dog's eye showing how an image is imposed on the retina. Vision is less highly developed than hearing in most dogs.

Below: The Irish Wolfhound is the tallest and heaviest of the hounds.

of the retina and are also the retinal cells which are able to react to colour. Colour is important in daylight; it is not important during the night when the rods are activated. Dogs have considerably less cones in comparison to man and most research into colour vision in dogs has concluded that they have either no colour vision capacity or, at best, very little. Obviously it is fairly difficult to determine if dogs can see colours, for what experiment could possibly prove it conclusively? Dogs could be rewarded with food when they choose one colour by pressing on a colour illuminated lever and not rewarded when another colour shows. However, the colour is not the only thing which may have changed; almost certainly the light intensity will vary with the colour and this may be the visual clue which the dog recognizes. Dogs can discriminate light intensity almost as well as man but there seems to be no reason why a dog needs to determine colour. After all, who needs to see that meat is red when you can smell it marvellously through ten thicknesses of newspaper!

Movement, however, is very important in dog vision. A dog is well able to discriminate form once an object is moving, or if the dog itself is moving. It may not notice its owner standing still on the horizon, or a stationary animal but, once either of them move, it is able to discern them, to recognize their form and to act upon this recognition by a behavioural response. It is a well-known fact that Labrador Retrievers (who

Right: This young Retriever was, like all puppies, born blind. After about two weeks its eyes were fully opened and now it can see perfectly.

Below left: Excellent vision is a pre-requisite for good sight-hunting. The Afghan's fast movement matches its visual capacities.

Below right: Dogs see moving objects much more clearly than static ones, so it is likely that this Retriever will catch the ball.

Left: A Pointer shows his deep sensitive nose – the quintessence of scent hunting and vital to his task of scenting out and indicating the presence of game to the hunters.

Right: Clear, bright eyes are a sure sign of a healthy dog.

Below: Pomeranians were developed for their liveliness and great companionship. Originally it was a much larger dog, but selective breeding has reduced its size and it is now recognized as one of the toy dogs.

have relatively poor sight, or, at best, average sight for a dog) are able to see birds that have been shot and are falling from the sky and can retrieve them quickly and accurately. However, if the birds have landed without the dogs seeing the movement of falling, their retrieval is much more inaccurate and lengthy. Movement is obviously important for a predatorial hunter. Dogs need to be able to discern the form of their escaping prey as it moves away and also to keep this sharp visual picture as they move after it. Their perception of shape even improves when they are moving relative to their prey.

Another important factor in vision is the eye placement in the skull and the manner in which this affects binocular vision (that is, the capacity for both eyes to see the same object at once). This varies greatly between breeds. For example, Collies have laterally placed eyes which give them good side vision (useful for watching a large flock of sheep on one side of the head) but poor frontal vision. Collies have no 'stop' (the dip in the skull below and between the eyes) and the high bridge of the nose allows very little overlap of the visual fields of both eyes (this overlap is vital for good binocular vision). Greyhounds, with long noses, have a similar head shape to Collies but they have a more pronounced 'stop' and their eyes are closer together and more forward in the skull. This gives a better overlap for the field of view of each eye – and thus better binocular vision, which is a

Above: The noble Irish Wolfhound is a gentle hunting breed, which is very rarely used for hunting nowadays.

great attribute for accurate focusing on the prey prior to the kill. Greyhounds also have a wide visual range – nearly 200 degrees for each eye. This means that they can see more out of the corner of their eyes than can man. The differences can be likened to that between a normal camera and one with a wide-angle lens. Dogs with deep-set eyes, like Bull Terriers or the Spitz breeds, lose some of their wide angle vision but gain in safety, in that their eyes are less likely to be damaged in fights or when digging.

A real visual refinement is stereoscopic sight – that is, three dimensional visual capacity. In man, this is well advanced but, in most mammals, stereoscopic vision is lacking. Stereoscopic vision has nothing to do with eyeball shape or position but is associated with how the nerve impulses from the half of the retina nearest the nose actually cross over to the other side of the brain; the impulses from the other half of the retina keep to their own side of the brain. This cross-over of impulses allows man to distinguish 'depth' of field – that is, the capacity to tell which objects in a field are close and which are far away, without relying on size to give the clue. Dogs do have this capacity in part but to a much lesser extent than man.

It is, of course, impossible to determine what visual impulses actually 'mean' to a dog. We do know that the nerve impulses terminate in the same area of a dog's brain as they do in man – that is, the visual cortex, an area on either side of the rear of the forebrain. How the dog 'uses' this area of the cortex we cannot tell.

Development of vision

Puppies are born blind – really blind! Not only are their eyelids closed but the visual cortex is so poorly developed at this stage that the pup could make nothing of light stimuli even if its eyes were open. Over the next one or two weeks (often about ten days), the eyes gradually open, as the cells which stick the eyelids together break down. At first, the cornea is often grey and hazy and it is obvious that the pup cannot see well. He is slow to turn his face towards interesting sights and generally appears 'bog-eyed'. Indeed, until he is about three weeks old, light and vision hardly seem to evoke any responses in a pup, who relies much more on sensations of warmth, smell, and noise to find his way around. Even at four weeks old, pups appear to have difficulty in discerning objects which are distant and it is probable that a pup's visual range at this age is only one or two metres.

By six weeks old, pups appear to see well, can discern distant objects and are able to 'intercept' moving objects such as their mother or littermate, who may be moving across their field of view. This shows that by now there is good development of the brain links which connect vision with movement (and its correction). By six weeks, too, the retina is mature in its form and pups show avoidance behaviour when presented with visual danger but precise form discrimination is much slower to develop and pups are not fully visually accurate until they are at least four months old.

All these developments are the result of growth

of nerve cells and improved nerve pathways in the brain. The wiring in a new house can be considered as an analogy. Not only do the wires have to be installed but also the light fittings and switches and finally the connections have to be made – often by trial and error – until the correct switch and light are coupled up and the system works well.

Breed variations in vision

Once again, man has played a major role in selecting and breeding from dogs which have an important visual ability. With Collies and other herding breeds, vision is an important part of their work. Whereas their visual capacities seldom reach those of man, their sight in comparison with most dogs is superb. It is a cruel trick of fate that Collies, Shelties and many other of these herding and sheepdog breeds are often afflicted with developmental eye deformities and other congenital and inherited problems, such as progressive retinal atrophy. Partly, of course, it has been particularly noticed in these breeds because of the importance of vision to them. Any diminution in sight is immediately noticed by owners and breeders.

Although sheepdogs have overall better powers of vision than other dogs, they still have the limitations of canine sight already described. Their capacity to respond to movement, however, is particularly good and they can react to hand signals given by someone standing more than one kilometre (half a mile) away.

Another group of dogs with particularly good vision is the gazehounds. Indeed it is probable that the name Greyhound is a corruption of 'gazehound' although other possibilities for the derivation of the word include *Grais*, meaning Grecian, or the old English word *Grech*, meaning grey. These dogs have excellent sight, in common with Afghans, Whippets, Italian Greyhounds, Deerhounds, Borzois and some other aristocratic breeds – many of which are quite rare. All these dogs have a combination of superb sight and graceful, rapid movement and, even more important, possess the capacity to link the two facilities together to produce an excellent, self-guided missile, which homes on to its prey with incredible precision. These breeds, along with the somewhat exotic and rare Salukis and Irish Wolfhounds, show similar character dispositions. They tend to be rather aristocratic and aloof and often seem to be looking away from human activity, staring to the distant horizon as if they are expecting a hare, elk or other fast prey to appear suddenly. Generally, they are friendly to other dogs but see a cat as natural prey. They are also quite quiet dogs, showing little tendency to bark.

As may be expected from their shape and size, they do need plenty of space and exercise and, with the exception of the Whippet and Italian Greyhound, the opportunity to run flat out over long distances at frequent intervals. It is unfortunate that the larger members of this group need so much exercise and also food, which, with the recent exception of the Afghan, perhaps accounts for them not being popular household pets. In fact, this is a pity, because

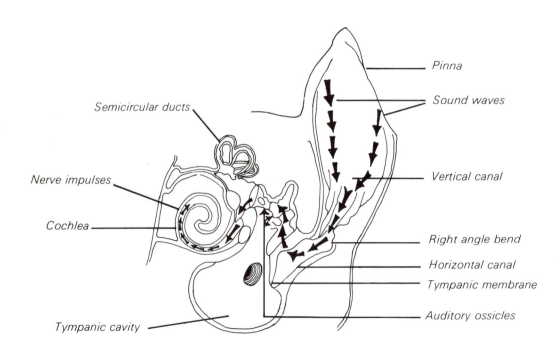

Below: The dog's hearing mechanism. Dogs are able to detect low intensity sound better than human beings and can also hear things which are out of a human's frequency range.

Semicircular ducts

Nerve impulses

Cochlea

Tympanic cavity

Pinna

Sound waves

Vertical canal

Right angle bend

Horizontal canal

Tympanic membrane

Auditory ossicles

Right: His head cocked to one side, this Rhodesian Ridgeback pup is 'all ears'. By putting one ear in front of another, he can more accurately locate a sound source.

Below: A young Alsatian pricks up his ears to catch a maximum of sound waves.

they are exceptionally gentle, well behaved and placid dogs with dignified and quiet habits. On odd occasions, though, they do decide to take lengthy, uninvited trips, disappearing over the horizon in search of 'ethereal hares'.

Hearing

The ability to hear is well developed in the dog and, in some respects, it is much superior to that of man. Man needs hearing to help him communicate but he does not need it to the same extent as does the dog to help him find his prey and to avoid enemies.

The mechanisms of hearing are similar in all mammals. Sound waves are 'collected' by the pinna (or ear flap) and are then channelled down the ear canal. The canal has a right-angle bend in dogs but this does little to reduce the intensity of sound waves. The waves strike the ear-drum (or tympanic membrane), which is made to move by them. This movement is then transmitted by three connecting bones, the hammer, anvil and stirrup (so-called because of their shape), to a tightly coiled tube known as the cochlea. This mechanism is much like the beat on a drum – only in reverse. In the case of the ear, the sound waves move the drum skin, which in turn pushes against the drum-stick.

The cochlea is filled with a fluid which, when moved by the stirrup, causes tiny hairs (distributed along the length of the cochlea) to move. As the hairs move, they set up tiny electrical impulses in cells at their base. These impulses then travel up to the brain.

Dogs can hear low frequency sound waves

about as well as man but, when the higher frequency sound range is entered, the dog has much greater acuity of hearing. Indeed, not only can dogs hear better than man when the pitch of sound gets higher but they can continue to hear sound much higher in the pitch than man. Shrill squeaks, that we could not hear, will be detected by the dog. A dog's upper limit of hearing is in the range of 30,000 cycles per second whereas man hears nothing over 20,000 cycles per second. This explains the silent dog-whistles to which a dog will react.

It is uncertain how well dogs can discriminate between sounds of different pure pitch but it is probable that they can do no better than man in distinguishing one 'note' from another. The limit of this discrimination is probably only about one musical tone.

The range of sound and its intensity are only the minor part of a dog's hearing. A far more important part is the 'character' of sound. The quality of sound to us may be typified by the difference between a clarinet note and the noise of the pop singer, although both may be producing the same note on the musical scale. The difference to a dog is that between the footfall of his owner at the door and that of a stranger. One noise evokes excited squeaks and the other aggressive growls. It is, of course, very difficult to research the dog's capacity to recognize sounds of different quality but our own practical experience will tell us that dogs do seem to have a superb capacity in this respect. The recognition of not only the sound of cars of the same make but an individual car's sound is easy for many dogs and explains the early warning which many household pets give of their owner's arrival home.

During the last World War many dog owners noticed that their dogs were able to hear sounds such as air raid sirens and bomber planes long before they could. Dogs soon learnt that specific sounds were associated with well known activities, like a rush for the air raid shelter, and they would be half way to the shelter before their owner even heard the warning. This behaviour is difficult to explain and many people have tried to do so by considering the possibility of telepathy. More probably, the explanation lies in the fact that the siren or bomber plane was emitting, as well as the sounds audible to man, some sounds which had a pitch above that of man's range. The dog, however, will have been able to hear them because its audio capacity in the high ranges is not only wider than man's but also more accurate. By the time the sound threshold had

Below: Something has clearly caught the attention of this group of Rough Collies. All are watching and listening attentively, their heads cocked to one side so they do not miss a sound.

risen high enough for man to detect it, the dog had heard quite enough to tell him to get moving, as the family did when they heard that sound!

Often one hears dog owners remark that their dogs can understand every word they are saying. In a sense, they are correct. Man's spoken words not only convey a meaning to another human but the way those words are spoken carries a clue of the speaker's mood. Usually, when we say, for example, 'I can't stand that man', we say the words in a way that emphasizes the meaning of the words themselves; we speak in a louder, sharper and more varied pitch than usual. Dogs detect these auditory clues without understanding the meaning of the words. Furthermore, we may suddenly stand up, raise our shoulders and move our arms when we are annoyed. All these are actions which speak louder than words to the dog and are likely to tell him to 'slink off to the garden and chew his bone – his master's in a bad mood'.

A simple experiment will demonstrate just how important the tone of voice is to a dog. Usually, a dog owner will speak to his dog in a deep, gruff, annoyed voice when he is reprimanding him for something, and in a bright, light and higher-pitched voice when asking, for example, 'Do you want your supper?' But try saying these (or similar well-recognized phrases) to a dog while using the reversed tone of voice. The dog will almost certainly react to the tone and not the words although he may be misled by the words 'supper' and 'bed' which he knows and recognizes. Unless the words are said in a very changed way, he may be uncertain and just end up staring at you, mystified!

Development of hearing

Like vision, hearing seems to be totally lacking at birth. Very young pups have flattened ears with closed ear canals. By the tenth day after birth, the ear flaps begin to be more independent of the head, the ear canal opens and pups show positive reactions to sounds. These reactions are very difficult to investigate. If, for example, one tries to determine whether a sound is linked to a food response reaction, there is the problem of trying to eliminate the smell stimulus which will also accompany the food. Sophisticated behaviour experiments do suggest that pups can hear when they are ten days old and, at eleven days react to food if a 'food sound' is made. By the seventeenth day, they have also learnt to respond by withdrawal to sounds linked to pain. It is no accident that the 'alerting sound' of the agitated mother is a high-pitched squeak. Once again, the enhanced audio capacity in the higher pitches is demonstrated.

Probably, puppies do not have any inherent understanding of the meaning of sounds. They

Above: This beautifully groomed Bedlington Terrier looks as delicate as a poodle, but is a tough breed.

Below: Scottish Terriers are elegant when well groomed. They are very alert but can be aggressive.

Bottom: The Jack Russell Terrier was named after Parson Jack Russell, a member of the British Kennel Club.

do not have an inborn sense, for example, that the mother's growl means, 'No, leave me alone. Your teeth are too sharp for my nipples.' They have to learn this with the association that a growl goes with a nip on the neck. They do, however, seem to have an inborn capacity to respond actively to any sound, whether familiar or not. This response is usually just one of waking up, sitting up and generally alerting themselves. It is difficult to imagine how this response could be 'learnt'. It will, in fact, be over-ruled by other stronger stimuli, such as intense hunger or extreme fatigue; very hungry pups will continue eating even if their mother is barking loudly!

Many pups, and some adult dogs, too, behave in a very positive way to strange sounds. They cock their heads on one side, prick up their ears and furrow their brows. The ear-cocking is an attempt to 'collect' more sound in the ear flaps; the brow-wrinkling which goes with this is not analogous to the worry or uncertainty seen in humans with furrowed brows but is the effect of the muscles cocking the ear flaps. Turning the head to one side is a method of locating more accurately the source of the sound. By doing this, they are putting one ear in front of the other, so that the sounds reach the two ears at slightly different times. The brain is able to detect this difference and to compute the source of the sound much more accurately than man.

It is important not to mix together the sense of sound and the behavioural activity of making sound. In pups the two are quite separate. Newborn pups make mewing or squeaking noises which they cannot hear from one another. It may be that they can hear themselves, probably through the skull bones (although it is most unlikely that it is important at this age), and certainly their mother can hear them. To her, their noise is an important signal.

Congenital deafness is not uncommon. It is often seen in the Dalmatian and in White Bull Terriers, where it would seem that the gene for lack of pigment is somehow linked to that for lack· of hearing. However, it does not commonly occur in other white breeds, like the West Highland White, so the mode of inheritance is also a breed phenomenon. Congenitally deaf pups are an embarrassment and danger both to themselves and society. Once deafness is recognized in a pup (not always easy until it is three or four weeks old), the pup should be humanely destroyed by a veterinarian.

Variations in hearing between breeds do exist but they are rarely obvious. In general, the breeds with long pricked ear flaps have better hearing than flop-eared breeds with excessive hair round the flaps. Thus, good hearing is an attribute of Foxhounds, Greyhounds, Alsatians and many terriers, while some Spaniels, Poodles and Shih Tzus may not hear so well in comparison.

Below: This terrier, with its pricked ears, has sharp hearing.

Above: This curious Hairless breed – the Mexican Hairless Dog – originated in Mexico, where it is probably suited to the climate

Sensation and pain

Humans can recognize several touch and pain sensations. An initial light touch, pressure, joint movement in the limbs, heat, cold and eventually pain are all quite separate sensations which we feel and to which we react. It is probable that dogs can feel these separate sensations too, but we really don't know this for certain. Much of our knowledge about sensation in dogs is purely observation, with just a little bit of anatomy and science. The rest is guesswork and so we have to be particularly wary of the old trap of putting human thoughts into animal actions.

We do know that dogs differ from humans in certain points with respect to the pathways of the nerves which carry these sensations. Dogs, like cats, have a very special nerve pathway which humans do not possess. It consists of interconnecting nerves which are able rapidly to convey the sensation of fine touch. Dogs are particularly sensitive around the face, the eyebrows, chin and muzzle; this sensitivity enables them to build up another aspect of their mental picture of an object. As well as being able to see it, smell it and sense it, they can feel its texture very accurately because of this extra-refined touch sensation. Perhaps this explains why a dog's first contact with a strange object is not only to smell it but also to investigate it by touching it with his face. Dogs have specialized tactile, or sinus, hairs – the whiskers – round the muzzle. These long, strong hairs are surrounded at their base by a very complex system of blood vessels and nerves which are an efficient way of changing movement into nerve impulses. Probably, these whiskers are involved in this special touch capacity and have nothing to do with telling the dog how close he is to objects.

Some experiments conducted in the United States of America showed that even newborn pups can recognize surfaces of different textures. They can also recognize heat and cold, as proved by the fact that they move away from cold and very hot surfaces and crawl towards comfortable, warm ones. Adult dogs also have a fine capacity to distinguish heat and cold. The fact that dogs are capable of withstanding extremely cold environments does not mean that they don't feel the cold, or that they are being stoical. It just means that the sensation of cold is not especially important to them and they do not show a particularly strong behavioural reaction. Certainly, they are more adaptable to cold environments than man and their tolerable temperature range is much greater than man's – definitely starting much lower and probably extending slightly less into higher temperatures.

Pain

The very word 'pain' is an emotive one. Many people believe that dogs do not feel pain in the same *way* as humans. Perhaps that is true, but what such people really mean is that they think

Right: The whiskers around this Irish Wolfhound's muzzle are sensitive, as they are in all breeds.

dogs don't feel pain to the same *extent* as humans – and that is probably incorrect. Dogs do not have the same highly developed nerve tracts for carrying pain sensations as those of man. However, they react just as quickly to an unpleasant stimulus.

It is extremely difficult to determine what stimuli are really painful to dogs. Like humans, dogs react more violently to a painful stimulus when they know it is coming, than if they are unaware that it is about to occur. If a person is held down by a group of torturers and told that a red hot poker is going to be placed on his back, he may faint at the thought or scream in real pain when a slight prick is given to his back. But the same person could accidentally spear himself with a garden implement and hardly feel a thing. This is largely true for dogs, too.

A dog, having previously had its toenails cut too short, may on the next occasion howl or bark as soon as the owner approaches him with the clippers. Yet the same dog may scratch and cut itself severely on brambles and gravel when out on a romp chasing after rabbits and behave as if nothing had happened. So much depends on the association the dog has between the pain caused and the circumstances which surround the painful stimulus. It is, however, wise to work on the theory that dogs can feel pain to the same degree and with the same psychological connotations as man.

There is a popular misconception that 'pedigree' dogs are more sensitive to pain, more susceptible to disease, and more 'highly strung' than mongrels. This is not true. There are Crufts champions as tough as old boots and scrub mongrels as shy and delicate as field mice. So much depends on upbringing, socialization and the life the dog leads. In many cases, mongrels have longer with their litter mates and meet more animals or other dogs, as well as unusual situations in the street, than do household pet pedigree dogs. This may well make them more generally relaxed and resilient but it will not make them less sensitive to pain than more closely-confined dogs. With regard to disease, the distemper virus does not ask to see the pedigree before it decides to attack!

Locomotion and balance

It is easy to forget how important the senses are to movement, until, that is, the light is switched out, noises cease, smell disappears, or, most important, our sense of balance is lost.

Movement and the fine control of motion are vital to the dog. Compared to a dog, the speed of a horse is brutish power with little fine control. At the end of a race, a horse needs time to slow down, while a dog can stop dead in its tracks. At all times, it possesses the power and control to deviate its movement, often with precise accuracy. These facilities are those of predatory animals – animals who not only need to pursue their prey but also direct its movement, so they can corner and kill it, often when the prey is also moving. Yet if things get tough, the pursuer must have the agility and speed to beat a hasty retreat so he is around to fight another day.

Above: Killing imaginary prey is a much-played game by most dogs. Note the finely controlled balance of these Italian Greyhounds as they indulge in a mock battle over a scarf.

Right: All dogs can swim, but Labradors seem particularly at home in water. Their heavy coats shed water well.

Man, in directing the form and capacities of his dog by selective breeding, has produced breeds with tremendous variations in their movement – the elegant striding Saluki, the waddling Bulldog and the prancing Toy Poodle. These breed variations in gait are one of the most interesting aesthetic features of dogs and a point of great importance in the show ring. Some breeds, such as the Dalmatian, have a beautiful striding gait which, although not quite a trot, is akin to the horse's movement and is a most natural complement to the horse and carriage, a use to which the Dalmatians were put in the nineteenth century. Few terriers or toy breeds have a graceful or pleasing movement – but they were not bred for this. Most terriers have a very stilted, jerky, tripping walk which can be most inelegant at speed. Because of their short body length, they have little ability to stride out and often two feet remain in contact with the ground at even quite fast speeds. This is inefficient in terms of locomotory energy and sometimes terriers will compensate when running at speed by using three legs – actually holding up one hind leg for several paces and then putting it down and changing to the other hind leg. Sometimes a hind leg is spared in this way because of a joint or bone defect (such as a slipping kneecap, which is

Right: Borzois, or Russian Wolfhounds, are extremely elegant and regal, with a quiet disposition. Like other large dogs they require considerable food, exercise and space.

common in smaller breeds) but when both hind legs are favoured indiscriminately then this can be considered as normal.

The gallop of the Greyhound, Deerhound or Alsatian is a rapid method of locomotion, where the body is propelled through the air in a series of low leaps. This movement is dissimilar from the gallop of the horse, as the dog has a much more flexible back. The hind feet are brought so far forwards by the back concavity that they land on either side of the fore-feet and well in front of them. Unlike the terrier, at any one time there may be no feet at all remaining in contact with the ground and any slight damage or pain in one foot can reduce the dog's speed tremendously.

Not only is movement important in itself but the way a dog moves and also the positions it adopts are important for communication with other dogs, as will be considered later.

For pure speed alone, the Greyhound is a difficult dog to beat. Fit Greyhounds can easily maintain speeds of about 59 k.p.h. (37 m.p.h.) for perhaps as far as one kilometre (half a mile). Whippets can average 56 k.p.h. (35 m.p.h.) over short distances and may sometimes be faster than Greyhounds on short courses. There are some unconfirmed reports of tremendous speeds for Salukis – up to 75 k.p.h. (45 m.p.h.). Certainly Salukis, Afghans and Borzois are not only fast but possess tremendous powers of deviation and

44

jumping while continuing to maintain speed. Greyhounds are also pretty good at turning and dodging when they are coursing. Much of this accuracy of movement stems from the dog steering itself and using its tail as a 'rudder'. If one of these breeds has a tail injury or has part of the tail amputated, then its speed round bends is seriously impeded.

The endurance of dogs is another amazing factor. The long-distance capacities of Eskimo sledge dogs are well documented. One such was a 127-hour journey of 1080 kilometres (675 miles) undertaken in 1925 by twenty relays of dog teams and drivers between Nenana and Nome (Alaska) to deliver vital diphtheria antitoxin. Most dogs are likely to last out longer than their owners when hunting or retrieving and, in quite an average day's rough shooting, a gun dog may commonly travel 112 kilometres (70 miles), much of this over rough ground or through undergrowth. Sheep dogs also travel tremendous distances in the course of a day's work – 160 kilometres (100 miles) per day for about six consecutive weeks was recorded for one Collie.

The scale of a dog's movement can be almost unbelievable. Greyhounds cover about five metres (18 feet) in a single stride when racing and Alsatians can 'long jump' over six metres (20 feet). These attainments are phenomenal when one considers them in comparison with man. A Dachshund, only 20 cm (eight ins) to the shoulder, can easily jump three or four times its own height from a standing position, which is the equivalent of a man jumping six metres (20 feet) in the air. Similarly, dogs are usually happy to jump down from even greater heights.

Climbing is not an attribute which we generally consider very well developed in dogs but some individuals and some breeds in particular are good climbers. The rather rare and probably primitive Basenji has a good capacity to climb, as do some other breeds like the American Coonhound. The dog does not have good climbing apparatus, like the retractive and sharp claws of cats, but can sometimes compensate by grasping the trunk of a tree by wrapping its legs around it.

Manipulation of objects is not a propensity which is shown by most dogs, although there are some who are quite dexterous with their feet and use them for performing quite delicate operations. Dogs have little control of individual toes, like humans have with their fingers, and can only use their feet as a single force. Performing Toy Poodles can hold balls between their feet and even roll them along but they are using the whole foot and have no capacity to bend their digits to grasp objects as do humans or monkeys. Puppies sometimes use their paws for batting one another during a play-fight, but this behaviour is rarely continued and developed in later life, except

perhaps to hold down a bone while chewing it or to extend a paw to 'explore' some strange creature or object without making prolonged contact by mouth.

What dogs lack in dexterity with their paws, they make up for by the efficient use of their mouths. Behaviourally, the mouth is an important part of the body. Its strength is tremendous; not only can dogs crack enormous bones, kill animals and carry objects but they can support the whole weight of their bodies by their mouths. Dogs use their mouths for carrying, and some mothers commonly move their puppies around by grasping them by the scruff of their necks and lifting them in their jaws. The

Above: Many dogs are adept at balancing and some, such as this Cocker Spaniel will 'beg' in this way, without having been taught or encouraged.

retrieving breeds are most developed in this carrying use of the mouth and are 'soft-mouthed', in that they can carry shot game delicately without bruising the flesh.

All dogs can swim – a capacity which is inherent even in pups. They propel themselves along by a striding motion of all four legs, producing the stroke known as the 'dog paddle'. The enjoyment from swimming and contact with the water seems to vary tremendously and is mainly an individual love, or hate! Some breeds, such as the Newfoundland, seem more at home in water than out of it; indeed, Newfoundlands have a long history of use by sailors and sea-shore dwellers for sea rescue, and their endurance in cold, heavy seas is legendary. Another 'water' breed is the Chesapeake Bay Retriever, which was developed (probably with some mixing with Newfoundland blood) for retrieval of water fowl. Both these breeds have a remarkably dense and oily coat which gives them a distinct advantage in cold sea water. It is hardly surprising that the Labrador Retriever is also an accomplished swimmer, as it was developed in Newfoundland for dragging drift nets full of fish to the sea-shore for easy beaching. A more surprising natural 'water' breed is the Poodle; that is, not the Miniature and Toy Poodles but the Standard Poodle, which is an excellent game retriever and works well in the water.

Behaviour

The mechanisms by which the dog is aware of its environment, how it is notified of the presence of other animals, its basic movements and the use of its body – all these have to be considered together in the enormous subject of dog behaviour.

The subject has fascinated zoologists and psychologists for centuries; it has fascinated man in general ever since he started to associate with dogs. We have closely domesticated the dog and so our opportunities to study his behaviour are frequent. This is particularly interesting, because the dog shows strong behaviour patterns not only to other dogs but also towards humans. In fact, he is so domesticated that he has accepted a human as part of his 'social round', sometimes developing a greater behavioural bond with humans than with members of his own species.

Several very important and strong behavioural patterns are shown by dogs – eating and drinking behaviour (ingestion), sexual behaviour, attitude to puppies (maternal) and communication with other dogs and humans. A study of these will enable us to understand much of what our dogs do, why they perform certain actions and show different behaviour traits.

Besides these 'basic function' aspects of behaviour, there are many complex and often deep-seated characteristics of dogs which are difficult to categorize simply. It is these activities which vary so much from breed to breed and from individual dog to individual dog – and which give each dog its own highly specific character.

Before launching into the deep waters of dog behaviour, it is useful to define one or two terms which behaviourists use so that we can more precisely understand the relevance of some canine activity.

An activity which always results from the same stimulus is called a reflex. Reflexes can be very simple and basic – such as scratching an itch or eating when hungry. Very often the dog's need to obey a stimulus is so basic that the dog may not even know it is happening. If a flea bites a sleeping dog, the dog may scratch the itch without even waking. In this case, the brain is not involved in the process, the whole reflex is subconscious and the nerve pathways which bring about the reflex are quite local.

Most reflexes however do need consciousness. Dogs cannot eat, drink or bite when they are asleep, for the brain is involved in these

Above: As they bask in the sun, these Whippets belie their true character, for they are extraordinarily agile and active and are extremely fast movers.

Right: The 'on-the-back' pose is a common play position for any dog. Play is an important part of dog behaviour and development.

processes. Most behaviour is just a complex mixture of different reflexes; rabbit-hunting behaviour is a complicated hotch-potch involving sight, smell and hearing as the stimuli, and movement as the activity which brings about communication with the dog's running, jaw movements, retrieval and, ultimately, appetite and eating.

An activity can be either inherent or learnt. Inherent behaviour is born with the dog, a simple example being the desire to eat. Usually, inherited behaviour patterns are the simple ones – eating, drinking, territory marking and so on. Even the degree of intensity of these behaviours can be inherited; Dachshunds are greedy, Setters are not. Sometimes quite complex behaviour activities are inherited or, to be more exact, the capacity to develop these behaviours is inherited. For instance, Collies are born with the inherent capacity to herd sheep but it takes practice and opportunity to develop that potential and 'bring-out' the full depth of herding behaviour in the dog.

Other behaviours are learnt. These are sometimes called acquired behavioural activities. No dog is born with the tendency to beg for food from its master and yet, once the dog has learnt that begging brings food, it will regularly show this behavioural activity. This is an example of an association but it is not as classic as Pavlov's important experiments in connection with learning in dogs. His experimental dogs were

Above: This magnificent Bulldog obviously believes it is entitled to creature comforts.

Despite their aggressive appearance, Bulldogs are docile and affectionate.

always fed at mid-day and, when the bells in St. Petersburg (now Leningrad) chimed twelve o'clock, the dogs always salivated in readiness for their food. The dogs had associated feeding with the sound of the bells chiming and this conditioned reflex was so strong that the ringing of the bells at any time, even without feeding the dogs, brought about the salivation.

A mistake commonly made is to think that a dog is always showing intelligence, when it is only showing a conditioned reflex. True, complex reflex behaviour may be associated with something which we can interpret as close to human intelligence but the two should still be separated. Canine 'intelligence' and the working of a dog's mind will be discussed towards the end of this chapter.

Another tendency that we indulge in is to put human thoughts into a dog's behaviour. It is a natural reaction, when dealing with an animal that can get so close to us, to try to get 'under the dog's skin' and consider it in human terms. Using human emotions to describe an animal's activity is called 'anthropomorphism' (Greek, meaning 'in the form of a man') and it is a mistake that behaviourists are always trying to avoid. Even to say that 'a dog is fond of bones' is a comment open to dispute. What we should really say about the bone-seeking dog is that it shows a variety of behaviour reactions which we interpret as pleasure when it is given a bone. Such reactions may be tail wagging, jumping up to get at the

bone and whimpering or barking in anticipation.

The biggest misinterpretations are often made when we describe the reflexes and reactions which accompany pain and discomfort. The problems which surround the study of pain reflexes in dogs have already been described and to interpret the reactions which dogs show to unpleasant stimuli is a behaviourist's jungle.

Anthropomorphism, however, is a pleasure to many dog owners! They wish to believe that they know how their dog's brain is working and they want to put their thoughts into the dog's actions. Coupled with the pleasure derived from being the pack-leader and gaining submission from a dog, it is one of the greatest pleasures of dog-owning.

Eating and drinking

Eating and drinking are such basic functions that it is easy to forget that there is an important form of behaviour associated with ingestion.

Dogs don't worry about their figures; they don't stop to chew and to savour their food, nor do they eat savoury things before sweet; they just eat and eat. Dogs in the wild are accustomed to feast and famine. Having killed their prey – sometimes alone but more often with the rest of the pack – they will gorge themselves until quite satiated. This behaviour of making the best possible use of available food is typical of predatorial animals because, unlike grazing animals, the food is not always present. Most household pet dogs retain such behaviour and so the owners must regulate the volume of food they receive in order to avoid obesity. Dogs can also exist for very long periods without feeding (a period of two months survival without food is recorded) and tolerate quite extended periods of fast with no obvious ill effects.

The quantity of food eaten by a dog will also vary according to his company. The spirit of competition is very obvious in feeding dogs and a slow feeder will usually eat a greater quantity of food quicker if he is fed with others. Even if a solitary puppy (or an adult) is satiated with food, he will start eating again if food and other puppies are brought into contact with him. Curiously enough, this increased eating behaviour, when in a group, does not mean that pack dogs eat more than solitary dogs; the extra eating stimulus wears off after a short while.

Much of this 'king of the feeding bowl' behaviour is wrapped up with pack dominance and aggressive behaviour in a group of dogs. Often it is the dominant pack leader who corners the majority of the food.

Consequently it is usually he (or more rarely she) who is the biggest and strongest in the group, and care has to be taken that the dominated dogs or pups are not so pushed out by stronger peers that they do not grow well. Giving several feeding bowls to a group of dogs will help.

The 'dog-and-bone' behaviour is an interesting example of social dominance which can be so pronounced as to become the classical 'dog-in-the-manger' attitude. A dominant dog in the pack usually chooses his own bone and fights off would-be thieves. If you give a dog a bone and he growls at you when you approach him, he is displaying exactly the same behaviour and is treating you as another member of the pack. The important thing is that you can, if you wish, remove that bone from him. If his growling and teeth-baring put you off then he has won the food dominance battle. Food dominance, however, does not necessarily make him dominant over you in all things but it is a good start in the pack order, so it is important that you win this battle and take the bone away from him, even if he growls, whilst being prepared to retaliate if he tries to bite. But do not keep on doing this and do not tease him by removing his bone just to exhibit your dominance. If you keep reinforcing your dominance, you will eventually make the dog cowed, spiritless and distrustful.

Puppies and feeding

Searching for food is virtually the first behavioural action shown by a newborn puppy and, once he has found the teat, the urge to suckle is tremendous. This desire is an example of

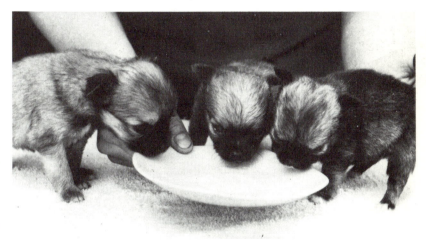

Top: Pups may have to be pushed towards a feeding bowl as they often tend to back away.

Above: Three long-coated Chihuahuas are given their first feed of milk and breakfast cereal.

Below: A puppy can be encouraged to take its first feed by offering it on a finger.

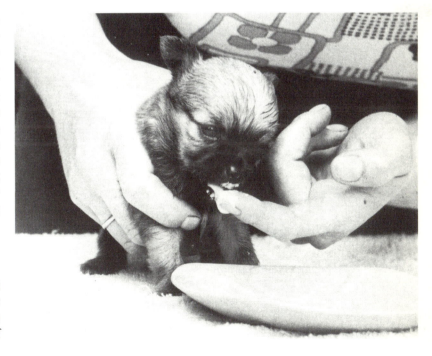

Above: Active large dogs, such as this Alsatian, need lots of food.

Above right: Smaller dogs need careful measured feeding to avoid obesity.

Below: Suckling may continue for a time after a pup has been weaned.

innate behaviour; no-one taught the pup to suck, it is just a basic instinct common to all puppies. As always, there are variations between individuals in this respect and some rather weak, often premature, pups may have to be held against the teat to give them time to grasp it in their mouths and commence suckling. Pups of some breeds can be rather slow to feed and do not show a strong ingestive drive. Poor feeding is rarely a problem in the robust breeds, such as the Labrador, but can be marked in some of the toy breeds, such as the Cavalier King Charles, particularly when they have got past the suckling stage and commence lapping.

Vigorous suckling is seen in puppies showing a strong hunger drive but is not entirely related to the fullness of the belly! Puppies do show so-called non-nutritional suckling; that is, they remain fastened to the nipple even when they have full stomachs and are falling asleep. Dozing off and eventually slipping off the teat may be enough to wake them up, at which point they start suckling again. Non-nutritional suckling can be so intense it can be classed as a vice, as shown when puppies suckle one another's tails or navels. It can also be a sign that pups are not getting enough food from the mother and, if this happens after they are three weeks old, it should be taken as an indication on the part of the owner to start additional feeding.

Right: A plastic washing-up bowl makes a satisfactory feeding bowl for this Great Dane bitch. Judging by the teeth marks, it is also used as a plaything.

Below: Although puppies have to develop a keen competitive spirit to ensure a good feed, the bowl should be large enough to assure a place for all. This one is not!

Above: This young puppy is happy to feed from its bowl, but will still suckle for comfort.

Below: Bones can help prevent tooth decay and mouth disease as well as provide essential vitamins.

Along with suction, the movements of a pup at the teat are to rhythmically pummel the mammary gland with the fore-feet, to nose the gland periodically and also to pull back the head while still holding the teat in the mouth. All these motions are designed to extract milk efficiency and to act as a stimulus for the mother to let more milk down into the nipple. By two weeks of age, all these actions have led to tremendous development of the neck and shoulder muscles of the pup which shows as a thick neck and a pronounced crest behind the head.

Even in newborn puppies, the competitive spirit has entered into feeding. The strongest puppies will fight for the full teats (often the rear ones) and if a pup finds his teat drying up he will leave it and try to displace a litter-mate from a teat which is still giving plenty of milk. Survival of the fittest is the first rule of nature.

Lapping does not seem to be instinctive behaviour and some puppies are very slow to lap. The natural stimulus for pups is probably the behaviour of the bitch to vomit up for the pups. This is sometimes seen in pet bitches but is not universal behaviour by any means. Pups will often lick the face and mouth of the bitch who then vomits semi-solid, partly digested food. The pups lap up the vomit by extending their tongues. This is a quite different procedure to suckling, when the tongue is curled into a spoon-shape so

it almost surrounds the nipple like a tube. Some pups are slow to learn to lap; holding their noses in contact with the food causes them to choke and dip their lips and nose. The food 'reward' is then the stimulus which gets them lapping. Under natural circumstances, it is probably a hunger drive, which would reinforce the stimulus to lap; poor lappers would soon find that there was need to develop the habit as the milk supply gradually faded.

However, puppies will continue to suckle for a long time even when semi-solid and solid additional foods are provided. Much of this suckling drive may be a desire for contact with the bitch; this is part of the care-seeking behaviour which we shall be discussing later. When the pups are six or seven weeks old, most bitches are unwilling to let them suck for even very short spaces of time and, although the pups may chase the dam and search for her mammary glands, she will often run away from them, growl or play in an attempt to divert them.

Puppies use their ingestive behaviour as a method of exploring their environment. This 'feeding exploration' continues in later life. Commonly, once an adult dog has smelt, seen and touched an object, it will explore further by biting it and tasting it. There are few foods, indeed few objects, which pups will not at least try to eat, including wood, bones, newspaper, earth and nearly all vegetable or animal matter. This means that great care has to be taken with poisons or potentially poisonous and dangerous substances, such as certain plants, paints (both wet and dry), powders, mineral substances and objects like electric light flexes. A puppy's powers of ingestive discrimination are very poor!

Food discrimination and abnormal ingestive behaviour

Dogs are generally indiscriminate feeders and, whereas much research has been conducted into the palatibility of various feeds, the results are certainly not clear cut.

Although essentially carnivorous and therefore committed meat-eaters, dogs also eat a tremendous variety of foods, often with great relish. These dietary idiosyncrasies tend to be very individual: the Pekinese who has an insatiable penchant for oranges or the Cocker Spaniel who loves peanuts. Usually it is the pet dog who develops these cravings, presumably because he has had the opportunity to explore exotic foods and flavours which are more usually the province of humans. It is rare to find much extensive non-carnivorous behaviour in dogs kept in non-pet situations, such as Foxhound packs. As will be discussed again later, dogs are very much creatures of habit and this extends to their feeding behaviour. They are perfectly

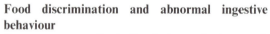

happy to eat the diet to which they have become accustomed day in and day out.

In general, dogs prefer salty meat or savoury, flavoured foods and will often shun sweet or acrid foods. There are obvious exceptions to this: garlic and onion, for example, appear to be particularly attractive to dogs and are always worth trying as inclusions in the diet of a poor feeder.

Although dogs will happily eat meat which is certainly not fresh, they will occasionally shun flesh which is patently stinking. Dogs seem quite happy to eat all meats raw and, with the possible exception of liver or meat suspected of being contaminated or full of parasites, there is much to be said for feeding it raw as some vitamins are not heat-stable and so are partly or completely destroyed by cooking.

People never cease to be amazed and revolted by the capacity and desire of dogs to eat substances which, to humans at least, are repulsive. It is beyond me to explain these desires or to understand what it is about these unsavoury substances which excite dogs. A common occurrence is a dog scavenging in dustbins for rotten food and seeking such delicacies as long-since dead birds, hedgehogs or farm animals. Similarly, a high proportion of dogs will eat cow or sheep muck, garden compost or rotten leaves with relish.

Although the term 'depraved appetite' is often used to describe this sort of activity, it is so common in dogs and occurs in so widespread a dog population that it cannot really be considered abnormal. Some people have tried to explain this behaviour by suggesting that the dog is somehow (quite unconsciously) 'recognizing' that it is deficient in a mineral or trace element which is present in the material. There is little scientific evidence to support such a hypothesis although rotten meat and faeces do contain lots of vitamins from the B groups. Sometimes giving raw liver reduces these tendencies, but equally, sometimes it does not. More worrying and aesthetically unpleasant for owners is the dog who persistently eats dog faeces – either that of other dogs or his own. This also may be treated by feeding raw liver, although it is possible that boredom is the major factor which causes this unsavoury behaviour.

With the exception of the last type of behaviour, there is little risk of parasites being contracted by such practices, although many people attribute parasites to this cause.

The habit of grass-eating in dogs is curious, poorly understood and difficult to explain. Many dogs – both wild and highly domesticated – do this and it is not an indication that a dog has become more domesticated or is losing his canine behaviour. The grass either passes through the dog in an undigested form or is vomited back,

sometimes with worms, which has led some authorities to suggest that grass-eating is an attempt by the dog to rid himself of worms either through vomiting or by inducing a mild diarrhoea. But, some parasite-free dogs eat grass while others, with worms, never do.

Drinking

Dogs take in about half their daily requirement of water within their food. The rest is taken in as desired, often in about six to ten drinking sessions per day. There seem few important behavioural patterns associated with drinking, the function being purely to replace efficiently water lost in the urine and faeces, and during breathing and sweating.

Some dogs prefer liquids other than water, such as tea or even coffee, when offered such luxuries by their owners. As with food, however, a dog will commonly drink the liquid to which it has become accustomed.

The habit of drinking filthy ditch water, either instead of, or even in preference to, clean water is inexplicable. Possibly, sometimes a more earthy flavour is more interesting to a dog than bland water, although it would seem more likely that it is just that the dog is thirsty when out on a walk and any fluid is acceptable to quench his thirst.

Below: Puppies do not have control of their own elimination until they are several weeks old. During this time, they are tended by their mother, as shown by this Jack Russell Terrier bitch, who is licking her pup to encourage it to urinate.

Above: Even when a puppy is ten weeks old, a mother will occasionally ingest its faeces. This is all part of the 'cleaning-up' behaviour which accompanies maternal activity.

Elimination behaviour

Almost as important as ingestion, the behaviour which accompanies the basic functions of faecal excretion and urination is well-developed in dogs and linked to sexual behaviour and communication – two subjects to be considered later.

For the dog, elimination is not only just a method of getting rid of waste products, it is deeply tied in with communication. Members of other packs can tell what dogs have passed that way, what sex they are, even what stage of the sexual cycle bitches are currently undergoing. Male dogs, in particular, mark out their territory by urinating and defecating and can receive information about other dogs by investigating their waste products. This marking is part of the roaming route taken by male dogs who often travel a circuitous journey in their daily tracks. Such daily 'route marches' are very important to male dogs and are a major part of the stray dog's life and system of communication, as he meets other male strays who join him to check around the pillars and posts. The purpose of these male groups is obvious as one observes them: during the route they may get the scent of a bitch on heat, whereupon they will attempt to seek her out and mate her. The first important reason for these routes then, is to check that no bitches in heat are left unmated.

The sites a dog chooses for elimination are not arbitrary. He or she follows quite a well-set routine and an owner can do much to dictate the pattern. Once the sites have been set, it is difficult to dissuade a dog from returning to them. A large proportion of the eliminative siting is reliant on scent. This is why it is important for puppies to be supervized in elimination during the house training period, to make sure the place chosen is not the lounge carpet for, once it is established, the puppy will tend to return to that site and the scent of it will be an attraction to visiting dogs.

In adult dogs, the leg-cocking behaviour of males is bound up with marking territories, as it means the urine scent can be deposited at nose level. Most adult male dogs cock their legs although some never do, even though they may be sexually active. Controlled to a great extent by the male sex hormones, the leg-cocking behaviour is nevertheless definitely learnt from other dogs. If a normal leg-cocking adult male is castrated, he may lose this tendency; equally, he may not always do so, which proves that it is not simply a sexual characteristic. The leg-cocking behaviour is so strong in some dogs that it continues despite amazing obstacles. There are several cases on record where dogs have either lost a hind leg, had one amputated or damaged and yet continue to cock the *good* leg! This means that they have to lift themselves off the ground in a sort of handstand position and balance in this fashion while they urinate. Similar balancing has been seen when a dog has suffered severe back injuries and cannot bear weight on one hind leg. Very occasionally some bitches will show a leg-cocking behaviour when urinating. It does not appear to mean that they are affected with any hormone problems.

The stimulus for leg-cocking seems to be the smell of other dogs' urine; possibly, by urinating on it, the dog is trying to mask its smell in an attempt to show dominance or to extend his territory. Dogs also urinate on objects to mark them as possessions; this is especially common with food or bones – often a dog will urinate on food when it cannot eat it all at once but wants to make sure no other dog will take it. Male dogs also only discharge very small quantities of urine at a time, constantly managing to keep some 'in reserve' for the next lamp-post.

At this point it is apposite to consider a curious and partly inexplicable marking behaviour; that of rolling in strong and often vile-scented material such as dead animals, birds', animals' or even other dogs' muck. Dogs commonly urinate on or near these materials but sometimes they roll on them – such behaviour occurs in adult dogs of both sexes. Why they do so, cannot be simply answered. Possibly, they find the odours pleasant or, perhaps, they are trying to mask the odour by placing some of their scent on the material. Dogs sometimes roll on their toys, perhaps to mark them as possessions.

There is an area of modified skin on the back of the dog called the tail gland. This is an oval area of skin with thick, stiff hairs which produce lots of yellow secretion from the grease glands at their bases. Some scientists believe that this secretion is an important marking scent for dogs. The scent itself *we* cannot smell, but then neither is our scenting capacity as good as dogs, nor has it such a wide range.

Other scents associated with elimination are those produced by the anal glands and these will be discussed further in Chapter Nine. We are uncertain of the functions of these glands. They may lubricate the faeces to aid in elimination or they may be scent glands. Certainly, they are associated with emotions and fright because often a dog will empty them when suddenly scared. Possibly the smell has the same action as it does on the skunk; it repels his foes.

Adult dogs have very good control over their elimination processes but, of course, this does vary between individuals. An owner must respect the limit of his dog's capacities. Bitches can hold urine for incredibly long periods, especially when on strange or dangerous territory; periods of thirty-six hours between urinations are commonplace. However, this voluntary control, which is reinforced by complex patterns of human dominance, reward and a desire-to-please, can be lost under some circumstances. The classic example is when a dog is frightened; dogs which are suddenly scared often urinate and defecate involuntarily. This is part of the 'fight or

Below: The bitch emits a scent which attracts the pups to her nipples, but before long they know where to go for feeding.

55

flight' reflex, which is a complex nervous reflex controlled by the involuntary part of the nervous system and so is outside the dog's capacity to inhibit. Essentially, the nervous system is telling the body to get rid of this excreta so that a lighter bodyweight can make it easier for the dog to escape or put up a fight.

The control of elimination is also lost when dogs are showing extreme submissive behaviour. If you, the boss – the pack leader – severely scold your dog, he will show strong submissive signs which may include rolling over on his back, raising a hind leg and dribbling urine. Of course the most cruel thing you can do is to scold him even more for this, because it will make the whole thing worse. He will get even more submissive and dribble even more and he will be completely confused by your reactions. After all, he has displayed his complete surrender to you and given you the honour of showing you that he recognizes you as the pack leader.

Dogs, particularly young ones, may also lose control when very excited and urinate, for example, when you return after a long period away. Again, this is an involuntary action. If you scold the dog, he will become confused, submissive – and urinate again!

Finally, dogs often lose their house training cleanliness when they are under stress – if they sense unhappiness in a household, or antipathy to them or to humans they know. Once again it would be cruel and counter-productive to scold them for this lack of control.

Elimination in puppies

Newborn puppies do not defecate or urinate at will and, in fact, do not have control over their elimination. Until they are about twenty days old, elimination is controlled by the bitch, who stimulates them by licking them around the area of the natural excretory orifices. She then licks up the urine and faeces produced and so keeps them perfectly clean. This marvellous and convenient (for the breeder!) behaviour is important in wild dogs, as at that age the pups would not be able to move away from the nest to eliminate and so could be a serious health hazard to themselves as well as providing a splendid give-away scent stimulus for predatory animals. The dam usually licks the pups when they wake and when they are feeding, which are the classic times for elimination in later puppyhood (see Chapter Eight). By twenty days, the pup can perform itself but the mother still cleans up after it; by about twenty-five days after birth, the pups move away to a selected area near the nest so that their bedding remains clean.

Puppies of both sexes squat to urinate but it soon becomes obvious that the males squat less deeply than the bitch puppies.

Sexual behaviour

Together with eating and catching prey, as with all animals, the patterns of sexual behaviour are particularly strong. Indeed, in human parlance,

Below: This Jack Russell Terrier bitch is exhibiting normal protectiveness for her pups when they enter a strange environment.

one refers to sex drive as a 'base tendency', but perhaps we would be better to say 'basic tendency' because of its primitive importance in all animals.

Sexual behaviour is intimately involved with all the senses so far discussed – elimination behaviour, communication and pack order – and also, obviously, in maternal behaviour, which will be considered separately. It is quite impossible to consider sexual behaviour here without thinking of how it links up with these other patterns.

Man does a lot to try to alter the sexual behaviour of dogs, much of which is an embarrassment and nuisance to him. The fact that he generally fails is exemplified by the frequent resort to spaying bitches and putting sexual restraints on male dogs.

Sexual behaviour is not always a function of the hormones of the dog's body. The sex hormones play a major part in starting off sexual behaviour certainly, particularly in puppies, but once a sexual behaviour pattern has been developed, it often continues, even if hormones which started it have long since disappeared.

Some aspects of sexual behaviour will be dealt with later in Chapter Nine. There are tremendous variations in sexual behaviour between individuals and between breeds, from sex-mad males at one end of the scale to frigid bitches at the other! Just as with humans, there are few very set behavioural rules to sex; it is not always easy to draw an exact line between what is normal sexual behaviour and what is abnormal.

Overt sexual behaviour occurs at a very early age in puppies, who may mount and produce pelvic thrusts when they are only five weeks old. This behaviour occurs in both sexes and either may be mounted indiscriminately. It is difficult to explain the reason for this behaviour which obviously occurs long before dogs are fertile. It may be simply practising for later on – the phenomenon commonly observed in animal biology ensuring that animals are 'behaviourally experienced' by the time they are physiologically capable. Another possibility is that sexual dominance shown by mounting is an expression of pack dominance. Commonly, the mounting activity will be seen by older pups who may behave sexually towards other animals or children during play. It may even occur when playing with the bitch, which is a difficult fact to reconcile with possible dominance activity. Usually, the bitch will react by aggressive behaviour, however, and humans who are mounted by pups should do so too, or else the pattern will become imprinted in the pup and the habit will be hard to stop.

Often, bitch puppies are the partners who are mounted in the sex game and, as they get older, their passive role in the game gets more pronounced. That of the male gets more active and, usually, dogs are capable of fertile matings anytime between six to ten months old. The onset of first heat in bitches also varies greatly.

The breed differences in sexual activity are not always clear-cut but we can make some valid generalizations. The pack dog breeds, such as Beagles or Foxhounds, often show adult sexual behaviour earlier than the more solitary breeds. Possibly, the behaviour is more obvious in packs, anyway, and there are more opportunities for sexual behaviour which, in turn, stimulate the development of the gonads and hence result in early fertility. Certainly pups who have been deprived of sexual contact with other dogs during their early life tend to be very late in showing sexual competence.

In the developing of breeds, man has tended to choose and use dogs that are sexually mature at an early age. Breeds that mature earlier are going to produce more of their kind at an early age so there will obviously be more of them! Some breeds, such as Greyhounds, Chows and Salukis, tend to be late sexual developers, and may be two years old before either sex reaches competence, although males tend to become sexually mature earlier than bitches.

The capacity of a member of a breed to recognize another of the same breed and preferentially mate with it is sometimes seen. This may simply be a matter of size identifi-

Below: The Chow Chow is one of the slowest breeds to develop sexually.

cation. Although there is no biological reason why the semen of a male Chihuahua cannot fertilize the egg of a Great Dane and produce a normal puppy, mating between these breeds is obviously – and thankfully – highly unlikely! There are even (admittedly rare) cases on record where males of a particular coat colour have refused to mate any bitch other than those of his breed and coat colour. Salukis in particular are shy breeders and confine their sexual attention very much to members of their own breed.

Dogs which are shy breeders are a real headache for dog breeders. In some cases this behaviour is linked with social dominance. If a dog is introduced to a strange bitch in heat then, although he may be sexually attracted to her and she to him, neither of them know whether the other is a dominant or submissive member of their own packs. They are unaware, as it were, of their potential partner's 'social background' and so it may take them a little while to sort out their orders, thus giving them the appearance of being shy breeders. Possibly, it is submissive males and dominant females who tend to be in this category. In any case, there is much to be said for allowing a breeding pair to get to know one another for some little while before a serious attempt is made to get them to mate.

Sometimes a dominant or very experienced bitch will mount and make pelvic thrusts on a timid or inexperienced male, although subsequently they may mate quite normally with good fertility and make excellent mothers.

Courtship and mating behaviour

In the wild, and in the free-ranging pack, the males learn about sexually interesting bitches from their daily rounds and begin to pay them attention as their heats start. Bitches involuntarily emit their own invitations by means of the chemical messages, or pheromones, which are discharged in the urine. A dog may pay an increasing amount of interest in a bitch as her season progresses, up to the time when she is receptive to the male and allows him to mate. This short period is known as oestrus. An in-season bitch may be courted by quite a large number of dogs, and much fighting and display of pack-order behaviour may occur before one dog mates the bitch. A male noses around the bitch and may advance towards her and run along with her unless she stands still. Both the bitch and dog may raise their tails and rumps but crouch down towards one another with their forelimbs bent, before suddenly jumping up. This play behaviour may be quite prolonged and can occur several days before the bitch is fully receptive to the male. Eventually the bitch will stand still with her tail raised – often to one side – and the male will investigate her vulval regions. He will then mount her and mating proper begins. Sometimes, during the early part of copulation, the male will bite the bitch's neck and grip a fold of her neck skin with his teeth.

Once mating is finished, and it may take up to half an hour, the dogs part and separate. Multiple matings do occur but in pack

Right: The St. Bernard is a remarkably good-natured dog and makes an excellent companion for children, but its huge size prevents it becoming widely popular. Here, a best-in-show winner, sits quietly, setting a good example to the puppy.

Below: Vizslas are gentle dogs at all times and this recently whelped bitch is clearly enjoying her maternal role.

conditions they are nearly always with the same dog and are separated by a day or so, although more frequent copulations sometimes occur. The biological aspects of mating will be dealt with in Chapter Ten when we consider breeding.

Sexual inter-relationships

Studies of wolves and wild dogs have shown that sometimes there are life-long pairings between males and females. This is not the case in domestic dogs, although some males show strong preferences for specific bitches and vice-versa. It is a general rule that the male is dominant over the female in sexual affairs and mating behaviour. If the female does exert dominance, she faces the male, so mating becomes virtually impossible. It may be that in litters there are some female pups which are dominant over some male pups and, if this social dominance continues into adult life, it can be a natural barrier to mating.

The homosexual behaviour shown by male and female dogs is quite a common sexual aberration and may be a result of a very close relationship between dogs. If two dogs of the same sex are raised together, then the normal complex intersexual socializing patterns cannot occur and so the dogs have no concept of male and female sex differences. In fact they will prefer dogs of their own sex because they are used to them. Often these curious behaviours disappear even with quite late socialization.

A dog's surroundings do much to influence sexual activities. Males are particularly sensitive to strange surroundings and are unwilling to mate with bitches if they are visiting them for the first time. This is why the female is brought to the male in selected breedings; she is much less influenced by her surroundings than the male.

Oversexuality is common in many male dogs, particularly in the larger or more active breeds, who may be kept in confined quarters for long periods. The sex maniac Labrador or Boxer is a common problem for many owners who are

Below: The German Short-haired Pointer is both kind and adaptable. Here, a bitch licks affectionately at one of her exuberant puppies. The breed can be trained to point, hunt and retrieve.

Above: Growing-up together! Although only a very young puppy, this Labrador demonstrates its tolerance of children.

Below: Dogs and cats have a common characteristic – that of being able to communicate and socialize with other animals. Here, the Cocker Spaniel puppies seem unperturbed by their feline bed-fellow, as they pursue the popular puppy pastime of chewing their basket.

constantly having to scour the countryside to find their dog on his sexual rampages. Boredom and lack of dog socialization is a common cause of oversexuality.

Maternal behaviour

This natural extension of sexual behaviour varies greatly between bitches. In the wild, one would imagine that good mothering ability would be vital. Poor mothers would soon lose their pups and quite probably the tendency for bad mothering ability would die with those pups. At least, one would assume this to be the case and most dog breeders would agree that good mothering is an inherited tendency.

In the domestic dog, good mothering is still very important but not absolutely vital. If a mother fails to protect her pups, there will be no marauding prey to kill them. If she leaves them at an early age and refuses to suckle them, then man comes to the rescue with the feeding bottle and

the hot water bottle. This accounts for the unfortunate occurrence of bad mothers who are still kept as breeding bitches because of their other redeeming qualities.

Pregnant bitches continue to socialize and run with the pack until quite close to whelping. Even with a family pet, there is usually no change in a bitch's behaviour except a general tendency to take things more easily. Two or three days before she is due to whelp, the bitch seeks a quiet place and makes her nest. The behaviour of whelping will be considered in detail in Chapter Ten.

Once the bitch has settled after her whelping, she exhibits a very close affiliation with her puppies and guards them very closely. Usually, she will permit only very close acquaintances – human and canine – to come near her and her puppies, without showing strongly protective behaviour such as growling, curling round the pups, often biting intruders and, if she is continually disturbed, moving the pups. Even very close canine friends may be most unwelcome at this time and they will usually respect her need for privacy and solitude with the pups. Constant interference may result in a bitch killing and eating the pups.

A bitch may also kill her pups if they are deformed or sickly. Bitches seem to be acutely aware of the very slightest deviation from normal in their puppies, the stimulus for this being the changes in behaviour and form. Bitches have been known to kill puppies with tiny abnormalities, such as bent legs, kinked tails or missing toes. This uncanny behaviour is a good example of very severe natural selection.

The behaviour of suckling, stimulation of elimination and feeding of the older puppies has already been discussed but the bitch's attitude to the pups is not simply one of a feeding and cleaning machine. She nudges them back when they move away from her and may squeal, herself, or make a high-pitched whine, which is probably heard by the pups and is an indication to them to return to her. This care-giving behaviour is very strong in some breeds, mainly the pack breeds, where there is an obvious need to protect the pups against other members of the pack who might not be well disposed to them.

At a later age, when puppies are perhaps sleeping away from the mother, she may flaunt herself before them when she wants them to feed, or when she wants to play with them. Many bitches are prepared to share their own food with their puppies but this response is very variable; the bitch may growl and even attack them gently if they attempt to steal her food.

Even when the puppies are quite old, the bitch is still very much concerned if a puppy squeals in distress and she, too, may squeal. Strangely, however, it is very rare for a bitch to help a distressed pup and, indeed, after a short while, she generally ignores the noise altogether.

Not much can be done with a bitch who is a bad mother. Rather than persevere with her, it is probably best to start supplementary feeding as soon as possible. On occasions, a different bitch may take on maternal behaviour and show care-giving activity to the pups of another bitch. This is usually seen in bitches who are themselves very good mothers and it is a good potential sign. Even the dog may pay quite a lot of attention to the pups, vomit for them and stimulate elimination. Other male dogs show very little pup orientation and appear to be afraid of puppies.

False pregnancy

This unproductive behaviour is such a common phenomenon that it can be considered as normal. It is discussed in more detail in Chapter Nine but it is a result of hormonal changes which are essentially identical to those of pregnancy. False pregnancy is more common in bored and under-exercised dogs. There are both breed and strain tendencies, the behaviour being particularly common in toy breeds, Poodles and Spaniels.

Social behaviour and communication

A major characteristic of all animals – and one that distinguishes them from members of the plant kingdom, for example – is that they behave socially to one another. Dogs are no exception and, in fact, are amongst the most sociable of animals. Much of a dog's strength depends on his capacity to react to other dogs and to do things together with them – to help him to hunt effectively, to feed and to defend himself against enemies.

Most important for man, the dog is capable of not only communicating and socializing with other dogs but also with humans. This is uncommon, although certainly not a unique position in the animal world, shared mainly by primate apes, horses and cats.

Dogs live not only in packs but also form a canine equivalent of 'cliques' within these packs. These little bands will often perform the daily route marches, described earlier, together and even form their own hunting groups with a pack. Probably, they form the nuclei of new packs when they get big and mature enough, forming splinter groups which leave the main pack to start afresh. Thus we see a more complex and efficient socialization pattern in dogs than in many other animals. When, for example, the Arctic lemming breeds to produce an enormous group, the very size of the population causes feeding and communication problems. Eventually, the herd may show the well-known self-annihilation behaviour. To prevent this,

dogs only allow their pack to get to a manageable size, then they will split up, moving off to fresh geographical locations so that they dilute their total population over a wider area. Thus the overcrowding problems which cause such devastation to the lemmings are avoided.

Social behaviour can be considered to be co-ordinated (co-operative) *or* competitive. Both these types of activity are needed for a balanced community although it is mainly the former which appeals to man when he, too, is accepted as a member of the pack – usually as leader.

Co-operative behaviour in the pack

Most groups of dogs, whether in a pack or just a group in a home, spend the majority of their time fairly close to one another. Very often, they do the same things at the same time; it would be

Above: The stately and gentle Irish Setter has an excellent temperament and is a popular family dog.

Below: In general, dogs will socialize with most animals, particularly if they have known them when they were puppies.

Above: Basset Hounds, like Beagles, enjoy pack life and despite their short legs, they need plenty of exercise.

Left: A splendidly alert Foxhound.

Below: Springer Spaniels will socialize easily with dogs and humans.

unusual for only half a kennelled group to bark at a stranger, and the other half to remain silent. Sometimes, however, one or two dogs in a group do isolate themselves perhaps to chew a bone, or because, as newcomers to the group, they have not yet been accepted and their order in the pack determined.

There is an obvious advantage for all members of a group to behave similarly at the same time, and such behaviour may also be complementary. The classic example of this is pack hunting, where a group will not just blindly chase after the prey but some members of the group will surround the animal and cut off its retreat, so achieving a highly efficient kill. Pack hunting is also important when the prey hunted is dangerous or bigger and stronger than the individual dogs. Although Great Danes are large in comparison to other dogs, one on its own would have little chance against a wild boar; in a pack they combine to make an excellent and formidable hunting force.

The desire to be sociable in dogs is probably not inherent, although this is difficult to prove either way. Pups huddle together for many reasons, including the warmth this gives them from one another and their mother. If pups are reared in solitary confinement, then their socializing desire will be found to be much reduced when they are eventually placed with other dogs. This makes it appear that dogs just like being together because they are reared together. Because companionship has become strongly imprinted in their youth, it continues in later life.

The frustration and virtual despair shown by some dogs when isolated is most noticeable; this is particularly true of the pack breeds. Beagles are very often extremely unhappy when kept on their own and for this reason can sometimes be failures as domestic pets. Of course, there are exceptions but many solitary pet Beagles will mope around, eating either poorly or unnaturally ravenously, and quite possibly doing lots of damage in the house. If another Beagle is purchased or it is taken to a large kennels, these problems disappear and it becomes a normal happy, healthy dog again.

Beagles are not the only breed to show a very strong need for pack company; the trait is seen in Foxhounds and Harriers as well as in many other hunting dogs and, also, quite commonly, in terriers. This is not really surprising; these dogs have been selected and bred for their hunting capacity and *not* for their ease of association with man or other animals. Little wonder that they miss this association when kept in 'dog isolation' and so exhibit signs of boredom.

The desire to 'follow the leader' and keep in line can be very strong in dogs. One dog of three in a home decides to chew his bone and before

long the other two will find bones, too. If, however, there are no other bones to be had, then a fight may well take place over who has the bone. The winner, however, will emerge as the odd man out rather than the victor, and probably before long he will stop chewing and join his two associates in romping round the garden.

Extreme frustration can be shown by a dog deprived of the capacity to behave within a group. If two or three Dachshunds are taken for a walk with a number of large, fast dogs, they will be happy as long as they are moving with the pack. If the faster dogs scent a hare and disappear into the distance in pursuit, the Dachshunds, of course, cannot keep up; they will

then often show their frustration by high-pitched yelps.

Dogs bred for their capacity as solitary workers rarely show intense need for group behaviour. The Spaniel breeds are usually quite happy on their own and, in fact, groups of Spaniels kept together will often remain apart from one another, each busy on its own. The same propensity is shown by many of the toy breeds who have been selected for their preferential capacity seemingly to enjoy human company.

The importance of scent in communication has already been discussed. As we cannot interpret scents in the same way as dogs, it is

Above: The gaily carried tails of these Bassets clearly display the hounds' excitement as they hunt together in the pack.

Above: An encounter between a Chow Chow and a Jack Russell Terrier. The terrier's position indicates submission.

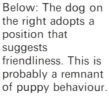

Below: The dog on the right adopts a position that suggests friendliness. This is probably a remnant of puppy behaviour.

difficult for us to go further in trying to unravel the mystery of 'scent language of dogs'. However, we can see as well as (in fact, better than) dogs and hear quite well, so our opportunities for interpreting the visual and auditory signals given by dogs are quite good.

Dogs can distinguish the outline of other dogs, and this is particularly marked when they are moving. Dogs have their own 'body language' just as humans do. On meeting someone with whom we wish to be friendly, we will smile and shake hands. Dogs will move the whole or part of their bodies, not only to show feeling to one another, but also to man.

One pleasant feature about a dog's communication with whomsoever it may be, is that he is perfectly truthful about his feelings! When he raises his hackles and ears he means aggression and the growl reinforces his attitude to his adversary.

When a dog is rushing forward to threaten an enemy, both his movement and body shape are such that he gives the impression of being as big as possible. Although he may lower the front half of his body, he generally stands tall, raises his hind-quarters and walks with his shoulders out from his body. He will raise his ears and his 'hackles' – the broad line of hair down the centre of his body from his head to his tail. With his neck arched and his tail held high, he advances towards his adversary, probably with his lips raised in a snarl. All these changes in body shape tell the other dog that he is not having the paw of friendliness extended to him!

The exact behavioural opposite to aggression – total submission – is shown by postural changes which make the dog appear smaller. He crouches low to the ground with all limbs folded, head on his paws, tail curled round and ears flattened to his head. If he really wants to show extreme submission, then he may roll to one side, raise a hind leg and even dribble urine.

Most of these body postures are shown both to other dogs and to man but there are some special ones which seem to be reserved solely for communication with humans. One of these is rolling over on to the back. This belly-up position seems to be a mixture of submission, care-soliciting and an invitation for contact with the dog's tummy. Some dogs never show this behaviour to man but the breeds who commonly do are the hounds, terriers and toy breeds – some Dachshunds seem to spend more time on their backs when in human company than in an upright position! When the posture is displayed, it is universally a sign of friendliness and trust.

Tail-wagging is a behaviour which humans generally interpret as a sign of happiness in dogs. However, this is really an emotive human interpretation of a dog's behaviour – a dangerous thing to do, as we have discussed earlier. Dogs

EXPRESSIVE
SOCIAL RESPONSES
IN THE DOG

Arousal

Play-soliciting

Aggression

Submission

Above: The diagram shows the ways in which a dog uses its body to convey meaning. A and B are alert and attentive positions. C is a play soliciting bow and positions D and E are active and submissive greetings. Position 1 shows passive submission as does J, where the dog is rolling over and presenting the genital region – a sign of trust. Positions F–H show the gradual shift from aggressive display to ambivalent fear-defensive-aggressive postures.

Above right: When two dogs meet, their first reaction is to sniff each other curiously.

Centre right: An aggressive snarl from the large dog evokes a submissive crouch from the other.

Right: The vanquished beats a hasty retreat, averting his eyes as he goes.

definitely do show signs we interpret as contentment and, undoubtedly, tail-wagging is one; as a dog contentedly chews a juicy bone, he often slowly wags his tail. Some dogs wag their tails when they meet other dogs, possibly this is to waft about their body odours so that their particular smell can be recognized more easily by the other dog. When a dog holds his tail very high and the tip wags quickly and stiffly, he usually appears to be showing aggression; if the whole tail is held up and flagged from side to side, as Beagles do when they catch the scent of a hare, this is a sign of alertness and excitement. Often dogs wag their tails for no apparent reason – when they wake up, when they are out walking, or when they are just watching something. In these circumstances, the wagging is probably just a part of the posture which tells others that the dog is alert and generally interested in what is

going on around him. Many dogs are incredibly vigorous tail-waggers; most Labradors and Spaniels come into this category and can give the impression that it is the tail that is wagging the dog! Even docked breeds, like the Cocker Spaniel and the Boxer, will wag their tail stump and, indeed, often the whole of the back end of themselves as well!

However much we try to interpret the meaning of tail-wagging, there is little doubt that, when it is directed at humans, it is a sign denoting peaceful intentions and contentment.

Above: Smooth Fox Terriers have a commanding and confident appearance.

Below: This Dandie Dinmont puppy is already developing the self-assurance typical of the breed.

Facial expression

It is easy to put wrong interpretations on the facial signs and expressions in dogs. Once again, they are 'talking' an entirely different language to humans and it is impossible to make direct comparisons. The aggressive lip-curled snarl of the dog, for example, is very similar to the grimace of pain which a human will show when he has dropped a brick on his foot. The smile shown by many dogs does not really denote the pleasantness or humour of the human expression, but is a sign of submission.

Dogs show aggression not only by curling up the lips to display the teeth, but also by wrinkling the nose until eventually the front teeth are also exposed. At the same time, the ears and the corners of the mouth are brought forward.

The end result of the aggressive facial change is not dissimilar to the 'greeting grin' which is shown by just a few dogs. Of course the greeting

grin has no relationship at all to the aggressive snarl and is, in fact, slightly different, in that the corners of the mouth are not quite so far forward. Charles Darwin, that most observant of behaviouralists, was one of the first people to describe this expression. Probably the tendency to greet by grinning is inherited and there are some people who believe it may even be a rare example of dogs mimicking humans, particularly as it appears to be reserved for humans only. Individuals in breeds such as Dalmatians, Shetland Sheepdogs and Labradors have the capacity to grin.

The dog 'smile', where the corners of the mouth are drawn right back, is a submissive grin. Dogs may show this expression both to other dogs and also to humans but, again, not all dogs display it.

Opening the mouth is often a dog's sign of alertness and readiness for contact or play. As a play-soliciting facial expression, it is often accompanied by an upwards jerk of the nose. Dogs commonly exhibit this behaviour when they want to play with another dog in a group and often they place their nose under their prospective play partner's chin and jerk upwards. Humans get the same treatment when their dogs want to play – many a full cup of coffee has been spilt when a playful dog has nuzzled his master's elbow!

We have already concluded that tail-wagging is commonly a sign of contentment; there is, also, sometimes a facial sign of contentment which dogs show. This is not a very obvious expression but careful observation will show the lips drawn back (similar to the submissive grin), lowered ears and half-closed eyes. You may see this expression on your dog's face when you are rubbing his tummy.

A common mistake people make is to

misinterpret a dog's facial *shape* as a facial *expression*. Bloodhounds do look 'worried' to us but then they always have that worried expression caused by their forehead wrinkles. A Bloodhound playing or showing aggression *looks* just as worried as when he is sleeping or eating. Similarly the droopy mouth of a Boxer or Mastiff makes him look doleful even when he is quite happy and the wide open, bright eyes of a Papillon give him a cheerful appearance, even though he may be feeling very sad. These facial shapes are one of the many factors which attract different people to different breeds – really all rather unfortunate, as they mean so little.

Some breeds seem to have little capacity for exhibiting facial expressions. Facial changes are not very commonly shown by Greyhounds or Afghans, for example, and many of the Spaniel breeds are similarly rather expressionless. Probably, they make up for this apparent communication deficiency in other ways.

Vocalization

We have seen how a dog's posture says much; the noise that a dog makes is generally less important and is only an adjunct to other methods of communication. Dogs obviously do not have 'words' in their language and vocalization is more a way of expressing mood in a dog than actually telling a story. For a dog, the importance is not so much what he says but the way he says it!

Barking is a vocal response which seems to convey many messages – general alertness, soliciting alertness in other members of the pack, a degree of aggression, and defending territory are the important ones. The loudness of the bark generally indicates the intensity of the message to be carried. There seems to be no pattern to the barking which could, even in a vague way, be interpreted as a code similar to speech in humans. Although your dog may always bark in stanzas of three, this is not his code for 'supper please'. To believe this would be anthropomorphism at its most facile.

Barking is only one of the communicatory noises of dogs. In addition, we can recognize whines, growls, yelps, snorts, squeals and howls, and baying noises.

Yelping is the shrill distress cry which both puppies and adult dogs make if they are very frightened, hurt – or *think* they are going to be frightened or hurt! In the case of puppies, the bitch is immediately alerted by these noises and investigates the situation. If an adult dog yelps, others in the group become interested and will stand or run around watching the display. However, they make no effort to contact the yelping animal or make the same noise themselves. The same, in fact, is true for puppies;

Above: The natural folds of a Bloodhound's face suggest a doleful attitude.

Below: Beagles are happier when they are living in a pack with other members of their breed.

Above: This Lurcher could be said to be smiling. The facial expression, with its half-closed eyes and drawn-back corners to the mouth, radiates contentment. Not all dogs have this ability to smile but those that do often display this expression both to other dogs and to humans.

Above: This Wire-haired Fox-Terrier has a bright and alert expression which indicates that it is ready to spring into action as soon as it is commanded to do so.

Below: Golden Retrievers are generally friendly and good natured. Despite the fact that this one is putting up with some rough play from a young friend, it is still wagging its tail with pleasure. There is no trace of aggression in its expression.

a single shrieking pup in a litter may be the object of interest but the call will not be taken up by the others. This is in marked contrast to barking, howling or even whining, which seem to evoke a copycat response in the rest of the group. Yelping appears to be an individual personal distress call.

Whining or whimpering, on the other hand, often evoke a group vocal response and is a mild discomfort or emotional upset noise. It is also a noise that may be associated with frustration or loneliness, although these emotions may be accompanied by other sounds, too. Puppies whimper when they are cold and hungry but, as long as they are kept warm, hunger alone rarely causes them to whine. The whine is the most usual vocalization of puppies at any age up to five to six months old, although pups can bark as early as four weeks if they are suddenly disturbed.

Growling is definitely an aggressive sound; it is sometimes associated with guarding territory. Pups very soon learn to growl and, as early as three to four weeks old, may growl if a strange person approaches their bed. This appears to be another sound which is learnt and practised commonly during play-fighting of a litter of pups, the growl getting louder, higher pitched and sharper as the play-fighting gets more intense. Growling is usually the first sound emitted by a dog if he senses danger – later this turns into a bark. It is a sound which has strong arousal capabilities and will usually excite and alert a group quicker even than the bark.

Howling is a very basic and, to us, generally an unpleasant noise. It is usually emitted by dogs when they are very lonely and is probably a 'company-soliciting' request noise. It, too, is a sound taken up by a group and, in such an event, it is often a means of long-distance communication between groups. Kennelled packs of dogs howl at night or in the early day, when there is little air movement. Although we may not be able to hear the response from another far-away group of dogs, it is probable that the dogs' acute sense of high pitch hearing can detect the reply. The sound pattern of howling is always similar. The first noise is a loud, fairly high pitched, drawn out, clear cry which gradually falls in pitch and is then followed by several short lower pitched cries. Wolves, coyotes and some other wild dogs display this howling behaviour when wishing to communicate over long distances and the capacity to howl is particularly strong in breeds which are rather close to wolves in ancestry, such as Siberian Huskies and Alaskan Malamutes.

We commonly hear howling in kennelled groups of dogs, such as in quarantine kennels, Foxhound packs and breeding kennels and yet it is a comparatively rare sound in domestic homes,

Above: Shetland Sheepdogs – Shelties – are a friendly breed and often show welcoming greeting grins. Few breeds grin in this way. This particular greeting grin is reserved solely for humans.

Above: Alertness and anticipation clearly show in the face of this open-mouthed Golden Retriever waiting for a ball to be thrown. And (above right) having caught the ball, the dog will play with it for a second or two and will then expect its owner to retrieve it and continue with the game.

even when pet dogs are left for considerable periods. This is probably because howling is a behaviour which is strongly subject to social facilitation – that is, a response is heightened because of dogs in the group continually stimulating one another by responding. Howling is also a behaviour trait which is learnt by socialization and dogs raised in a group from birth, like breeding kennel dogs, have had plenty of chance to keep re-learning and practising the howl.

Howling is also a sound with sexual connotations. Males isolated from bitches which they know to be in heat may howl continually and the bitch may respond in like manner. Even toy breeds, which under normal circumstances very rarely howl, may react to in-season isolation by howling.

A variation in howling is baying – the sonorous howl-like bark produced by pack dogs which are excited when following game or by some other arousing stimulus. Only certain pack hunters make this noise; Pointers and Setters, for example, rarely do so.

Finally, there are a variety of dog sounds – snorts, squeals, grunts – none of which would appear to have any particular code importance, although the nasal snorts of Boxers seem to be 'attention seeking sounds'.

The degree of vocalization varies much with the breed. The classic example is the Basenji which is virtually mute; at best, he produces a sound which has been described as yodelling, but in no way can he produce anything that remotely resembles a bark. Another relatively quiet breed is the Greyhound, and in fact almost all the gazehounds – the Whippets, Deerhounds, Afghans, Salukis and Borzois – are not noisy at all, only barking or whining under extreme provocation. The Chow and many of the Spitz

breeds are also comparatively quiet dogs.

Terriers have a reputation for excessive barking which may be an expression of boredom if they are unable to utilize their excessive energy.

Body contact

For many dogs, body contact with socially accepted dogs and people is obviously very important. Even from a very early age, puppies show a desire to contact one another and there is some evidence that the 'piling' phenomenon shown by a litter of puppies has greater significance than just keeping warm. The distance that one dog keeps from another is an important part of the socialization pattern and will be discussed in greater detail later but, once social friendliness is agreed between dogs, then there are great variations of importance of body contact. Some of the pack breeds, like Beagles,

Left: This Basenji has an expression of extreme alertness.

69

Above: Puppies pile together, not only for warmth, but also to fulfil a desire for body contact.

Below: Although small in relation to their quarry, Elkhounds hunt their prey by surrounding them and attacking *en masse*.

The pack order and social dominance

In any group of animals, a social hierarchy is established in order to give a stable arrangement and relationship between individuals, and so that fighting is kept to a minimum. This is particularly important in predatory animals, as there is a need for the pack to have a concerted policy of attack – and defence, in case of danger. Dogs have a well-developed pack order and a complex social system, based on the communication method already outlined.

The pack-order system starts at a very early age in puppies, when they begin play-fighting around five weeks old. Within a short time, probably only a month or so, an order of dominance has developed, although it can change considerably by the time the group is six to seven months old. Usually, among domestic dogs, the litter group has separated by the time they are six months old and so the chances for variation in the pack order are considerable.

The method by which pups determine their pack order is quite complex, but it mainly depends on play-fighting. Dominant puppies are those more often seen shaking their litter mates by the neck, racing towards them and bowling them over. When the litter mates submit by rolling on their backs, the dominant pup will generally grab them by the throat and bite them. They are also the first at the feeding bowl, as well as the one to beat the others to the bone and to keep it once they have gained command.

Curiously it is not always the biggest, loudest or the male puppy who is the dominant one. Indeed, size and sex appear to make little difference to the order until the pups have reached adulthood.

In adult dogs, however, sex and size are important, and usually bigger males are dominant. The pattern of dominance gets more complex when pups grow up in a group, and their age and family relationship become important. For instance, a bitch puppy, however big and dominant in her group of peers, will rarely become dominant to her mother even when she is fully grown and physically stronger. In this case the dominance of the mother exerted over her pups while playing is retained right through into adult life.

Similar complexities occur when different breeds or different sexes and ages are mixed together in one group. Usually the adult rule of dominance of sex and size applies but there are often bouts of play-fighting, aggressive show and real fights, particularly if the breeds are of a similar size. A common occurrence is for the individuals of the different breeds to form splinter groups within the pack and there is no doubt that dogs can recognize individuals of their own breed. These breed packs, however, may not be totally fixed in all aspects and the

are often in such intimate contact that it is as if there was an invisible biological glue sticking them together! Conversely, Spaniels and Chows rarely seem to find contact important between themselves, although their need for contact with their owners may be quite strong.

Many pet dogs, who have had little chance for advanced dog socialization and are often juvenile in their behaviour, commonly show extreme comfort-seeking behaviour with their owners. This may be shown by lying on their owner's feet or wanting to lie on his lap.

pack isolation can be broken when stimuli such as food or a bitch in heat are introduced. Then the dominance orders are upset and fighting breaks out in an attempt to arrive at a new order. A human analogy would be the management sort-out which would have to occur if three separate companies were amalgamated and brought together under one roof. No doubt there would be a lot of aggression and arguing as to which director was to be chairman, which executive was to be the company secretary, and a host of minor arguments to determine the allocation of secretaries, desks and so on!

In general, dogs of most breeds can co-exist fairly well in a mixed breed pack but problems do arise with the aggressive breeds; that is, breeds that are aggressive to other dogs. In general, this includes the terrier group – Bull Terriers in particular; Dobermann Pinschers, Alsatians and Mastiffs can also be aggressive to others.

The pack order in non-aggressive breeds, such as the Beagle, is somewhat simple. Here 'might is right' – always! The dominant dog is the one who leads the others in the chase and at all other times. There is no questioning the situation; all members of the pack take it for granted.

Some investigation into dominance in different breeds has resulted in the conclusion that the pack order is fixed and rigid in breeds such as Basenjis and Fox Terriers, where males are nearly always dominant. In other breeds, such as Spaniels and Beagles, males are not always dominant. Although the pack order is set, a newcomer is fairly quickly accepted with little fighting, even if a group is very large.

The dominance of man over dog is such an important subject that it will be considered separately, after the important behaviours of aggression, submission and friendliness, which influence it so deeply.

Aggression

'Aggression' in a dog may be described as the sum total of all the individual aggressive actions we have mentioned already. Stalking, chasing, 'enlarged body profile', snarling with teeth displayed, growling and eventually head on attacks are all recognized signs. Aggressive dogs fix their eyes directly on to their adversary who usually avoids this direct stare by looking away – a similar avoidance of looking someone in the eye is seen in submissive humans who are feeling guilty.

Very often, the postural and vocal signs are enough to elicit submission in the adversary without the need to fight, but if the dominance is not accepted then fighting may occur, with teeth used as the major weapons. A dog may slam against the neck or side of an enemy in an attempt to knock him over but the main damage

comes from the bites which are directed to the underneath of the neck, the belly, armpits and, in the case of a dog who tries to run away, the back and base of the tail.

If the canine subject of the aggression refuses to accept his adversary's dominance, then he initially faces the other dog and displays similar signs. He may stand still and allow the other dog to circle him, watching all the time out of the corner of his eye until he can see him no longer. He then turns rapidly to face him again. This circling and standing still behaviour continues in both dogs until eventually either dominance is accepted or fighting ensues.

The most common reason for a show of aggression is defence of territory. This is seen not only when another dog is considered as a possible

Above: Dogs will fight to establish the order of dominance if it is not immediately evident.

Below: Boxers possess a strong sense of territory and make excellent guard dogs, but they are generally a friendly breed once they have accepted a family as their own.

invader but also when other animals and humans come within the animal's invisible home zone. The intensity of the territorial defence signs decrease with the distance from the 'nest' or the dog's home until, on neutral ground, it becomes so weak as to be non-existent. Indeed, dogs who would be aggressive to one another if they met on home ground may be completely friendly if they meet somewhere which is foreign land to both of them. This can be used to advantage when you wish to introduce a strange dog to your own. Rather than letting them meet in a snarling flurry of teeth and fur on your front doorstep, let them meet first some way down the road and then walk them both home together.

Sense of territory does not end at the front gate however. The family car, caravan or tent is considered within the territory area, even if it is actually resting on strange ground a long way from home. The physical size of the territorial limits seem to be very important – the smaller the area recognized as 'home' the more intense the aggression to strangers. This is commonly seen with dogs who show an intense defence of their owners' cars and yet may show virtually no territorial defence when a stranger arrives at the gate of their owners' large gardens. Similar intense behaviour is sometimes displayed by a show dog guarding his small bench area. Chaining up a dog seems to reinforce his sense of territory, presumably because he is physically limited to an area, which makes it psychologically more definite territory than a whole garden where he may be free to wander.

The aggression displayed towards visitors to a house is usually dropped once they have entered and been greeted by the dog's owner. Intense barking directed against regular callers such as tradesmen or postmen may be due to the fact that, although they call, they are commonly not greeted by the householder and they rarely enter the house – in the dog's eyes they are always therefore considered potential foes! Inviting the postman or milkman into the house for an occasional cup of coffee may not only ensure a more regular and efficient service but also a quieter dog each morning.

Territory marking is intimately tied up with elimination and the sense of smell, and occurs not only with respect to larger areas but also to the owner's home. A dog introduced to a new home, whether another dog is present or not, will commonly make his mark by urinating on the floor. It is unfortunate when this occurs in the house of a friend but there is one consolation: it is only performed once and so the embarrassment is unlikely to occur again!

Besides the territorial behaviour around homes, gardens and cars, the space which surrounds a dog at any time is also regarded very personally. Sometimes a dog may bark at a

person if the territory is defended – its hackles may rise, but it may still wag its tail in friendliness. The dog is thus doing his duty in defending the territory and yet is happy for the human to enter his 'social' or 'personal' zone of space. If the gate was opened and the person went to the front door, in all probability the dog would give up the territory defence and show all friendly signs to the human.

Some dogs may act aggressively towards a person but, if that person ignores their aggression and walks towards them, they run away a little, turn and resume their aggressive actions. This behaviour recurs, as the person continues to advance. What is happening is that the 'unsocial' zone around the animal is being encroached upon and his flight distance is being threatened. This upsets him – and he wants to increase the distance between the intruder and himself each time until he feels safe once more. However, he won't take positive action, such as biting, until the person enters his personal zone. At this point, the threat becomes reality.

The friendly, highly socialized dogs also have

Above: Dog behaviour has been immortalized by many artists through the ages. This eighteenth century Chinese porcelain shows dogs 'conversing' by mouth contact.

Below: Ears back and barking furiously, this German Shepherd Dog defends his territory to the last, proving his effectiveness as a guard dog.

these zones. The 'unsocial' zone of our aggressive dog is a social zone in a friendly dog – the space that he not only *lets* you enter but actively encourages you to do so. He is even happier when you enter his personal zone and eventually touch him.

The zones and the invisible barriers which divide them change with the circumstances. No barriers exist for the dog's master but they may for his friends and certainly will for enemies of his master. Sometimes dogs let you enter their social zone but, when you put your hand out to stroke them, they move away a little, indicating that they don't want you in their personal zone. Later on, when you have sat down and been accepted, they may come over to you and rub themselves against you; then they have decided to break down the personal zone barrier themselves.

Aggressive tendencies in a dog can start at a very early age and much of their subsequent development depends on the dog's environment and the social contacts which it makes.

It is undeniable that some breeds are naturally aggressive – after all, many have been bred with this in mind. Bull Terriers and Staffordshire Terriers are typical and were initially developed for the vile sport of dog fighting. This was abolished in Britain in 1835 but, to some extent, the aggressive heritage within these dogs remains, although, as selection is now placed on form and physical development, such tendencies are becoming less pronounced.

Aggressive behaviour, like many other behavioural traits, however, is definitely inherited. Successive breeding for aggression will result in dogs of enhanced aggressive tendencies, just as successive selecting and breeding for head length would lead to dogs with larger and longer muzzles. This is discussed further, under behaviour and breeding.

It is important to remember that the aggression shown by these breeds is, anyway, directed against other dogs and not against other animals or man.

Terriers are generally somewhat pugnacious and often ready to pick a fight with almost any type of breed. Many of them were selected originally for their capacities as ratters, rabbiters or earthing dogs for the hunts, and so will show aggression at any small 'game', which can well include another dog! The hunt terriers and Jack Russell Terriers are particularly quick to fight, as may be seen by the countless small scars that commonly adorn their muzzles.

It is important that the dominance order is allowed to develop in a dog group. A common and unfortunate situation is when there are two dogs in a household who are aggressive to one another, so the owner does not allow them to meet. In fact the less they meet, and the more the

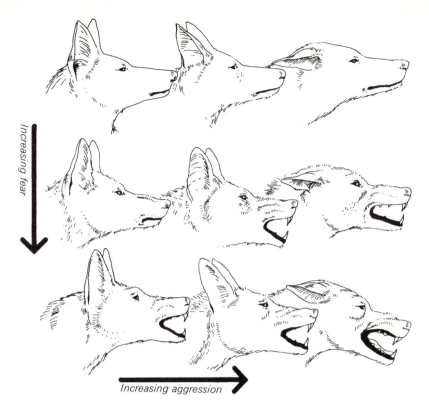

Increasing fear

Increasing aggression

Above: A dog's facial expression reflects its mood exactly. Unlike many humans, if a dog is angry it is unable to disguise this in its face.

owner makes sure they are kept separate by avoidance tactics, the worse the situation will get. The situation will spiral and the whole thing will be made worse by the owner's anxiety, which the dogs may even sense. The only answer is to allow the meeting to occur, possibly on neutral ground as already discussed, and risk a fight. Once the aggression is directed to sorting out the pack order, the problem is solved for all time.

Whereas an aggressive Cairn can be an unpleasant and vicious adversary, its very size means that it is unlikely to be a serious threat to very much except a rabbit or rat. The same cannot be said, however, of a Rhodesian Ridgeback or Alsatian bent on winning a battle of its own making. It is unfortunate that so many

Left: Only the most foolish intruder would attempt to move past this aggressive Elkhound.

Above: The black spots are the Dalmatian's most distinctive feature and can provide superb camouflage although they were never intended to.

Above right: Many people find the lean, athletic body lines of the Whippet unattractive, but its good manners and delicate grace are most endearing.

Below: The appearance of the Bulldog belies its nature. They are generally very friendly.

large breeds have gained the reputation of being aggressive. Probably there are less fights per capita with these big breeds than with terriers but, because the damage done is proportional to bodyweight and not to the degree of aggression, they become more noteworthy.

So much of a dog's aggression depends on the upbringing. Weaning a pup at too early an age – say three to four weeks – and isolating it from its litter-mates will result in a dog which is poorly 'dog-socialized'. The influence that this has on dog-to-dog relationships in later life is variable. Possibly, when introduced to other dogs for the first time since litter life, at about six months old, the dog may be very friendly but, more likely, it will be aggressive. Conversely, leaving a pup in the litter for a very long period, with very few human contacts, will probably make it, at least initially, very aggressive to humans. These young dogs may also be very afraid of humans and become 'fear biters'. These are dogs who avoid human contact and have a strong sense of the 'social' and 'personal' zones we have already discussed. Once their 'social zone' is crossed and their 'personal zone' is entered, they will attack humans in an exaggerated manner. Of course, dogs that have socialized late with humans are not always 'fear-biters', just as 'fear-biters' are not always dogs that have been introduced to humans late in life.

At the risk of upsetting some breed dog owners, it has to be said that there are some dogs with a tendency to human aggression and 'fear-biting'; these should be socialized with humans at as early an age as possible. Some strains, although by no measure all, of Alsatian, Old English Sheepdog, Dobermann, Airedale, Rottweiler and Rhodesian Ridgeback have

regrettably produced some aggression problems in recent years. It must be emphasised that this is only a small percentage of some strains and it is not a universal problem by any means but earlier, rather than later, socialization with humans, coupled with a firm hand from the owner, will do a lot to help.

Dogs display fear in the same circumstances as humans; that is, they are frightened of things, dogs and people that they know can hurt, and sometimes they are frightened of things that they have never met before, thus expressing fear of the unknown.

The signs of fear in a dog are often similar to the behaviour he shows of passive defence. He crouches, or runs away, licks his lips, puts his tail between his legs and avoids looking at the 'fearful object'. He may eventually become paralyzed by fear and roll over in the submission position; he may also urinate or defecate. If he runs away, he may seek his own kennel or defence territory and may even get close to his master in an effort to enter his master's own 'personal zone', where he expects to be safe.

Fear of anything is often brought about by association. If a dog is hurt or upset by a person, an animal or an object on one occasion, then this will commonly be associated with fear at a similar later contact. Age plays an important part in this. Very young pups have little concept of fear and it is not until the pup enters the late socialization period of its development at about two to three months that it begins to associate things with pain and discomfort. If a four-week-old pup was subjected to pain every time a bell was rung, the association of fear with a bell ringing would be unlikely to persist into later life unless the stimulus was continued well into the late socialization period. However, if the experiment was repeated in an older dog of four months, then a fear association would definitely result from the bell ringing and it would probably persist all the dog's life.

Fear associations are slower to occur and more difficult to produce in older dogs. The eight-year-old dog will have heard bells ringing plenty of times without being hurt and, although he would naturally be wary if he gets hurt and bells ring, the fear reaction is less pronounced. Puppies get very frightened if they are suddenly subjected to unpleasant shocks. Very suddenly picking up a puppy when you are standing behind him (so that he cannot see you), can provoke an intense yelping reaction in a puppy, which may even verge on hysteria. It is not altogether surprising – suddenly the very ground has been taken away from beneath him and he is being held by a stranger, someone who doesn't smell like his brothers or sisters or his mother.

Puppies (and also adult dogs) are usually very inhibited when they are picked up and held. They keep quite still and may tremble involuntarily. Only when they are well into the socialization period, at about seven weeks old, do they seem to enjoy human contact and react by licking. The inhibition displayed will be even more intense if the puppy is held by the scruff of the neck, in the way the mother may hold the puppy to move him about in times of danger or if she wishes to punish him or show dominance. Scruffing a puppy and shaking it by the neck skin is an excellent method of punishment and it is even useful for adult dogs. As long as a large handful of loose neck skin is taken, it is also a good method of lifting a dog in an emergency. If you have your hands full of shopping and the dog's

lead breaks or you are driving along and the dog tries to get out of a car window, the one-handed neck grab is particularly useful as it also immobilizes the dog – something that a grip on a leg or tail will never do.

The stimuli which a puppy meets during his socialization period play a big part in determining how he will react to potentially fearful situations in later life. Although, as already mentioned, unpleasant stimuli may result in fear reactions, it is vital that the socially developing puppy *does* get exposed to a whole variety of such stimuli so that he does not become over-protected and frightened of everything later in life. It is important, however, that no single

Above: The Old English Sheepdog is one of the most appealing of all dogs. The popularity of the breed has recently increased.

Below: Shetland Sheepdogs are rarely used for herding nowadays, but they still retain their herding instinct. They require careful and regular grooming.

unpleasant stimulus is met too often. Meeting other dogs and strange humans, eating the odd bitter shrub leaf, getting stung by the occasional wasp and being nipped by a mousetrap are just as important experiences as a nice warm bed, good food, a quiet environment and contact with kind owners. All these experiences – good, bad and indifferent – lead to a well-balanced dog in later life.

A quite intense fear of changes in surroundings or fear of strange and unfamiliar objects, animals or people can develop when a puppy is about four to five months old – that is, during the 'juvenile period', between the social phase of development and adulthood. This is particularly commonly seen in the slow maturing breeds, such as Alsatians, Dalmatians or Great Danes, and can give rise to quite excessive phobias and fears. Fear of the unknown is common in many dogs and humans and can sometimes be overcome by gentle yet enforced socialization and experience.

Dogs are definitely capable of sensing fear in other dogs and in humans. It is difficult to determine exactly what signs people are showing when they are afraid of dogs but probably it is a combination of postural uncertainty, avoidance of eye contact with the dog and, possibly, scent changes given off with the fear sweat. There is also the vague possibility that dogs are capable of determining fear by telepathic messages; this will be discussed later.

Friendliness

It is often assumed that friendliness is the direct opposite of aggression but this is not strictly true. Subordination is really the opposite, and not all subordinate dogs are friendly; similarly, not all aggressive and dominant dogs are unfriendly.

Friendliness is shown in adult dogs in two ways – firstly, by play and, secondly, by 'care-

soliciting' (sometimes called care-seeking or etepimeletic) behaviour.

Play is not the sole province of puppies and juvenile dogs. Adult dogs play, in the same way that adult humans play games such as golf or cards. To humans, games can be seen as a substitute in some ways for fighting – beating an opponent on the golf course or on the card table is a civilized and refined fight, rugby or boxing are perhaps a little less refined! Dogs have not developed this refinement and their play is really inhibited fighting and, even though bites and snaps are commonplace, no-one gets hurt except by accident. A slightly more refined play is seen when dogs pull on either end of a stick or piece of material; in this case, the object of their battles is mentally a rabbit or piece of meat which they are ripping to death or fighting over for possession. Even more refined play is shown in chasing a ball or fetching a stick; possibly the stick is some prey

Top and above: These Border Terriers delightfully demonstrate that play can be fun for adult dogs.

that the dogs are chasing and killing, or it may represent a dead bird that is being retrieved. The shake which some dogs give to a stick after they have caught it suggests that the former possibility is the most likely.

Play among adult dogs is a sure sign of friendliness and certainty that the pack order between the dogs is fixed. If it is not, then aggression between them manifests itself in a real fight. Uncertainty of friendliness is shown by the two dogs who never play together but reserve an icy-cool 'atmosphere' between each other as they avoid entering one another's 'personal zones'.

A curious play game amongst adults could be described as 'playing trains'. This is initiated by one of the pair soliciting play by facing the other, head on, with his shoulders low and giving a light growl. He then turns rapidly and runs off with the second dog in hot pursuit. The two chase one another very closely with many about-turns, until the lead dog eventually rolls over as if he had been shot, thus exposing his underneath for the second dog to attack in play. This complex chasing game may represent a simulated aggression chase between the two dogs – in which case it is the slightly dominant dog who is the initiator of the chase and also the hunted one. Alternatively it could be that chase is a play hunt in which the dog in front plays the part of the prey which is ultimately 'killed'.

In play-soliciting behaviour directed towards a human, much will depend on the bond or relationship between the person and the dog. Bringing a ball, stick or other plaything is the usual approach. Sometimes a dog may paw at the person's leg, give excited growls or yelps, vigorously wag his tail or jump up towards the person and then suddenly withdraw – all the time facing him. All these signs so obviously say 'come and play' that the owner immediately recognizes the friendly overtures of his pet.

Breed variations in friendliness are not so pronounced as with other behavioural and temperament traits. Indeed, all breeds of dog are naturally friendly to man, or else they are unlikely to have been developed in the first place. Even the guard dog breeds are friendly to their owners and other humans not recognized as territory breakers. The toy breeds are obviously especially friendly to humans – their only problem being that they can get so attached to one person that they appear unfriendly to everyone else. Apart from the toy breeds, several breeds in particular are renowned for their love of human company – the Setters, Springers, Labradors, Retrievers and Boxers perhaps being prime examples – although every dog owner knows that his dog is the friendliest of all.

Above: One of the participants in the romping group is beginning to show signs of dominance, as he attempts to put his fore-paws firmly on his play adversary.

Below: Temporary submission! But you can be sure that the underdog won't stay in this position for long.

Top left: King
Charles Spaniels
make excellent pets.

Left: Springer
Spaniels are popular
gun dogs with
considerable appeal
as domestic pets.

Above: Uneasy
bedfellows. The
Miniature Smooth-
Haired Dachshund
eyes the intruder
with suspicion, but
seems reluctant to
make a move or
give up his bed

Care-seeking behaviour is quite rarely seen between adult dogs and more commonly it is shown towards humans. The dog seeks care just like a puppy demands affection from its mother when it crawls forward on its tummy towards her, commonly with its neck extended and making crooning noises. It tends to approach her abdomen and, as it reaches her, it may then roll over on its side. Its tail, held low down to the ground, is wagged gently from side to side.

If the approach is made to humans, the dog will generally jump up and paw at the person and it will commonly lick his face. The dog may gently bite the person's feet or hands or some article of clothing, as it squeaks with excitement.

Specialized activities

Some of the more simple characteristics of dogs have been described but a dog's use to man depends on more complex activities and behavioural patterns. In other words, dogs are not useful just for single activities and simple manoeuvres but for a whole group of activities rolled into one. Some of the most complicated activities are displayed in the behaviour shown by gun dogs and herding dogs. Such activities rely on the special sensory powers for this efficiency and, when these are combined, they make up the complex characteristics and capacities of dogs.

Hunting behaviour

Hunting, killing and retrieval of game is one of the most basic of specialized activities. Dog owners should never forget that they have a predatorial animal in their care – a pet Yorkshire Terrier that chases and kills a wounded wild animal is behaving perfectly naturally. Even the toy dogs and utility group retain pronounced hunting capacities, although these are not developed in their usual life.

Hunting includes the basic behaviours of exploration and aggression, mixed up with some herding. Exploration includes scenting and the chase. There are very few dogs who will not hunt and chase anything that moves. Initially, hunting involves stalking the prey and pointing towards it, whether the hunted animal is a deer or a garden toad. The dog then chases the prey and may show some herding behaviour by running round behind it and cutting off its retreat. The kill itself may consist of tentative nips and bites or a full blown attack in which a small creature may be shaken and thrown about. Rarely does a dog exhibit the playing behaviour which a cat shows towards its prey; the canine instinct is to effect a quick kill.

Whippets show a complex behavioural tendency as they run after their prey; they often open and close their jaws in a slashing motion as if whetting their appetites for the kill.

Having dispatched his prey, a dog often carries it around for a time. He may return it to his master but frequently he will guard his capture, fighting off anyone who wishes to steal it from him. Guarding the prey is not a totally all-embracing mania for most dogs; however, many may fight half-heartedly for retention of 'choice cuts' but are commonly content to share much of the killed animal with others of their group and are happy to help their pack members tear the prey apart.

Burying bones, or even meat, is not a universal behaviour in all dogs. Burying appears to be an attempt to store food. When a dog is ready to leave a bone, he may bury it to prevent others in the group stealing his prize. The tendency to bury is not a breed disposition either, although many gardens full of buried bones do belong to the owners of terriers! There appears to be no truth in the suggestion that bones are buried to make them more digestible or to improve their flavour; many dogs also retain far from perfect memory of the burial site.

Digging is quite a mania in some dogs. This behaviour is related to hunting prey which has gone to earth – animals such as rabbits, badgers, foxes, rats and other small mammals. Digging out earths and chasing prey down their natural tunnels is a very strong inherent behaviour in the terriers, particularly the hunting terriers such as Fox Terriers, hunt terriers and Jack Russell

Above: The Greyhound is an extremely old breed. Although bred as hunting and racing dogs, they make excellent domestic pets.

Left: Terriers, such as this Jack Russell, are extremely active and athletic dogs.

Terriers, who are bred for their earthing ability and capacity to corner a prey (often considerably larger than themselves) until the huntsman arrives. Dachshunds are amongst the most vigorous of digging dogs and can dig holes of enormous proportions in a very short time. They will chew, sever and pull up or dig under any tree roots which cross the path of their tunnelling.

Tracking and herding

Tracking has been mentioned when scenting ability was discussed. In the case of hunting dogs, tracking is part of the search for their quarry, but the same cannot be said of trackers such as Bloodhounds or St. Bernards, which are used to finding humans. Their displays of affection towards the people they find is an indication that they are not 'hunting' them. Probably, the origin of this behaviour lies in the scent following of dogs during their communal daily 'route march'.

Herding is highly complicated behaviour, which is a mixture of hunting, aggression and guarding territory. Some of the sheep and cattle dogs may have been developed for their capacity to guard flocks at night; it is, therefore, aggression that plays a part in their behaviour and selection. Herding the animals into corners and between obstacles, and also singling out animals from a group, is a much more highly developed activity than guarding, and probably has hunting as part of its origin. Possibly the herding dog is acting as one of the hunting pack, with its master as the pack leader. In this case, it is prepared to take orders from its leader but the final part of the hunting behaviour – that of killing the prey – is inhibited.

Herding dogs show stalking and herding tendencies at a very early age and tend to run amok in flocks unless controlled. After the correct training, such dogs do not disturb the flock but can inhibit the movement of the sheep by 'showing-eye'. This means mesmerizing the sheep with a fixed stare at which they will stand quite motionless. Somewhat inexperienced sheepdogs will nip the heels of sheep in an effort to get them moving but, as they learn the 'tricks of the trade', they just rush in as if to nip. This has the required effect of getting the sheep moving.

Cattle herders, such as Corgis, rely almost solely on the fear that cattle have of dogs, to keep the herd moving. They will nip the heels of cattle and, being small and agile, can avoid any kicks which happen to come their way. This heel-nipping behaviour explains the unfortunate tendency of not only Corgis but also other heeling and herding dogs to bite the legs of children who run away from them and snap at postmen delivering mail! Not much can be done to cure them of this, although a brisk slap accompanied by a frightening shout may help.

A curious aberration of herding behaviour has been observed in some members of the Collie and Shetland Sheepdog breeds. This is herding of humans. They will often pace around the house, attempting to 'herd' everybody in it together and they do not seem happy until all the members of the household are in the same room!

Above: The Jack Russell is not accepted as a breed by any of the Kennel Clubs.

Below left: The Welsh Corgi is a very old cattle herding breed.
Below: Sheep herding is the chief occupation of the Border Collie.

The capacity to herd is an inherited behavioural tendency which can be fully expressed by good training. Occasionally, excellent herding is seen in a non-sheepdog or non-heeler breed but this is unusual.

Intensity of activity

Dogs appear to have a considerable reserve capacity of energy. Much, of course, depends on their state of physical fitness but most dogs will continue to exercise until they literally drop. There is considerable breed variation in the need for exercise and also the type of exercise taken. Some dogs will extend themselves by taking enforced exercise of twelve hours a day for several days. Then, they seemingly make up for this burst of energy by spending the majority of the next few days sleeping.

Possibly, this is related to a dog's natural tendency to hunt vigorously until it captures its prey, before gorging itself, after which it sleeps and rests until it needs to eat again. Whatever the reason, the capacity to act in this way would seem to make dogs more adaptable than man, as they do not need such regular and extended sleep.

When tired and in comfortable home situations, dogs will sleep very deeply. Studies of their eye movements have shown that they show similar rapid eye movements, beneath closed eyelids, to the movements of human eyes and this suggests that their brains shut off in a similar way when sleeping. Dogs certainly dream and it is a common sight to see their legs 'running', as they emit excited squeals and barks as if chasing an imaginary dreamland hare! They are also slower to wake up from these deep sleeps.

Unlike humans, dogs spend a lot of time in half-sleep. This means sleep from which they are easily roused and are immediately capable of defending themselves or their territory, another important adaptation for life in the wild. It often appears that domestic dogs rest for the greatest part of their day and yet are easily activated. Probably their total rest quotient is similar to humans but they make up for shorter periods of deep sleep by having much longer half-sleep time.

Behavioural development in puppies

As already discussed, puppies are not born with a fully developed set of behavioural activites. Just as they are immature in their form and function, so they are also immature in their behaviour and temperament. Like children, how they develop will be affected by their environment and the individuals they meet. To develop into well-balanced puppies that have fully realized their breed potential, they need the correct blend of social contacts – dog, animal and human. A short study of a puppy's behavioural development gives a greater understanding of the temperament of adult dogs and of the many problems which may arise or have arisen in a dog's behaviour.

Behaviouralists recognize four stages in a puppy's development to adulthood, although these stages obviously merge into one continuous process. The neonatal stage is the first and lasts from birth up to about fourteen days old. During this time, only the most basic behavioural activity is displayed, as the pup does not leave the nest and is unable to move around on its own. The transition stage from day fourteen to three weeks old sees a rapid development of the puppy's senses and also his capacity to move around. By the end of this period, the pup can see, hear, smell and move quite well. In the third stage, the pup begins to be aware of and react to its surroundings and its litter-mates, whilst

Below: Retrieval is a complex part of hunting behaviour, but training starts at an early age. This Labrador has been initiated to retrieving in his owner's back yard.

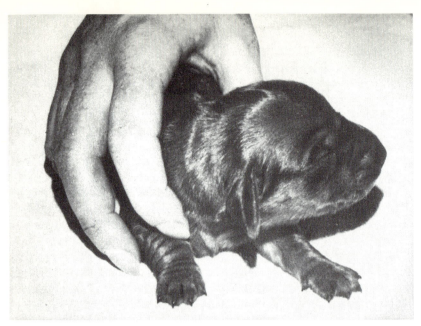

Above: Newborn puppies are blind, but will search for their mother by extending their heads and crawling forward slowly. This is known as the 'rooting reflex'.

Below: At five days old, this puppy is still blind, but is now making a positive effort to get up on its legs.

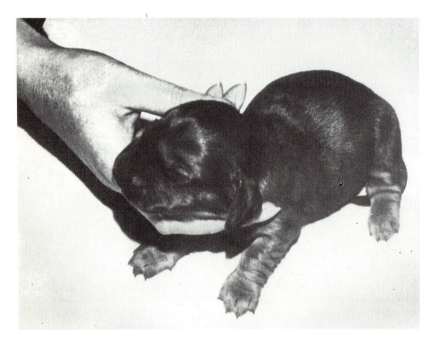

old and social contact is of little or no importance until then.

From three weeks onwards, the pup becomes increasingly aware of its mother and litter mates. It soon starts to venture from the group and begins to explore its environment and the responses of its animal contacts. By four weeks old, a pup can walk well, recognize its mother and try to follow her as she moves about. No longer is its activity confined to rooting for food and nuzzling at the mother. The total waking time increases with short periods of play after feeding, which gradually lengthen until they may take up two to three hours a day in an eight-week-old puppy.

Play is a vital part of a puppy's development, just as it is in the growing-up process of a child. Part of play is exploration, finding out what strange things smell like, feel like, look like and taste like, whether it is a plant leaf or a litter-mate's foot. Deprived of the opportunity to investigate, pups become not only bored, centring their energies on fighting other pups or whining, but, at a later date, when they do meet the big, wide world, they are unduly sensitive to the new strange stimuli and may be scared. Such puppies may retain the timidity to new things well into adulthood.

But play is more than just chewing a twig. It involves fighting over the twig, pulling it backwards and forwards and running after it with the others in a group, when the pack leader has managed to claim possession of it after a fight. During the play fight, the pups simulate stalking, chasing, herding, biting and killing the prey with head-shaking and leg-biting behaviour. Accompanying the fight are all the sounds of the chase and kill – the bay, the growl, the bark and, if play gets a little rough, a submissive whine. As important as winning the play fight is losing it and a pup soon learns not to stay around too long if all the others decide to attack at once. Co-ordinated attack is rarely too intense but in some terrier breeds, quite serious injuries can be inflicted to litter-mates in such early games.

The importance of contact and posture is obvious to anyone who has observed a litter of socializing pups. Pawing is usually play-soliciting; soft-mouthing appears to be a greeting while hard-mouthing with biting is obviously fighting. Nuzzling under the tummy usually results in the nuzzled pup standing still in the same way the mother does, to allow the pups to suckle. This care-soliciting behaviour is sometimes retained into later life.

As early as four to five weeks, members of a litter start performing quite complex behaviour together, such as chasing a moving ball or running after a litter-mate who has cornered the one and only bone. Already the litter are a pack –

beginning to show quite complex behavioural patterns. This socialization stage lasts until weaning, which usually takes place at between eight to ten weeks old. The final stage in the pup's behavioural development is the juvenile period, which extends from weaning until the pup reaches full social maturity.

During the first three weeks of a pup's life – that is the neonatal and transitional stage – behaviour is rather basic. It seeks warmth, contact and food, and the most important reflex it displays is the 'rooting reflex'. This is a crawling movement with the neck extended in search of the bitch's mammary area. The mother is in full control of the elimination of the pup, which urinates and defecates in response to her licking, remaining quite motionless while she does this. Other than seeking the warmth of the mother and litter-mates, pups show no communication behaviour until they are three weeks

capable of not only eating, sleeping and playing at the same time but able to perform individual activities together in a co-ordinated way. They are learning to hunt and investigate together and are so preparing themselves for the daily route marches of adulthood. They will make a good attempt at defending their territory against invaders and show co-ordinated aggression by barking and growling at strange noises or animals.

Although pups are born with all the basics of the nervous system, the development of the brain and central nervous system continues well into adulthood. The cerebrum (the part of the brain which is involved in conscious actions) is present at birth but, over the first three months of the pup's life, its surface becomes more and more convoluted and furrowed. These furrowings give it a greater surface area and this, and other developments in the nerve cells themselves, make it a much more complex and efficient structure which is needed to cope with the greater demand placed upon it.

It is during this socialization period that the puppy reared under normal circumstances begins to meet man. Quite soon he learns to recognize the sight and smell of man and to realize that this is the animal who brings food, pats him, lifts him up and even shows some dominance over him. This early association with man is vital and if pups do not meet humans during their early socialization period, then it is found that it is almost impossible, or at best very difficult, to get them to socialize with humans and become domesticated and happy in a human

home environment when kept as a family pet.

Experience has shown most dog breeders that the best time for a pup to leave the litter is around eight weeks old. There are variations to this, which will be discussed later, but by this time the pup will have had plenty of litter-mate contact, enabling him to socialize happily with dogs at a later age, and yet will still be within the natural socialization period for contact with man.

The balance of contact between dog and human is a rather fine one, but it can be redressed on either side of the eight-week period to make up for obvious deficiencies. For instance, if a pup is weaned at five weeks instead of eight, then he could be insufficiently 'dog socialized'. However, if he is then given the company of other dogs, even if this company is not continuous, he is likely to develop into a perfectly balanced dog with respect to other canines. Similarly, a very late weaning at, for instance, twelve weeks need not be disastrous, resulting in a puppy which is intractable and afraid of man. As long as he sees plenty of people who pick him up, play with him and dominate him, he will be adequately socialized to humans.

Contact is in itself a very important part of socialization. It has been observed that personal contact is more important than the pleasurable stimuli, such as feeding. A small group of laboratory dogs were subjected to an experiment which involved daily blood sampling, the dogs being sampled each day by the same person. A different person fed them and cleaned out the runs, but did not often make any contact with the dogs. Although the daily contact with the same

Above: Twelve days old and the puppy's eyes are now open, although it sees only through a hazy cornea.

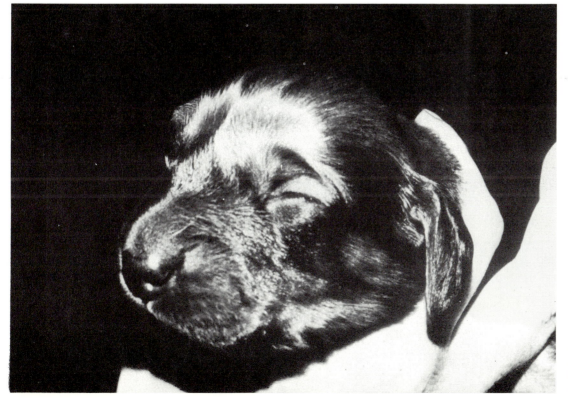

Left: At five days old, the puppy's ear flaps are now visible.

83

person involved a painful stimulus – that of blood sampling by needle puncture of a foreleg vein – it was soon observed that the dogs became very attached to this person and showed obvious pleasure when he arrived by wagging their tails, excitedly jumping up and barking happily. Their show of interest in the person who fed them, however, was very weak indeed. Dogs therefore are not guided only by their bellies; they show affection to humans for many other reasons!

Some breeds have inherent problems, which together with certain circumstances can lead to extremes of social imbalance. Although some of the late-maturing breeds should theoretically have a long socialization period, if humans enter their social world too late, they can be imprinted on other dogs so that they do not accept humans well. Some of the problems have already been mentioned with regard to fear-biters and aggression tendencies. The answer with some of these strains of later maturing breeds seems to be early and continuous contact with humans coupled with continuous contact with their litter-mates for as long as possible. In practice this is difficult to arrange, but a good compromise can be to wean early at five to seven weeks, *but* – and this is very important – the pup must then have as much contact with other dogs and as many strange places and things as possible or else it will become too dependent on its master. This will result in aggressive tendencies and 'spookiness' at a later date.

If dogs are delayed in their socialization with humans, problems may occur when they are ultimately trained for specialist behaviour and purposes. For this reason, dogs which are destined to become Guide Dogs for the Blind are weaned at a very early age. Their subsequent socialization with many people ensures that they are unlikely to get too attached to any one individual. They are also rather poorly dog-oriented in their social behaviour, which, coupled with their training to ignore other dogs, makes them unlikely to desert their blind owners and cross a street in search of dog contact. The fact that they are sterilized ensures that, even if the dog on the other side of the street is a bitch on heat or a courting male, they are not tempted to leave their owners.

Puppies will commonly get friendly with members of another species, such as cats or rabbits if reared with them. If their social contacts are solely with these other species, they may prefer their company to that of fellow dogs.

The relationship between dog and man is essentially an attachment between two different species. The special social attachment of dogs to man is a function of man's capacity to become pack leader and a measure of his control of dog breeding in selecting strains within breeds which show a heightened capacity to socialize with him.

Behavioural problems

Behavioural problems can be much more important than medical problems, both for the dogs and their owners. The mental trauma of owning a fear-biter, or a dog who wrecks the home if left for longer than an hour, or a dog-fighting dog can make dog-owning a pain rather than a pleasure.

We have already seen how many of these temperament problems can arise. Most of them are 'man-made' in that they are caused by bad upbringing. Breeding can also play a large part, however, and some strains of dog can be home-wreckers or aggressive, although their upbringing has been exemplary. If the only criteria considered, when selecting for breeding, are a dog's conformation, his coat colour or his length of stride, then temperament problems are bound to occur. Judges in the show ring are not immediately concerned about whether the beautiful Boxer to whom they are giving first prize has just eaten his owner's Persian carpet or killed the next-door cat, and the dog's physical form and appearance, or even behaviour in the show ring, will not reveal these problems. In fact, such bad habits really only have any great significance if they are passed on with the dog's genes, if he is used for breeding. Such a simple trait as home destruction is unlikely to be perpetuated but aggression and extreme timidity may be. The genetics of inheritance behaviour are very complex and there are few traits which can be stated simply as being dominant or recessive. In general, though, a bad temperament should be discriminated against in a breeding programme, even at the expense of losing some other point. After all, whether a dog is brindle or black-and-tan, is comparatively unimportant in

Below: Very young pups are unhappy and worried if placed on their backs. They extend their legs and squeak miserably as they try to right themselves.

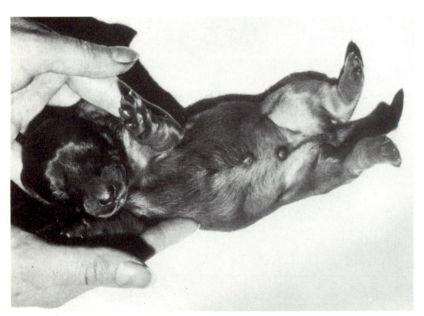

Above: Anxious to play, this youngster tries to entice its somewhat reluctant mother into a game.

Right: If it is very hot, puppies may lie out in a line. More usually, they 'pile' together for warmth and contact. Newspapers make an excellent bed for these Cairn puppies.

Above: Many prospective dog owners dismiss mongrels when making their choice, but this bright-eyed and alert dog is an ideal pet.

Below and below right: Thorough investigation of the environment is a vital part of a puppy's early socialization. All puppies are naturally inquisitive.

relation, say, to a child being badly mauled by an aggressive dog.

Displaced behaviour is a common problem with dogs nowadays. This is a behavioural aberration caused by the normal behavioural drive of the dog being inhibited and tends to occur when an animal is very bored or very excited. The bored Alsatian would like to romp across fields but, as he is confined to a small kitchen, he chews a hole in the kitchen door. The bored terrier, left alone in his tiny kennel, wants to be half-way down a rat hole or play-fighting with his canine friends, so he paces from one side of the run to the other for hours on end. When his owner returns, the dog may be so excited that he runs madly round in circles or he may even suddenly bite his owner or bite a piece of furniture. Keeping the dog occupied is the cure every time.

Excessive sexual drive is also commonly a problem encountered in bored dogs and some of the larger breeds. Sex mania in males is not unusual in some strains of Labradors, Retrievers and some other gun and retrieval dogs and in these cases there may be need for castration to make the dog socially acceptable.

Some of the timid breeds, such as the Toy Spaniels, Miniature and Toy Poodles, Pekinese, Pomeranians and even some Afghans and Collies, sometimes display excessive human attachment and dependence. The dog may become highly nervous and unhappy when separated from its owner or even when a situation arises where a separation is threatened. These dogs may pine if left and show spiteful aggressive tendencies to anyone who comes near their beloved owner. These unfortunate, over-indulged dogs have a perpetual juvenile attitude to all animals and humans. The damage is already done when they get to this stage – the

prevention would have been more extensive socialization with other dogs and people for a longer period. Cure is very difficult, but sometimes gradually introducing them to an increasingly strange environment, group of animals and humans may help them to become more 'outgoing' and sociable.

Some types of dogs can easily become dominant, and an over-permissive upbringing can lead to them being aggressive and domineering. Dogs which do need a firm hand and strict discipline are often the stronger breeds – the giant breeds such as Great Danes and Pyreneans being prime examples. However, nearly all the terriers, many gun dogs and even some small breeds such as Wire-haired Dachshunds can be very strong-willed and need a strong will to control them, so they do not develop into canine juvenile delinquents. Luckily this problem can generally be cured by firm words and actions but care has to be taken that

the dog is not so beaten into submission that he becomes cowed and surly. Usually, however, a lesson only has to be delivered once for the dog to understand that you are the pack leader.

Over-indulged dogs are just like spoiled children – and no-one likes either!

Canine intelligence

It is indisputable that a dog's brain is very active. Throughout this chapter the sort of things that go on in a dog's brain have been discussed and it would be wrong to say that nothing happens. There is, however, little or no evidence to show that dogs think in the same way as man. All we can witness is that the dog obeys simple commands from his owner or basic commands from his own body, that of eating when he is hungry or showing aggression when he feels that his territory is threatened.

Below: A breed of ancient extraction, the Saluki is gentle and affectionate. It is a true Gazehound – hunting almost entirely by using its powers of sight.

capacities which dogs have in the various behavioural fields.

Given that the capacity to learn is in *some* ways akin to human intelligence, can we say that obedience is a measure of intelligence? The answer is no, for a dog may have learnt to perform an action and may be capable of performing it well and yet not obey the command. Some terriers can learn quickly and usually perform well on command, but they are commonly obstinate or 'wooden' and refuse to act at a certain time.

Temperament influences a dog's capacity to be trained; shy or dominated dogs are sometimes slow to learn new things and wary of investigating strange experiences. Similarly, a dog which is highly dog-oriented but is not well socialized with humans can be intractable but it would be unfair to label it as 'unintelligent'. All it means is that its capacity to be trained can never meet its full potential.

Another influence on intelligence is the dog's environment. Recent scientific investigation has suggested that intelligence in humans is, on average, about fifty-one per cent dependent on genetics and forty-nine per cent on environment. This means that, on average, highly intelligent parents have a slightly greater chance of producing more intelligent offspring than less bright parents, as long as the environmental influences on both children are the same. If the children of the dull parents were pushed hard at school, subjected to hard mental effort and intelligent company they would, on average, be more intelligent at sixteen years old than the sixteen-year-old offspring of the bright parents who have never had such mental gymnastics to perform. The same is probably true of dogs. There must be *some* genetic advantage in being a Collie who is quick to lead sheep well, or else the breed would not be any better at it than Boxers! True, Boxers don't usually get asked to herd sheep but if one did, from weaning, it might do the job quite well!

Memory is often quoted as a measure of intelligence but we know this to be untrue. Even with humans, quite simple or even mentally retarded people can have phenomenal powers of memory. Perhaps because they do not have to use their brains to worry about politics or higher mathematics, they have more mental reserves to use for retaining actions and sensations from the past. A dog can remember something which stimulated him strongly, even if that stimulus occurred a long time ago. For example, a dog may re-enter a house after a long period away and go straight to the room where he found biscuits on the floor five years ago. We like to think, anthropomorphically, that he is being 'intelligent', but he isn't really. We may still remember the incident, although we had neither

Mental capacity is rather like art; it varies in beauty, form and concept depending on who sees it. Whippets and Beagles can catch hares better than a man without special implements or firearms. A single Collie can herd a flock of sheep, even without his owner's commands, better than ten men. We would have no chance in trailing the scent of a human the way a Bloodhound can. You can call these capacities instinctive if you wish but they are, in the broadest sense of the words, mental capacities.

If the definition of mental capacity is to be narrowed down and restricted to something approaching human intelligence, then the dog is obviously left far behind. Dogs can learn quite well by associating different stimuli with certain actions, although great variations are shown here by different breeds. Foxhounds may be able to associate the huntsman's commands with actions they are supposed to perform but their learning capacity is not exactly startling. In general, none of the pack hunting dogs are quick to learn and they are thus difficult to train. However, this does not necessarily make them less intelligent than an easily trained breed like a working Collie. Intelligence in a dog depends so much on the methods of measurement one uses. One dog may have a superior scenting capacity to another, who may have a superior sight capacity to another who may have a superior herding capacity to the first one ... and so on. How can comparisons or measurements possibly be made? So much depends on the specialized the reward of the smell nor the taste of the biscuit and, in the intervening years, have had much more to think about than the dog.

There has been much discussion and investigation into the possibility that dogs have a sixth sense or a capacity of extrasensory perception. With respect to the sense of smell, dogs have much greater perceptive ability than humans and this may explain some of the incredible feats of tracking and homing shown by dogs. It may be that dogs are sensitive to the earth's magnetic forces and so have an additional navigational sense. Probably, however, perception of the sun's position, landmarks such as stones with particular smells or even shapes are the guides which give them this ability. We must not be too sceptical of the possibility of a sixth sense, though; migratory birds and fishes show fantastic navigational ability which man has not yet been able to elucidate, so may not dogs have this capacity too, to a lesser extent?

Mental telepathy is another subject of great debate. The heightened powers of perceptual acuity of some of a dog's senses may explain a little of the less fantastic stories of telepathic communication between dogs and people. We may not realize it, but perhaps we produce different body smells or move in a slightly different way when we are about to do different things. Dogs may be able to discern these tiny changes and act on them. More difficult to explain are the cases of possible telepathic communication over long distances. Once again, it would be peremptory to be too sceptical of suggestions that dogs have senses which we cannot detect.

To return to our original discussion point – what goes on in a dog's mind? – we must try to decide whether dogs think in the same way as man. Are dogs thinking of food all the time, or of bitches in heat? Probably not. Possibly because they have greater sensory powers than man, they spend more time consciously examining their environment than he does, even though they may not be engaged in the act of sniffing. Most of the time we are unaware of the scent of our environment because the smells are not strong enough to reach our level of consciousness. But, if our scenting capacities were as acute as those of dogs, we might well spend more mental capacity in constantly analysing our environment. This is only one example of an enhanced sensory capacity in dogs; all the others are involved in the dog's mental activities.

It is most probable that dogs are not thinking of anything most of the time – or at least, their brains are not involved in thought processes. The mass of evidence suggests that dogs are not capable of originating thoughts unless they are stimulated to do so first. For instance, the smell of meat may make a dog get up, move around and search for his food bowl; hunger may make him act in the same way. Man, on the other hand, is capable of a chain of thoughts which do not need any external stimulus to start them.

Man's attitude to dogs

Why is it that dogs are so popular with man? We have tried in part to answer this question throughout this book, but the full answer is more complex than just having dogs as companions that help catch food, herd sheep or guard the home.

Dogs seem to be among the few animals who retain an open social structure; that is, they do not possess a very strong drive to socialize solely with members of the same species. Other animals can enter the dog's social world. This is rather like the difference between a socially open society in human life, such as a music-appreciation club, and a socially closed one, like an ethnic religious sect or an erudite academic society.

Furthermore, the dog's desire to please seems to be a species attribute and he is always happy to have a pack leader. Little wonder that some people show more affection to their dogs than they do to other humans. You may have had a bad day at the office, received a tax demand and had your car stolen but your dog will always make a fuss of you!

Below: The Irish Water Spaniel is a comparatively rare breed. Its coat has an unusual texture which is completely water resistant.

Sporting Dogs

Dogs, by nature, are sporting animals. Very few dogs can resist scouting around for a scent, chasing a rabbit, or showing excitement at the prospect of a brisk walk. Many sports actually revolve around this instinct to hunt and chase.

Under the classification of the Kennel Club in Britain, the registerable sporting breeds are contained within the Sporting Division. This includes the Hunt, Gundog and Terrier Groups. In America, classifications are rather different and the Sporting Group refers only to gundog breeds, which are included in the British Kennel Club's Gundog Group.

Many people feel that hunting, particularly through the use of another animal, is a destructive and deplorable pastime. Others would claim that hunting is a perfectly natural activity for man and animal, either singly or together. They would claim that hunting is an extension of a basic need to find food and is necessary to rid the countryside of unwanted, verminous predators. No doubt the arguments for and against hunting as a sport will continue as long as man hunts with the dog. However, in view of hunting's ancient history, it seems unlikely that this activity will suddenly vanish.

Hunting

It is impossible to conceal the predatory instincts of dogs. All puppies play-fight and that is the most obvious indication that dogs are born with

Above: Hounds from the Fitzwilliam Hunt are released in the early morning from their pound before going off for a day's hunt.

Below: This huntsman exercises the hounds in the kennel paddock during the summer to keep them fit for the new season.

the impulse to kill to eat. To ignore this is to rob the dog of the respect it deserves as one of the most successful predators in the evolution of animals.

We have already traced the development of the hunting prowess of dogs. This prowess has always been important to man. Within all groups of dogs there are breeds which have either a present-day hunting use or a history of hunting. However, over the last few centuries, man has turned to the gun as a more efficient method of killing the animals he wishes to eat. Nowadays, hunting with dogs is mainly confined to the pursuit of verminous animals such as foxes, rats and hares. Although the destruction of vermin by hunting has taken on social and sporting aspects that some people find objectionable, in general, dogs *do* destroy vermin very efficiently. There is also some evidence to show that there is less behaviour stress for the vermin in being pursued by a dog, which could be described as a 'natural' enemy, than in being hunted by man, with his traps and his guns.

Although the Gundog Group consists of 'hunters' in the broad sense of the word, in the last few centuries they have mainly been used in association with the gun and we shall consider them later in that context. It is only breeds contained in the Hound and Terrier Groups that are selected and bred primarily for their hunting behaviour. And, within these groups, there are only a few examples of breeds which are currently employed solely for hunting. Certainly, all dogs in these groups retain a heightened hunting capacity, but nowadays the vast majority are bred as show or companion dogs. Indeed, this change of emphasis has been so extreme that, when a dog is needed solely for hunting, it is almost impossible to find a suitable pure breed and we have to resort to interbreed crossing to produce the desired result. For example, the comparatively new sport of racoon hunting in America has led to the development of the American Coonhound, which is a 'cross-bred', although the Coonhound is eighty per cent Foxhound in origin. Pure Foxhounds would not have been suitable for coon-hunting. American Coonhounds are not recognized even by the American Kennel Club, although they are registered by the United Kennel Club.

A similar story applies to the popular and effective hunt terrier, the Jack Russell. Although there are a few exceptions, many Fox Terriers and other recognized terrier breeds are just not suitable for dealing with a fox when it goes to earth. Even at the beginning of this century, the insatiable demand for sticking to breed standards had affected the Fox Terrier breed. However, some people preferred terriers with less perfect looks, but more 'guts and go'. One such person was the Reverend Jack Russell, a mid-nineteenth

century Master of Foxhounds. Russell would use any type of wire-haired Fox Terrier dog that he liked the look of, for his Devon Hunt. From them, a definite Jack Russell Terrier type evolved which, although still variable in size and conformation, is generally a much smoother and smaller dog than those kept by the parson. This variability has prevented Jack Russell Terriers from being recognized by the Kennel Club.

Very early in their development, hunting dogs were chosen either for their sighting or scenting capacities. These characteristics are still con-

Above: While the huntsmen discuss future tactics, the Foxhound pack waits patiently for instructions.

Below: After a day's hunting the hounds are transported back to the paddock where they will be well fed.

Above: The hounds walk patiently across the countryside waiting to pick up the scent of the fox.

Below: These Foxhounds function as a pack within which the order of 'social' dominance will be well established.

sidered of prime importance. The appearance of hounds and terriers is perhaps less significant, in overall terms, than the way they are employed and the work they now do.

Foxhounds and foxhunting

A young Foxhound's life starts in the same way as any other dog's. The hound bitch normally has a large litter. Up to twenty-one puppies have been recorded but the normal litter is not so large. The number actually reared would probably be six or seven. The puppies are born at the Hunt Kennels and are reared by the mother under the care of the kennel staff. Weaning takes place at about six weeks and life is no different for them than for any other puppy. At about twelve weeks, the puppy's training begins when it is handed over to the 'walker'. This is the term used

to describe a person, who may be a local farmer, a member of the Hunt or someone with a special interest in the Hunt, who 'adopts' a hound puppy (or maybe more) for several months. During this time the hound experiences a measure of domestication, learns to walk on the lead, to mix with people and other dogs and to become accustomed, as far as possible, to farm animals. It is an essential part of a hound's early training that it learns not to worry or even to show any particular interest in farm animals or other dogs and cats.

The young hound is returned to the Hunt Kennels for the 'Puppy Show' which is held at the Kennels and is an important event in the Hunt year. On this occasion all the young hounds of that season are present with their 'walkers' and prizes are awarded for the hound which is considered to have been the best reared.

After returning to the Kennels the young hound joins the older and experienced hounds to adapt to pack life. During exercise periods, it will be coupled up to an older hound (i.e. the young hound's collar is linked to that of the older hound) so that it becomes familiar with, and learns to obey, the commands of the huntsman.

The Hunting Season is from November to March. It is preceded by a short period, lasting two to three months, during which 'Cub Hunting' takes place. This is when the young foxes are hunted in an attempt to cull the fox population which has increased during the breeding season. It is at this time that a hound has its first experience of hunting.

Hounds are not counted individually but referred to in pairs, known as 'couples'. Every hound is known, intimately, by the huntsman, who can describe its personality and characteristics in great detail – a remarkable feat considering that he may have between forty and fifty couples, and frequently more, in his care. Each hound is named and always responds to its name.

There is a unique vocabulary attached to hounds and hunting. An outsider will soon learn that hounds are never referred to as 'dogs', always 'hounds'. That they do not have 'tails', but 'sterns', that a hound 'stud dog' is 'a stallion dog hound', that a 'line' is the trail of scent left by a fox. To 'riot' is when a Foxhound hunts any animal other than a fox.

Life for a pack of hounds follows a strict routine. There is a feeding procedure which is adhered to rigidly, depending on whether or not the pack is hunting. For example, a hound would not be able to hunt on a full stomach so they are not given a heavy meal immediately before hunting. They are usually fed on a mixture of boiled meat, cereals, bran and gravy and this pudding-like mixture is fed in troughs, but there is no 'free-for-all'. The huntsman selects the shy

Right: Eager for any passing scent, these hounds are being taken, by trailer, to the meet.

Below: These young Foxhound puppies will eventually be integrated into the adult pack and will soon be avidly scenting foxes.

feeders from their lodges (kennels) first to ensure that all the hounds get a fair share. The source of meat for hounds is usually farm stock which has died from non-infectious disease or as the result of an accident. This 'flesh' is collected by the kennel staff from the surrounding farmers who either – by tradition – donate it to the Hunt or are paid only a nominal sum.

During the season, the Hunt will go out two or three times a week. Usually fifteen to twenty couples will be selected from the pack on each occasion.

When the bitch hounds are 'on heat' they are kept entirely separate from the rest of the pack. They are fed and exercised on their own and are not taken out hunting. When it is decided to breed from them, bitches can be mated either to a stallion dog hound in the pack or to one from another pack. This depends on the line of breeding and what special attributes the huntsman wishes to pursue. The quality of the pack depends on careful breeding to encourage the production of puppies with the good points which are required for their pack.

The bitch in whelp will not be taken out hunting after the first few weeks of her pregnancy. She will continue to live in the pack until about a month before her litter is due. She is then removed from the pack to a kennel of her own and will probably have quite a lot of freedom until her litter is born. She returns to the pack when her puppies are weaned.

Foxhunting is not such an ancient sport. Hounds originally hunted the stag and it was not until the middle of the eighteenth century that foxhunting became the vogue and kennels, such as the Fitzwilliam or Berkeley, took up the sport.

The origin of the Foxhound itself, though, is very ancient. Probably the hound was introduced to Britain from France by the Normans for deer hunting. These heavy Norman Talbot, or St. Hubert Hounds, were a common ancestor for the modern Bloodhound. It is from them that the hound inherits its 'nose' or ability to discern scent.

The controlled breeding and registration of Foxhounds is an old science, for the Foxhound Kennel Stud Book was opened in 1800 (seventy-three years before the inception of the Kennel Club) and has been published continuously ever

Above: Foxhound bitches on heat are segregated from the dogs of the pack.

Below: Hunting is thirsty work – especially for hounds.

and have tremendous 'bone' especially on the shoulders and the straight, almost spar-like, legs. This tremendous skeleton, covered in obviously plentiful muscle, makes for a superb and fast hunting machine with incredible stamina. It is not unusual for a pack to travel a linear 64 km (40 miles), meaning that an individual hound may cover 160 km (100 miles). Foxhounds are noble creatures in appearance. Their broad, slightly-domed head with its powerful, blunt, muzzle gives them an aristocratic look. But this noble head is not there for beauty. The well-developed nasal bones are needed for 'scenting', and the strong mouth both for 'giving tongue' when excited by the hot scent of a fox and, ultimately, for killing the quarry.

It is a popular misconception that Foxhounds are vicious. This is certainly not true and they are friendly to all creatures, with one obvious exception! They have been bred to hunt the fox, but any ill-temper shown towards other creatures, especially humans, is strongly deprecated and disciplinary action would be taken by any hunt staff in this respect. At a meet the hounds, and in particular the bitches, will commonly make a great fuss of followers and they are great favourites with children.

Although the breed is recognized by the Kennel Club, there are great variations in size, weight, colour and conformity of Foxhounds. Different hunts will select different hounds, depending on the terrain to be hunted. It is no accident that hounds of the 'Shire' packs of the Midlands, such as the Cottesmore, Pitcheley and Quorn, are big, long-legged and fast, for they are selectively bred for open country. On the other hand, smaller, shorter-legged hounds which are hardier, more capable of hunting in hilly or wooded country but have a very strong scenting ability, are ideal for the Border Counties.

The 'classic' Foxhound is tricolour – that is to say, it has mainly white legs, tan ears and face with a white muzzle and blaze, and a black and tan body, but other colours are common. Black and tan hounds are often found in Scotland and Ireland and sometimes totally white hounds are seen. The term 'badger pied' is given to a mainly light hound with grey, speckled, patches.

since. Foxhunting itself is under the control of the Masters of Foxhounds Association (MFA) which was formed in 1881 by the Duke of Beaufort. The MFA lays down strict rules and etiquette by which all who hunt are obliged to abide.

Most people, seeing a Foxhound for the first time, are struck by their size. They are big dogs

Beagles

The Beagle is something of a rarity among hunting dogs, in that it still performs the task for which it was originally bred – that of tracking the hare in Britain and Europe and the cottontail rabbit in the United States. The Beagle's history of hare-chasing can be reliably traced back to the fifteenth century, and there is circumstantial evidence that the breed existed in Greece, in a form similar to the present day, as far back as the third century B.C.

The nineteenth-century European Beagle was often bred smaller than today's dogs. It was referred to as the 'pocket Beagle' because it could easily be carried in the coat pockets (admittedly voluminous) of huntsmen. These dogs stood only 25 cm (10 ins) or less to the point of the shoulder, whereas the breed standard laid down by the Kennel Club today is 32.5–40 cm (13–16 ins). Beagles are found in any hound coat colour, of which the most popular is probably the tricolour – that is, a mixture of black, white and tan. Other colours commonly seen are lemon and white, 'badger pied', blue, tan and white, and black and white, but there are many other colours, mixes and mottles. At first glance, Beagles bear a close resemblance to short-legged Foxhounds but, in fact, they have a more domed forehead and perhaps a less noble bearing than the larger breed.

Beagles are within the top twenty-five most popular breeds registered annually – a fact probably attributable to their manageable size, cleanliness, attractive appearance and gaiety. They have an equable temperament and are well-mannered with children and other dogs, yet Beagles do have some drawbacks as household pets. They can be stubborn and wayward and, not uncommonly, they are also destructive. Frequently they have a desire to roam – although keeping Beagles with other dogs can often help to overcome this problem.

Beagling
Apart from a period in the seventeenth and eighteenth centuries, when fox-hunting was the sporting mania, beagling has been a popular sport for hundreds of years. It is now undergoing a tremendous revival in Britain and Beagle trials have an unsurpassed following in America.

Classically, the beagling season in Britain extends from September to April, with exercising runs during the summer at the discretion of the huntsman. Meets may be held during weekdays, but they are most popular on Saturdays, and their frequency depends very much upon the countryside available and the size of the field of followers. Hunting at the same location more

than twice or, at most, three times in a season is generally avoided. Meets are held on large farms and over land harbouring hares. This usually means open countryside, fields and arable land. The size of the pack varies, but a manageable number is twelve to fifteen couples.

Although beagling is not beset with the horse and tack expenses of foxhunting, the costs of beagling are still considerable. Hounds have to be fed, the salaries of the huntsman and kennel staff must be paid and there are ancillary expenses, such as transport and veterinary attention. Nonetheless, beagling is a considerably cheaper sport for its followers than is foxhunting.

Pack Beagles are kept in very similar circumstances to Foxhounds. They live in purpose-built kennels, which have feeding troughs and exercise yards. Usually the Beagles

Top: It is not unusual for the scent to be lost while beagling. This is known as a check.

Above: A group of hounds waiting patiently for the huntsman's next command.

Below: Before the 'off', an atmosphere of excitement spreads throughout the pack.

Above: The heavy Basset Hound is used for hare hunting and is followed on foot.

Below: The Basenji was originally an African dog. It is still used by the natives of Sudan for hunting antelope and beating big game.

every scent, but a good pack should be 'steady' (that is, ignore the scent of foxes, domestic cats, weasels and so on, and keenly follow only that of the hare, however 'cold'). Good Beagles follow the scent very closely, never deviating to follow other smells which may cross the primary scent.

Hounds searching for a scent to follow are generally very quiet but, once they have located a line, they 'give tongue'. The music they make gets more excited, louder and expressive as the scent gets hotter. The whippers-in and the field make an all-out attempt to keep up with the pack and a whipper-in will shout 'holloa' if he catches sight of the quarry.

The ultimate goal is to catch up with, and dispatch, the hare which produced the line. This is not an easy goal, when one considers the tremendous speed of the hare, its guile and its capacity to run in circles which can easily confuse the hounds.

If the hounds make a kill they are moved on to another part of the hunting territory, to find another scent. A completely blind day's hunting is by no means rare.

If the popularity of beagling continues to grow at its present rate, the already numerous British packs will certainly increase. Some packs have quite ancient origins and are associated with colleges, universities, the Services and other public and private institutions and societies. In America, hunting with Beagles is also very popular. The most common quarry is the cottontail rabbit but sometimes the European hare, the jack rabbit or the snowshoe hare are chased.

are taken to the meet in vans or small trailers. Like foxhunting, Beagle meets usually start at public houses, farmhouses or some similar home where the occupants are sympathetic to the sport. After a short time the whole party moves off, the Master followed by the hounds which in turn are followed by the whippers-in and the rest of the field.

Once out into the countryside, the Beagles cast about searching for the scent of the hare, and the huntsmen and field make every attempt to keep up with them. Unless one is extremely fit, following the pack's every run and double-back can be crippling. Beagles will naturally hunt

Field trials in the U.S.A. and Canada

Beagle field trials are a popular sport in North America and outnumber trials for all other breeds of dogs combined. The trials last for several days and often more than 200 dogs compete in a single event within the trial.

The sexes are divided and grouped by sizes. When trailing the cottontail rabbit they run as a brace, but they run in a pack when hunting the hare. The mounted judges give marks for style, speed and endurance. All the trial events are governed by strict rules. Beagle field trials provide as much fun and interest for the spectators as they do for the dog owners and for the dogs themselves.

Showing Beagles

As with Foxhounds, showing working Beagles is mainly an affair for the pack owners and followers. Shows are held under the rules of The Association of Masters of Harriers and Beagles in Britain, and in the U.S.A. by the National Beagle Club. At important shows, such as the

Peterborough Hound Show and the South of England Show, the dogs are judged on their form and on their fluidity of free movement in the ring.

Harriers

Harriers were especially liked for hunting hares and, although they were originally followed on foot, the pack is now followed by a mounted field. These hounds stand 47–52 cm (19–21 ins) to the withers and, with the exception of rather dished faces, fall very much between a Foxhound and Beagle in appearance. Harrier packs are now quite rare, as the sport was hit by the increasing popularity of foxhunting.

Basset Hounds

Like so many sporting dogs, the original stock of the Basset is not completely clear, although its countries of origin are certainly France and Belgium. Probably, the Basset was derived from the French St. Hubert Hound by selectively breeding for lower, heavy dogs with considerable endurance which could crash their way through scrub and undergrowth in pursuit of boar, deer, wolves and other game including hares, which it hunts today. Bassets have two very pronounced features. They have superb noses which at times can even rival those of Bloodhounds (there is probably some Bloodhound breeding in the Basset), and their 'music' is particularly 'melodious'.

In spite of their bulk, Basset hounds move surprisingly quickly in the hunting field, although a follower will find it easier to keep up with them than with Beagles. Packs are not common in Europe, although there are several in Britain. They hunt under the Rules of The Masters of Basset Hounds Association which, in 1959, decided to review their stud book and to make provision to include registration of the English Basset Hound. This is a product of interbreeding in the first half of this century.

Again, there is quite a difference in form and function between the Show Basset Hound and the working English Basset. In America, Bassets run at field trials similar to those for Beagles.

The facial folds and long ears of the breed often lead to the rather erroneous conclusion that these hounds are very solemn. Nothing could be further from the truth. Bassets are a vigorous and happy breed, generally clear of temperament faults but needing plenty of attention. They also need lots of exercise.

Coursing

The current sport of coursing is thought to have originated in the Middle East. In coursing, gazehounds such as Salukis, Afghan Hounds

and Greyhounds are used to pursue and kill game such as small deer, gazelles and hares. Nowadays the activity is confined largely to Greyhounds, and the quarry is hares. Sometimes, Whippets, Deerhounds and Salukis are used to pursue the game.

The term 'coursing' simply refers to the release of hounds in sight of the quarry, followed by judgement of the ability and style of the hound in attempting to catch and kill. We say 'attempting' because, on average, only one in four hares is

Above: Although they are primarily working dogs, hounds occasionally have their days of glamour in the show ring.

Below: Terriers are hard working dogs. This couple are typical working hunt terriers.

Above: The very last meet of the season for these Cambridgeshire hounds. Out of season, the hounds are exercised regularly so that their fitness is maintained.

Below: The judge at hare-coursing meetings is always mounted so that he has a clear view of the proceedings.

actually caught. Coursing in Britain became firmly established in 1776, when Lord Orford founded the first coursing club, called The Swaffham. The Waterloo Cup meet was first held in 1836 and the National Coursing Club, the body which controls coursing, was founded in 1858 and subsequently drew up rules for the sport. The coursing season runs from mid-September to mid-March.

Coursing has a history of hunting and, because of this, it is included here, although the racing element is really pre-eminent. Meets mày be 'walked-up' or 'driven'. With the former, the spectators, competitors and the 'slipper' (who holds both hounds) walk the field in a line. If a hare gets up, then the slipper waits until it is

about 80 metres (90 yards) from the hounds, before releasing them. At driven meets, beaters drive hares singly towards the slipper, who then releases the pair of hounds. Judges award points for speed, ability to outstrip the other dog, ability to 'turn' the hare from its course and other aspects of style.

Coursing has had a rough time in the last few years from the anti-blood sports lobby, and has been singled out for Parliamentary debate and legislation.

In America, coursing is a flourishing sport with highly standardized regulations. Captured American jack rabbits are released from one end of a 410-metre (450-yard) fenced run and given a 27-metre (30-yard) start on the pair of hounds, who try to execute the *coup de grâce* before the rabbit reaches the escape hatches at the end of the run. Betting is lively at these meets as, indeed, it is in other countries.

Coonhunting and trials and races

The relatively recent American sport of racoon hunting demands a lot from the American Coonhound. This breed was developed from Foxhounds and, sometimes, from Bloodhounds. 'Coonhunting' is usually practised at night when the racoon is active and hounds often have to swim through swamps to pursue the quarry.

Licensed night-time field trials involve meets in forests, where the dogs are released to pick up the trail of the racoon. Owners recognize the note of their own dog's voice as it starts trailing, and both the owner and judge then keep a check on the dog, until it eventually pursues the frightened racoon to safety in a tree.

Above: Otterhounds are now quite rare. These large, shaggy dogs are renowned for their beautiful 'music' and superb scenting abilities.

Right: Two nicely matched Beagles. As with Foxhounds, beagles are counted, hunted and shown in couples.

Above: The English Springer Spaniel is an adaptable shooting dog with a fair capacity for retrieval.

Below: The German Short-haired Pointer is the 'Jack-of-all-trades' of the shooting world.

Below right: Two Pointers at work on the moors. The bitch is on point and the dog is backing her.

Daytime races are also held. In these, the dogs are released in a river and have to swim towards a floating box which holds the racoon. As the dogs approach the box, it is pulled by a rope from the river's edge and taken to a tree. The first dog to reach the tree is the winner.

Gundogs

An aura of mystery surrounds gundogs and the work they do. There is an instant mental picture of grouse moors, wet heather, tweed trousers, deer-stalker hats and double-barrelled guns, with the glistening feathers of dead birds carried in the mouths of noble, steaming Spaniels and Retrievers. The image carries with it a certain social standing and an unfortunate air of pomposity and decadence. It is an image which is quite outdated and bears little relation to reality. True, there are the organized old-style shoots,

supported by titled gentlemen in expensive attire. Nevertheless, a high percentage of perfectly adequate gundogs are owned by small farmers, farm workers and, indeed, anyone who enjoys a walk with a gun in the hope of taking the odd pot-shot at a rabbit, pigeon or, if lucky, pheasant. Some gundogs are owned and worked by people who rarely, if ever, shoot although they may compete in the gundog working tests, which we shall deal with later.

The origins of the gundogs have already been discussed in our considerations of breed development, and it is reasonable to repeat that work to the gun is as recent as the gun itself. Most gundogs were well on their way to their present state of development a long time before guns were in regular use for bird-hunting.

In America, the gundogs division of the American Kennel Club, called the Sporting Group, consists of the Pointers, Setters, Spaniels and Retrievers. All these are designated gundogs in the British Kennel Club classification.

It is a fallacy to think that *only* the gundog breeds can make useful gundogs. Many mongrels, first crosses, utility breeds and even some toys make quite handy flushing dogs (flushing is the act of scenting a bird, rabbit, etc., tracing its hiding place in the undergrowth and then disturbing it to make it fly or run away). Some of the herding dogs can be trained to make adequate retrievers. After all, hunting – and that is the basis behind the sophistication of a good gundog – is a very fundamental behavioural characteristic of dogs.

Uses of the gundog breeds

Gun work can really be considered in three stages. Firstly, finding the quarry and showing the huntsman its position; secondly, flushing out the game and, thirdly, retrieving it once it is shot. The first task is one for the Pointers and Setters and is really only of great importance in open country, such as grouse moors, where the pointing of the birds is of the utmost significance.

Right: Labradors have a legendary endurance. They originated from the east coast of Canada and, in the early nineteenth century, became very popular with English shooting men. They are now common in every country where good shooting dogs are appreciated.

In such terrain, if the dog were to flush the bird straight away, the guns might be far off and would stand no chance of hitting the birds, which would be well out of shot range.

The dogs must range out well in front of the guns, testing the air with their superb noses for the scent of the birds. Once they detect the bird and its position, they stop moving forward and point towards it, with their heads held high and, classically, with one foreleg held up as if their step forward had been stopped by an instantaneous freeze! At this stage the dog may be only a few metres from the bird, which will be mesmerized by the dog's presence and will also remain frozen. The guns have now moved up behind the dog. On a quiet command from the gun, the dog moves forward and 'sets up' the bird – that is, the bird loses its nerve and flies up, thus presenting a possible target for the guns.

The Pointers and Setters are well suited for their work. They are quiet dogs – noisy and babbling dogs would disturb the game – and have an excellent capacity for self-control and for accepting very subtle signals from their masters. They must also have plenty of stamina, since a day's shooting on moors, criss-crossing over heavy ground, means travelling great distances. The Pointer is the epitome of fine game-bird scenting, although the three Setter breeds now share that quality, too. The English Setter is the most popular and is both tough and graceful. The Gordon Setter is the heavier Setter, of Scottish ancestry, and the Irish Setter is the beautiful 'Red Setter' of light, but long, bone. Two serious faults that can occur in Pointers and Setters are to circle the birds, so that the guns find they are shooting towards themselves or the dogs, and to make 'false points' towards the cold scent of a bird that has long since disappeared. Both these faults are often made by non-pointing breeds, if used for this purpose.

The German Short-haired Pointers and their

Below: There may be differences in colour and size but all the Retrievers have one thing in common – the capacity to bring in the game without damaging it. From left to right – Labrador, Flat-coated, Golden and Curly-coated Retrievers.

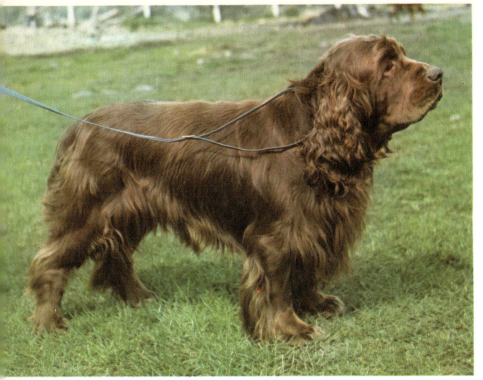

Above: The Sussex Spaniel is, alas, very rare. It was bred to push through and under brambles.

Left: Selective breeding almost ruined the Field Spaniel at the end of the nineteenth century.

Below: The only thing we can say with certainty about the origins of the Irish Water Spaniel is that it is one of the oldest of breeds.

Long-haired and Wire-haired close cousins are useful Pointers, but are the 'jacks of all trades' in the shooting world. This position they share with Weimaraners, the grey-coated, flop-eared hunting dogs from Germany which, like the German Pointers, can point, set, flush and retrieve, both on land and from water.

Hunting game in heavy cover, undergrowth and even woodland is very different work from the delicacy and finesse of pointing and setting. For this a sturdier, lower dog with strong legs and heavy chest is needed, yet it must retain the sensitive nose required of all good gundogs.

Imagine a thick hedge with a ditch on either side running right along the top of a long field. This cover could be the hiding-place for families of pheasants, partridges and many other game birds, as well as for rabbits. A strong, low dog, with an intense desire and ability to pursue these creatures along and out of the hedge and ditch is needed, so that potential sport is not missed. This 'flushing' capacity is the province of a whole battalion of gundogs – the Spaniels, the Retrievers and others, such as the German Pointers, Hungarian Vizslas and Weimaraners.

The English Springer Spaniel is an excellent working Spaniel, which has become popular all over the world. The breed was originally developed to 'spring' game into nets, but these liver, tan or black and white bomb-shells of energy are also good retrievers. The slightly smaller and more finely muzzled Welsh Springer does a similar job. The Cocker Spaniel, long-eared, feathery, and an energetic flushing and retrieving gundog, weighs about 13 kilos (28 lbs). Today it is a popular show dog. Clumbers are much heavier, weighing up to 32 kilos (70 lbs). They have tremendous bone, body and endurance but are less energetic and popular than the Cocker. The rare Field Spaniel, which looks much like a cross between a Springer and a Cocker, and the Sussex Spaniel are really few and far between. So, too, is the Irish Water Spaniel, which bears more than a fleeting resemblance to a Poodle. It is longer-legged and has a dense, oily, coat that hangs in tight ringlets.

An interesting and refined point of 'shooting over' a dog, whether it is a Pointer, Setter, Springer or Spaniel, is the habit taught to the dog of 'dropping to shot'. Once the dog has flushed or pointed to the game and the huntsman is ready to shoot, the dog drops to the ground, thus giving more room for the gun to aim at the bird. Even more refined is the dog who then jerks his head up to see where the bird has landed so that he can make a fast and accurate retrieval.

A flushing dog can exhibit many faults. One is to 'give tongue' so that the bird is sprung well in front of the dog; another is 'weak hunting', when the dog does not thoroughly search all the undergrowth for his quarry.

Right: Cocker Spaniels are amongst the most popular of all breeds as family pets. Although they were trained to the gun originally, only a few of the breed are now so used.

Below: Even while at rest, the Pointers have an alertness and obvious willingness for work.

Whereas Spaniels and other gundogs do retrieve, in recent years the collection of shot game has been the *tour de force* of the Retrievers. The essence of good retrieval is speed, accuracy and gentleness. No one wants to eat a battered pheasant retrieved by a hard-mouthed dog, or to see a wounded duck scuttle away to a painful safety while the dog searches a flooded ditch some distance away. All the Retriever varieties are not only good at collection but are also vigorous flushing dogs. This has accounted for their supremacy in the shooting field over the last fifty years. Their rise to fame is really quite an achievement when one considers that not only have they ousted the entrenched gundog breeds to a great extent, but that they were not originally developed as gundogs at all. This says a lot for their adaptability – a feature which has taken them into homes as pet dogs, into the Services as tracking dogs and into the lives of visually handicapped people as guide dogs.

The most popular retriever is the Labrador, which may be black, yellow or more rarely, chocolate coloured. This smooth, yet powerful,

dog hardly needs description. It is one of the most numerous of registered dogs all over the world and one which has a most equable temperament at all times.

The Golden Retriever is a little more lightly boned and bodied but it has the same equable character and good hunting capacities as the Labrador. The dense, feathered but wavy coat needs a minimum of attention. Flat-coated Retrievers are even lighter-boned, with a slightly longer muzzle, but they are much rarer than Labradors and Golden Retrievers. This is a pity, since they possess the same grand properties as the Curly-coated Retrievers, which are especially suited to water retrieval. Finally, there is the Chesapeake Bay Retriever, which is a water Retriever *par excellence*. It is not a common breed and is said by some to be a relatively mediocre gundog on land. This would hardly be surprising, since it is probably the closest of all Retrievers to the original Newfoundland stock.

Dogs do not always have the luxury of seeing the shot bird land and it is by a combination of guiding arm movements from the gun and by the dog's own nose that he is able to search for and to find the game. Often a bird will fall wounded and then it is the duty of the Retriever to find the bird rapidly and return it.

Training a gundog

Gundogs inherit their ability, like so many other aspects of behaviour, from their parents. Pups from good gundog parents have a head start over ones from mediocre stock. In general, gundog puppies are treated in the same way as other dogs – plenty of human contact, socialization with other dogs and other animals and a chance to explore. Exploration should take place where the dog will ultimately work. There is no advantage in delaying taking the young Spaniel for a hunt through brambles or a Retriever for a slosh across a brook, even though some old-fashioned 'guns' say that pups should be kept from the field until they are eight months old.

When a pup is only three months old, it can be given short lessons in simple field commands and trained to come to the whistle, with a reward of some titbit to lend a little food association to the whistle sound. 'Stopping to the whistle' is often taught by arm movements from the handler, so that the dog can be stopped at any time even when it is in 'full flush'. Simple lessons, such as 'sitting' and 'staying', are vital and are not always easy to teach a young puppy, who is usually eager to join his master in a hunt.

Retrieving is a basic and inherited behavioural pattern in many breeds of dogs but a good retriever is something more than a dog which brings back any old thing. He must accurately sight the bird, collect it only on command, gently return it post-haste and deliver it rapidly to his handler. A young dog is usually taught with a dummy – a piece of wood, possibly covered in fur or feathers, and later a dead bird or a stuffed rabbit. Sophisticated equipment is available that launches a dummy by firing it with special cartridges that reproduce the noise of the gun. By gentle and patient training, the dog can be taught to retrieve well without such faults as losing the bird, eating it, damaging it by hard-mouthed retrieval or even, most annoying of all, keeping a little way away from the handler and refusing to deliver. Very gradually, young dogs are introduced to the sound of the gun, first by getting someone in the distance to loose off a

Below: The Labrador delivers the game to its handler in such a way that the bird is undamaged.

Left: English Setters are tough and graceful. They have good scenting capacities and are good pointing dogs. As pets, they need lots of exercise which makes them suitable for households with active and interested children.

Above: Golden Retrievers are superbly good tempered with children, and also very popular as gundogs. They have incredible stamina and a basic commonsense.

barrel, then by bringing the sound steadily closer. This whole procedure may take a few weeks, and it is important to ensure that the dog is quite steady to the report and not 'gun-shy'.

The whole process of gundog training is a lengthy and exacting task for both dog and handler. It contains some elements of specialized knowledge and technique and, like all dog training, lots of sound common-sense. Nowadays there are trainers who run special schools for the job and who undertake, often at high cost, to gun-train dogs.

Field trials

British Field Trials are recognized by the Kennel Club and are held under a strict set of rules. The title of Field Trial Champion is awarded to a dog which has won a certain number of open stakes, the number varying with the section, of which there are four. There are three major sections – Spaniels, Retrievers, Pointers and Setters – with a subsection for German Short Haired Pointers and other all rounder gundogs.

Field trials are held under 'live conditions'. Dogs are assessed for their performance under normal shooting conditions in the field, using natural game – not with 'planted' birds. So, the British Field Trial is a very good and just competition for dogs – rather like a day's ordinary shooting, but with judges present. There is, however, some method and recognized procedure to each Trial Section. Pointer and Setter trials are held out of the normal shooting season, since the birds are *not* shot. Blank shots are fired to give the dog the sense of achievement. The dogs are allowed to 'quarter' the moors or fields in pairs to locate the birds. The first dog points the bird and his handler 'claims' the point by raising his hand; he then accompanies the judge to the area, where the second dog joins them and points in the same direction, behind the first dog. The first dog goes forward, the bird

rises, and then both dogs 'drop to the wing' as the blank cartridge is fired over their heads. A fresh beat is then taken and the day continues with draws which decide which dog goes on to compete in second and subsequent rounds. The judges decide on first, second, third and reserve, taking into account that some dogs may have had a 'bad field' and little game to point.

Spaniel trials are held in all sorts of game and shooting countryside, but usually with plenty of scrub and undergrowth. The dogs are judged for their flushing ability and tenacity, for their ability to wait until asked to retrieve, and for their retrieving ability. This is a much more subjective sort of competition and two judges assess each dog.

Retriever trials are also held in the shooting season. Three or four judges assess the capacity of dogs to keep to heel and to wait until the birds are shot. The handler is then asked to send out his dog and the dog's speed and tenderness of retrieval are judged. All these assessments are subjective. 'Style' is notoriously difficult to assess. Faults, such as whining before being sent to retrieve, unwillingness to enter water and a hard-mouthed retrieve are considered serious.

The general-purpose trials (for Pointer/Retriever breeds, such as German and Short-haired Pointers) involve the gundog's skills of pointing and retrieval. These trials are conducted on live, unshot, game.

Trials are run for different grades of dogs such as puppy, novice or open stakes. Each year a championship stake is held for the section winners. A field trial champion is no 'artificial gundog'. He is a real working specialist whose place in the ordinary shooting field is assured.

Field trials in America are very different and in many ways are similar to the British gundog working tests. American field trials are enormously popular and include sections for Pointers and Setters, Retrievers and Spaniels, with some variations in rules for different breeds

within these sections. The trials are run under rules laid down and sanctioned by the American Kennel Club. Pointers and Setters are judged on their work in pointing birds which have been 'planted' in the field.

Retrievers are asked to collect 'planted' ducks and pheasants. In the Spaniel trials, where the dogs competing are virtually always English Springers, 'planted' pheasants are hunted, flushed, shot by 'official guns' and retrieved by the dog. Competition in American field trials is fierce but the work itself bears little relationship to the normal hunting conditions of gundog work.

British gundog working tests are becoming increasingly popular, particularly as the opportunities for field trials become less and the expense of mounting 'live trials' increases. The technique for both dogs and hunters varies considerably from the field trial. Such tests are run on dummies or dead birds which are 'planted'. In the gundog sense, the whole procedure is artificial and can only be adopted for Retrievers or Spaniels, as dead birds or dummies cannot 'fly up' for Pointers and Setters. Although tests are not officially 'recognized' by the Kennel Club, they are heartily approved of and are usually organized by breed clubs and societies. The element of luck or uncertainty is eliminated, since the courses are pre-set and predicted. A dummy can be thrown for retrieval – sometimes into water – or planted.

Although they can never take the place of field trials, working tests do offer an additional dimension to gundog competition and are excellent experience for novice dogs and handlers. They are not to be down-rated as mere playtime. Working tests have a bright future for dogs, handlers and also for spectators.

Racing dogs

Racing is a refinement of the chase in hunting. Racing dogs are essentially hunting dogs and the two best racers – the Greyhounds and Whippets – are properly placed in the Hound Group. These and the other fine racers – Salukis and Borzois – are gazehounds and were developed for pursuing their prey by sight across open plains, in contrast to the scent hounds – Foxhounds and Bassets – which lumber along, diligently scenting their quarry with their noses. The speed of racing dogs is astonishing. On a 'rate per bodyweight basis', the Greyhound would be at least twelve times as fast as a racehorse over short distances. In a race held in 1930, at Hooton Park in Cheshire, between a Rudge motorcycle, a Lea Francis sports car, a racehorse and a Whippet, the pace was set by the Whippet for the majority of the race and the motorcycle only just managed eventually to take the honours.

Greyhound racing

The sport of coursing is probably as old as man's association with dogs but organized dog racing is comparatively recent. In 1876, in a field just outside London, an exhibition race was held in which Greyhounds chased a stuffed hare that was mounted on a rail track trolley. There was little enthusiasm for the sport, either in London, or at similar races in Miami, Florida. It was not until 1909 that a track in Tucson, Arizona, began to draw the crowds. Soon more tracks and stadia in Houston, Tulsa and also in Manchester, in England, helped the sport to grow in popularity.

Nowadays, Greyhound racing is a flourishing industry in Great Britain, the United States and Australia. There are organizations, like the

Above: In some parts of Britain, gundog working tests are popular sports. The dogs are set tasks similar to the work they are expected to do while on a shoot. In this picture, competitors with their Retrievers watch the water test.

Above: Border Terriers are sensible, workmanlike and ideally suited as family pets.

Above right: It is quite likely that the Australian Terrier was developed for ratting and rabbiting, which makes it a popular choice as a farm dog.

Below: Whippets, as the name suggests, are fast runners and like nothing better than chasing rabbits across open country.

National Greyhound Racing Club and National Coursing Association of America, that run the sport with strict betting rules. Greyhound racing in Britain is either held under the Rules of the NGRC at licensed tracks or at unlicensed establishments called 'flapping' tracks. Dogs and bitches have to be at least fifteen months old to race under NGRC rules. They also have to be registered – information on their coat colour and markings is lodged with officials and identity is carefully checked to avoid mistaken identity or deliberate faking.

Hounds may be privately trained away from the track or kept and trained at the track itself. Training at the track is more economical and more convenient for the owner and trainer when racing the dog at that particular track, but it can be a slight disadvantage if they wish to race elsewhere. Exercise and training involve a great deal of road work (walking round for exercise, to keep the feet strong and the nails short). There are, also, gentle gallops to the trainer and formal 'trials' at the track. Only the owners and trainers can attend trials but the times are carefully recorded by track officials. A lot of folklore and mystery surround the feeding and training of Greyhounds – as it does with any racing sport. Traditionally, the diet of boiled meat, oatmeal and various 'secret additives' is prepared in Greyhound kitchens, but nowadays the feeding and medical care of the dogs is a little more scientific than it used to be. The weekly purges of sulphur tablets are almost gone – and the dogs are happier and healthier.

Greyhounds are bred in much the same way for coursing and track racing – one litter may furnish dogs suitable for both. Their instinct to chase the hare is a very natural one, even when the hare is an artificial object electrically propelled along a track. Greyhounds also have an insatiable spirit for competition. The length of flat races varies from 210–1100 metres (230–1200 yards); most are about 457 metres (500 yards). The Greyhound Derby is 480 metres (525 yards). The maximum number of dogs in a flat race is six but in hurdle races no more than five hounds can compete.

The dogs are given a veterinary inspection before the evening's race and checked for signs of a full stomach – feeding a Greyhound before racing is a sure way of slowing it down. Tests for possible doping may be performed before or after the race. Checks are made for bitches in season, which are not allowed to be raced. Numbered jackets and light cage muzzles are slipped on and the dogs led into the 'traps'. The stadium lights are lowered as the electric hare hums past. Once it is about 11 metres (12 yards) ahead of the traps,

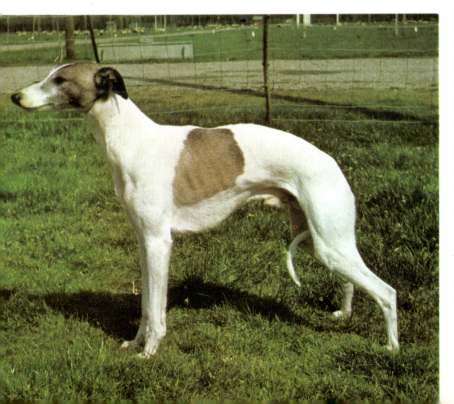

the gate opens and the dogs fly out in hot pursuit. The experienced hare controller keeps the hare always just in front of the fastest Greyhound.

The races are always run at an astonishing speed. A 480 metre (525 yard) race is run in about 29 seconds and only *split* seconds separate the winner from the slowest dog in the race. It is not just sheer power on the straight that makes the difference between a first-class dog and a loser but also style and skill in cornering, the ability to challenge a leader and careful positioning. Speeds of about 16 metres (54 feet) per second are reached. Six hundredths of a second between dogs constitutes a 'length' (one metre or yard), and 0.01 of a second a 'short head'. Photo finishes are needed every time to verify the positions. With such speeds, it can be understood why the mildest disease, the tiniest foot problem – or slightest doping – can have a marked effect on the performance of a dog.

All Greyhounds are great racers – but some are superb! Mick the Miller won the Greyhound Derby (now held at the White City Stadium) outright in 1929 and 1930. He also won the St. Leger 640 metre (700 yard) race for young dogs at the old age of six and finished his racing career of 48 races with 36 wins. His embalmed body rests in London's Natural History Museum. Trev's Perfection also took some beating. He won the Derby, Scottish Derby and Welsh Derby all in one year, which brought his earnings up to £3,500 for seven months' racing – good money, indeed, for 1947!

Not all dogs get to race for the big money and many are retired at three or four years old. Others may carry on until eight or nine, which is the average length of a Greyhound's life. Some dogs live to fourteen or fifteen. Retired racing Greyhounds can make good pets. Such organizations as the Retired Greyhound Trust do all they can to find suitable homes.

Whippets and 'rag racing'

The frail appearance of the Whippet is misleading and is partly due to his tendency on occasions to shiver. In fact, the Whippet is a hardy animal. It is also very fast – only the Greyhound is faster in longer races.

Whippets are a very modern breed. They were developed in the mining and manufacturing areas of northern England from Greyhounds and probably Italian Greyhounds. They were bred for 'snap racing' (rabbit coursing), in which the dogs were slipped on to rabbits in an enclosed area or pit. By the time rabbit coursing was abolished by legislation, on the grounds of cruelty, it had become a playground for crooked betting and cheating.

'Rag-racing' took over and the Whippet quickly adapted. The owners of the dogs (or

Above: This fifteen-month-old Greyhound is being jumped by her owner in preparation for a race at the Wimbledon Stadium in London.

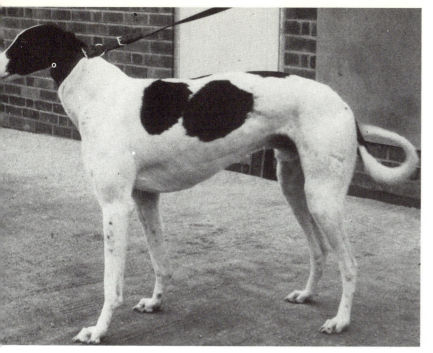

Above: A well-trained Greyhound has well-developed muscles in its chest, shoulders and hind quarters. They are ideally built for sprinting.

Left: In some localities of northern England, terriers are raced.

Below: The winning owner will have backed his dog to win.

'trainers') would stand a fixed distance away (nearly 180 metres or 200 yards) and wave a rag to induce the dog to run. Slippers threw the dog when the starting-gun was fired and the dog would race towards the rags, often hitting them in mid-air! Greyhound racing took the limelight out of rag racing. The racing Whippet suffered in the doldrums until the 1950s, when the sport started again in the north of England and spread steadily. The sport's keenest following, though, is in the North and Midlands. Nowadays traps are used, as with Greyhounds, but owners and trainers still wave their rags.

The Whippet is still an instinctive hunter. Many a quiet evening's walk with a Whippet along a hedgerow can yield a Sunday rabbit lunch with little effort from the Whippet and even less from the owner.

Terrier racing

Just for fun, terrier racing has recently started in Britain. All breeds compete and spirits run high.

The sport is beginning to become organized and traps are used for releasing the dogs.

Hound trails

Not quite a race and not quite a hunt – hound trailing is a popular sport which is locally confined to the hill areas of the English Lake District and the Scottish Border, parts of Wales and south-west Eire. Trails are sometimes held in conjunction with an Agricultural Show. The light-boned Foxhounds used for this sport are very fast and follow the scent of a 'drag-trail' made with rags soaked in turpentine, aniseed or paraffin and dragged round by a length of cord. Trails are laid over rough countryside. Walls, ditches and screes are common obstacles. The trails cover considerable distances – eight kilometres (five miles) for puppies and sixteen kilometres (ten miles) for older hounds, who cover a run of this length in about half an hour. The hounds are slipped by their owners who often then make for the finish of the trail to encourage their hounds home in record time. Strict rules and regulations are laid down by the various governing bodies which control the sport and hounds are officially ear-marked to avoid mistaken identity.

Sledge dog racing

This is not to be confused with the working activity of sledge haulage. Sledge dog racing is a modern North American sport which is a popular extension of the working capacity of dog teams. Sledge dog racing can be enjoyed wherever and whenever there is sufficient predictable snow, and so tends to be confined to Canada and to the northern states of America. In general, the dogs used in teams are the classic polar haulage dogs – Alaskan and Siberian Huskies – although there are a few other breeds occasionally used, such as Border Collies.

The number of dogs in a team varies from seven to fifteen, with the usual number being in the middle of the range. The accent is naturally on speed and light sledges are used for the popular 40 kilometre (25 mile) races. The great event of the year is the world championship at Anchorage, in Alaska, where three races of 40 kilometres (25 miles) each are held on three consecutive days. These races are naturally competitive each day and the speeds vary according to the conditions. Good times for the 120 kilometre (75 mile) total are in the 330–340 minute range (about $5\frac{1}{2}$ hours). The sport is gaining in popularity and seems to have a good future, although opportunities for it will obviously be limited.

Dogs in the Service of Mankind

There are about thirty-seven breeds registered by the Kennel Club in its Working Group but, in the broader sense of the phrase, many more breeds and dogs serve Mankind in different ways. They help in mountain rescues, in herding sheep and cattle, or in guarding the home and belongings; they guide blind and even deaf people; they are used in the investigation of crippling diseases and they are also trustworthy companions who help many people to face the loneliness and rigours of a demanding society.

The Working Group itself consists mainly of dogs that herd sheep and cattle, guard dogs for stock and home defence, rescue dogs and a small sub-group of haulage or sledge dogs.

Sheep and cattle dogs

As already mentioned in the chapter on the history and development of breeds, the function of a dog as a drover, 'collector' and guardian of stock is a very ancient one. Stock-control dogs are now distributed all over the world but they originated and developed in Europe and western Asia, where cattle and sheep were extensively reared.

The German Shepherd Dog (Alsatian) is the best-known of the sheep dogs, although it is rarely used for this purpose now. It is a highly intelligent and tractable dog but it has a relatively short history, having only become a standard

Above: Not so long ago, Bearded Collies were in some danger of dying out. If this had been allowed to happen it would have been tragic because, not only is it an effective working dog, but also loyal and affectionate.

breed in about 1900. It is now slightly larger and definitely much heavier than it was originally, and its use with the Services, with the police and for other work, which will be described later. These functions have now completely taken over its herding activities.

Collies are more commonly used for shepherding today. These dogs are of Scottish origin but, although people persist in calling Rough Collies 'Scotch Collies', Collies in general are widely spread throughout the world. As a set of breeds, the Collies are of medium size, with a very tough constitution, good eyesight and hearing and an innate desire for work. The largest are Rough Collies, who can weigh up to 30 kilos (66 lbs). Bearded Collies can be almost as big, and Border Collies weigh up to 20 kilos (44 lbs).

As with many working breeds, the Collies have been developed and crossed with the sole aim of producing the best dog for the job, with little or no regard for breed 'standards' of size, shape and colouring. Because of this, stable breeds have been few and slow to develop. So, the Border Collie, which is probably the best British sheepdog, was not recognized by its own country's Kennel Club until very recently. There is, however, a stud book kept by the International Sheepdog Society in which registration is greatly dependent on proven ability judged by success in working trials. Border Collies are now the typical working sheepdog. They are very compact, with a mainly black or grey body, although they often have a white chest mark, a blaze down the muzzle and white feet. The dog is known internationally and has been exported all over the world. It has been particularly successful in Australia, where inter-breeding with other dogs and the dingo have produced two 'new' breeds, the Kelpie and the Australian Cattle Dog which are now in wide use throughout the sub-Continent.

The Rough Collie, on the other hand, has been recognized by the Kennel Club for some time. With this recognition, has come all the change in appearance and ability which usually accompanies such fame. The Rough Collie is a very ancient breed, which was extensively developed in the Highlands of Scotland and was virtually unknown until the mid-nineteenth century, when the breed achieved fame in the show ring. Although the coat is very dense and often rather oily, it can look most impressive when properly groomed. The dog is basically rather tall and spindly but, when in full coat, it looks much bigger than it really is. The extremely long head and profuse coat are breed points that are now considered much more important than the inherent working capacity of all members of the breed.

A much rarer member of the Collie set is the Bearded Collie – often rudely mistaken by the

Right: Italian Sheep Dogs are rather rare and were bred for guarding flocks.

Below: A Border Collie – a breed newly recognized by the Kennel Club in Britain.

ignorant as a 'mongrel with some Collie in the mix'. Again with ancient Scottish lineage, this Highland breed was probably used for both sheep herding and cattle driving and only very recently has become patronized by people who wish to show it. The breed's name is itself very descriptive, but there is also a remarkable similarity to Old English Sheepdogs – and there are many indications that, about the turn of this century, the Old English was crossed with the 'Beardie', probably to swell its numbers.

The Smooth Collie is probably as rare as the Beardie. It is just like a Rough collie, without the coat. There is some evidence to suggest that the Smooth Collie was a cattle drover but that the Rough Collie was a sheep herding dog. This breed is not popular at present in the show ring, but holds its own very well in obedience tests and has a stable temperament – a point on which it scores over some of the Rough Collies.

Although not a Collie by name, the Shetland Sheepdog has much of the Collie in its form and nature. Today, the Sheltie – as it is commonly known – resembles the Rough Collie very closely, although its ancestors, from the Shetland Isles, did not. They were much more inelegant and craggy little sheep herders – as tough as the rugged islands of their origin. The breed began to appear in the mainland of Britain about the turn of the century and was quickly snapped up by breeders in the show world who started a 'Shetland Collie Club' – a title which did not go down well with Collie people. The name Shetland Sheepdog was soon adopted and the breed was recognized by the Kennel Club in 1914. There are now very few working Shelties, even in the Shetland Isles.

Apart from those that still work in obedience trials, these sociable and good-natured dogs live a well-ordered life as pets.

In comparison with many breeds, Old English Sheepdogs are probably not all that old, but they are the only *English* sheepdogs. Breed standards are of recent importance and the breed's origins are uncertain. What developed was a comparatively large driving and herding dog with hardiness and tractability. Its size (height: about 56 cm/[22 ins]) proved useful for guarding flocks and this guarding behaviour comes through strongly in the modern dogs of the breed. Despite its size, however, it is a remarkably agile breed and can lope along for great distances, with frequent easy turns and twists to explore the countryside. It now exists as a popular and fashionable house pet for those with the pocket

Above left: By running behind the sheep, an experienced sheepdog steers part of his flock away from a dangerously loose fence.

112

Above: Having rounded up the flock, the dog 'gives them the eye'. This keeps the sheep in order until it is time for them to be moved on again.

Above right: The dog has 'penned' the sheep against a secure fence.

Above left: Man and dog work together in perfect understanding when rounding up sheep. Good sheepdogs are worth a great deal of money but most shepherds are unwilling to sell their dogs.

Below left: The dog runs alongside the sheep to encourage them to keep on the move.

Right: The dog takes a breather having gathered the sheep together.

to feed it and the time and space to exercise it. Great care is needed by breeders to check the uncertain temperament which comes to the fore in just a few of the breed.

Two more important herders deserve mention before we leave Britain: the Cardigan and the Pembroke Welsh Corgis. The origins of both these dogs are in dispute. Some claim that the Cardigan is as old as the Romans, and that the Pembroke came with the Flemish weavers in the twelfth century. It is more probable that both have common origins and, at least in recent times, there has been some common breeding. In both cases, these long, low, tough and agile dogs proved excellent for cattle driving in Wales. They nip the heels of cattle, to keep them moving, and then drop down to avoid any backward kicks. They also become household pets, which is what they remain today. The name itself – 'Corgi' – probably derives from the Welsh language and means 'small dog'. Sometimes pups of the Pembroke Corgi are born tailless but, in any case, short docking is practical. In contrast, the Cardigan has quite a long 'fox-brush' tail.

Virtually every country in the rest of Europe has its own particular 'brand' of shepherd dogs. Most European shepherd dogs are bigger and more aggressive than British sheep and cattle

dogs because, until very recently, they had to contend with wolves, which were common sheep predators in Europe.

Belgian shepherd dogs, for example, classified as Groenendaels, Malinois and Terwerens, are large herders and guard dogs which all resemble a heavily boned Rough Collie or a light-boned German Shepherd Dog. The Malinois and Groenendaels often tend to be black or have a black head, while the Terwerens are normally a rich fawn or mahogany colour with a black overlay to their hairs.

France's shepherd dog is the Briard – a large dog measuring up to 68 cm (27 ins) to the shoulder, which leans heavily toward the Mastiff side of the Spitz/Mastiff shepherd dog origin. The Briard bears some similarities to the Hungarian Komondor and the Puli and may have a common ancestry with these breeds. Used as a pack dog and general army dog during recent European wars, the Briard is an intelligent and useful breed.

The Bouvier des Flandres is a large Belgian cattle-driving dog. It no longer works in its original capacity but, like the Briard, is used by the Services. It is 62 cm (25 ins) high, wiry-coated, and bears some resemblance to an overgrown Airedale. The Bouvier des Flandres

Above: Patience is essential for a good sheepdog. These two Collies await their moment of glory in some trials.

Below: This Bernese Mountain Dog is descended from a breed once used in Switzerland to draw basketmakers' carts.

also has superb bone development.

Another unusual herding breed is the Maremma Sheepdog from Italy which was also important as a flock guard. It would appear to have some close ancestry with the Pyrenean Mountain Dog, although it is not quite as massive.

Of all the world's sheepdogs, the Australian Kelpie is probably the most vigorous worker. It looks very much like a Smooth Collie and it is a tough dog whose job is to find, collect and herd back any stray sheep from the flock. Kelpies are invaluable to Australian shepherds and tales of the breed's capacities are legendary. It is quite common for the dogs to walk over the backs of penned sheep to traverse the flock before cutting out a small group. They often work entirely on their own, with no signals from their master.

Australia also has the Australian Cattle Dog – sometimes called the Queensland Heeler. This tough breed derived from Smooth Collies, and drives cattle by vigorous biting or 'heeling' at the lower legs. It is little wonder that Australia has totally banned the import of German Shepherd Dogs, when it has now developed its own superb breed to cope with cattle, sheep and a tough environment.

Sheep dog training
Before sheepdog training can commence, the dog must have the right genetic background; training then consists of the exploitation of the potential herding attributes of the dog and the suppression of unwanted tendencies. Many people wrongly believe that no formal training is needed; they think that training is just a question of introducing the young dog to sheep and allowing it to watch another experienced dog at work. In fact, pairing-up novice pups with older dogs is usually disastrous: the youngster is only confused by the commands and by the antics of the other dog and it will also become either subservient to the other dog or try to dominate it. If the partnership does work, then the younger dog may be unable to work without the older dog. Training a young sheepdog involves teaching it certain commands independently of other dogs and, in all ways and at all times, treating it as an individual.

Formal training usually starts at about six months old with the simple 'heel' and 'sit' commands. The pup is introduced to sheep in a small paddock, usually on a length of rope, and encouraged to get them moving gently. Any tendency for the pup to rout the flock or savage an individual sheep is briskly curtailed by bringing back the pup on the rope, scolding it, and giving the command 'lie down'. Once the pup's rough tactics are curbed, he is allowed to circle the flock and comes back to the shepherd.

The shepherd may have been training the dog for several weeks even to reach this elementary stage. Soon he teaches the dog to move to the right of the flock with the command 'away' or 'away here' and to the left with the words 'come by'. Once the dog is capable of quiet, controlled circling of the flock, he is taught to stop halfway round – that is, with the flock between him and the shepherd – by the command 'lie down', which is given in a strong, low voice. The last stage is to teach the dog to move the flock towards the shepherd with the command 'fetch' or 'steady on'.

With these commands, the dog should be able to move the sheep in any direction and can soon

Below: These Rough Coated Collie pups will grow to be as hard-working as their mother.

Right: The alert and majestic Rough Coated Collie is widely known as a Scottish sheep-herding dog.

be taught to guide them through gaps and into gateways and pens. All the commands can be, and often are, given by whistle – the length of blast or change of intensity of the note are the key. Each shepherd has his own command code – whether by voice or whistle, or even both – and this can be reinforced by arm signals.

The sheep move because they are naturally aware of the dog's presence and afraid of a potential nip. In fact, good sheepdogs do not bite – 'gripping', as it is called, is considered an extremely serious fault in trial work. 'Giving the eye' is more important. This is when the dog stares at the sheep to mesmerize them. Sheep dogs can halt a flock of sheep and keep them quite immobile by facing them and 'showing eye'. This power is more useful to the dog and hence to the shepherd than the ability to run the sheep.

Cutting out one or more sheep from the flock is an important and useful, but basically instinctive, capacity. It stems from the fundamental behaviour, shown even by wolves, to single out one individual from a flock or herd of animals for attack – often with the co-operation of other wolves. Everyone who owns a sheepdog or a dog with a herding instinct (and *very* few dogs are completely devoid of herding instinct) must remember that the dog retains this latent capacity and the desire to get sheep to run. It is for this reason that improperly trained dogs of the shepherd breeds are a serious potential danger to stock and that, once they have fulfilled their inherent desire to 'cut out' an animal or get the flock on the run, the behaviour will be intensified and repeated until stock-chasing becomes an insatiable vice. The shepherd breeds need careful, strict training, stern commands and plenty to occupy them, for it is often the bored dog which becomes a sheep-chaser.

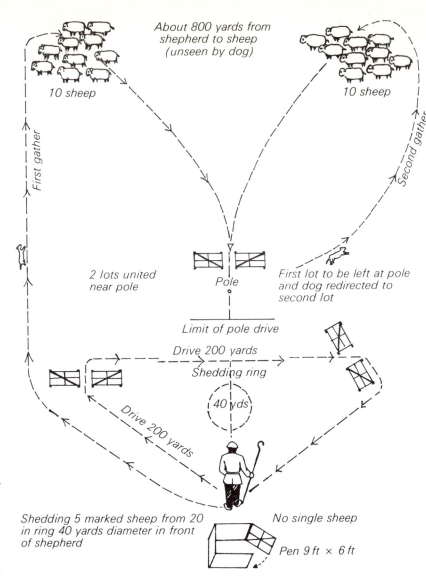

Sheepdog trials

Although sheepdog trials are famous as spectator attractions, they are serious and important competitions which do much to keep up high standards of shepherding and sheepdog breeding. The first recognized sheepdog trial was held in 1873 in Wales and, since then, these events have increased in popularity. The International Sheep Dog Society was founded in 1906 and it now keeps the Stud Book for Sheepdogs and also sets the rules and arranges overseas trials. Trials are held by local clubs, often at area and county agricultural shows, and can be at various levels – nursery, novice, Open and National, which are held for England, Scotland, Wales and Northern Ireland. Sixteen top dogs, four from each country, then compete in the International.

Although there are several variations to the shepherding course, the basic format is similar.

For example, a dog may be asked to leave the shepherd and gather up five sheep from the far corner of the paddock. He then fetches them between two hurdles situated about 180 metres (200 yards) in front of the shepherd and brings them round behind his shepherd, before driving them through another hurdled gap. Then he separates two pre-determined sheep from the flock. This is called 'shedding'. While the shepherd holds the gate of a pen by holding a rope, the dog pens all the sheep, takes them out of the pens again and then singles out one or two sheep marked with a ribbon. All of this has to be done with the minimum of fuss within a fifteen minute period.

Another course is to bring two lots of ten sheep together and shed the five that are marked. There are also more complicated gathering and fetching courses. The dogs are not judged by their speed of work but by their efficacy – in fact they are judged on style, the maximum effect with the minimum of disturbance and fuss.

Sheepdog trials are not gimicky occasions for off-duty farmers to get their dogs to perform

Above: Sheepdog trials have become an increasingly popular spectator sport in recent years. Much patient training must be carried out before the dogs can attempt to try the standard tests shown above. A recent series of sheepdog trials was shown on British television and, surprisingly, became a great success with viewers.

tricks or stunts. At all times they are intensely practical working tests for dogs and shepherds, which mirror the sort of work the dogs are expected to do amongst stock. Without sheepdogs, stock farmers of the world would need much more sophisticated equipment and would undoubtedly not be able to work so efficiently.

Mountain rescue

It is instinctive to think of St. Bernards as the major mountain rescue breed but, in fact, today the task is undertaken by a variety of strong, tracking breeds of which the German Shepherd Dogs are certainly the most popular. There are many legends surrounding the St. Bernard; a popular one recounts how on scenting a lost person within the snow, the dog would lie next to him in order that the warmth from its body would transfer to the unfortunate frozen traveller. The other popular belief is that St. Bernards always carried brandy in miniature barrels hung about their necks – inner warmth for the rescued soul!

Many mountain rescue organizations working in the Alps, Canada, America and other mountainous parts of the world have slightly modified the Services and police training methods for tracking dogs. In addition to German Shepherd Dogs, Labrador Retrievers and Husky breeds are sometimes used. Dogs are particularly useful for mountain rescue, not only because of their keen sense of smell and their ability to dig in snow, but also because they can travel over terrain which man finds difficult, and vehicles – impossible.

Guide dogs for the blind

'A dog is a man's best friend'. There are some who would dispute this claim, but there are many visually handicapped people who would heartily endorse it.

The use of dogs as guides for blind people originated in Germany to help war-blinded servicemen after the First World War. The Guide Dogs for the Blind Association was formed in Great Britain in 1934 and has expanded considerably since those early days. There are now five centres from which the Association operates. These are at Leamington Spa, Warwickshire; Bolton, Lancashire; Exeter, Devon; Forfar in Scotland; and, the most recent, at Wokingham in Berkshire. In addition, the Breeding and Puppy Walking Centre, which supplies all these establishments, is situated near Leamington Spa.

In the United States, the guide dog movements

Above: Both the Pembroke (left) and Cardigan (right) Welsh Corgis were once 'heelers', or cattle herding dogs.

Below: This St. Bernard takes time off to fulfil the breed's popular and much loved image as a rescuer.

also have a long history. The Master Eye Institute was formed in 1926 and there are a further four organizations and many more training centres.

There are a limited number of breeds which are suitable as guide dogs. Size is a governing factor. The dog must be of a size that enables a person of average height to walk comfortably holding the working harness. Temperament is another important aspect. In addition the nature of the work for which the dog is destined demands that it must be intelligent, adaptable, and of a friendly disposition, without being too effusive. It must not be aggressive or nervous and must not be unduly disturbed by sudden occurrences.

Which breeds? Which dog?

The breeds which are most commonly in use now are Labradors, Golden Retrievers and a Retriever/Labrador cross bred. German Shepherd Dogs, some Collie types, and a few other breeds are more rarely used. Labradors and Retrievers are dogs with a wonderfully gentle disposition and they can readily adapt to whoever is their handler. This adaptability is very important. The German Shepherd Dog is also a very popular and traditional 'guide' but its 'one-man dog' quality can be a hindrance, often making it harder to train.

The time taken to train a guide dog varies with the dog. It may take only five to six months, or it

Above: This splendid chocolate Labrador Retriever has a short, dense coat which is quite straight and water resistant. Its head is typically broad.

Top: A black
Labrador Retriever.
Note the handsome
'otter-tail' – a
feature of the breed.

Above right: A
Golden Retriever
with a full and
magnificent coat.

Above: Yellow is
currently the most
popular colour for
Labradors.

may take a year or more. The length of time taken in training bears no reflection on the eventual efficiency or reliability of the dog as a guide.

Dogs selected for training as 'guides' are found to be more satisfactory when neutered and this is now the normal policy for both sexes. When training, the dogs are taught to ignore other dogs while they are working. It is obviously easier for the trainer – later the handler – and also for the dog if his (or her) interest in the opposite sex is minimized. In the case of bitches, it rules out the times when, because of being 'in season', the guide could not work. To the householder with a pet bitch, this presents only a mild inconvenience but if you are dependent on the dog to act as your 'eyes' for your daily journey to the shops, the office, the railway station or just for a walk, this twice-yearly interruption of approximately three weeks would be a considerable problem and, in addition, a cause for anxiety, since it would attract the inevitable bevy of amorous dogs.

The dog seen in the street, guiding a visually handicapped person (not all guide dog owners are totally blind – hence the use of the term 'visually handicapped'), has progressed a long way from the pup born to a selected brood bitch. In the early days, many of the dogs were donated by breeders or by people who, for some reason or other, were no longer able to keep their dog, or by

Above: Guide dogs must be taught to ignore the 'charms' of other dogs they pass while leading their blind owners. This dog is being deliberately walked through an area where it is liable to come across other dogs. Thus, the young guide dog becomes used to strays and pets alike.

charitable organizations who contributed a puppy as their donation to a worthy cause. Although these were once marvellous sources of guides, they are seldom used today. Breeding Centres house a number of brood bitches who are known to be from good guiding stock and, for the most part, these are the sole source of puppies for training. Today the breeding is very selective, not only to maintain and advance the standards but also for reasons of economy. Training a guide dog is expensive. By careful selective breeding, the 'raw puppy material' can be produced which has a really good chance of continuing right through the rigorous training with little danger of failure.

Brood bitches are kept either at the Breeding Centre or, as is frequently the case, they live out

with a family as a pet, while remaining the property of the Guide Dogs for the Blind Association. This is one of the many ways in which help can be given to the Association, although cash is probably its most needed commodity.

The breeding manager decides when the bitch will be mated and makes all the necessary arrangements. The bitch will remain with the family, if they are able to cope, to have her puppies. If this is not possible, she will return to the Breeding Centre and be taken care of until her puppies are weaned, usually at six to eight weeks old. At this age, the Breeding Centre staff will decide which puppies they want to keep and which are to be sold as pets. Those they decide to keep are sent out to puppy walkers.

Training begins

The breeding manager tries to select puppy walkers who live in busy, built-up, areas. The puppy goes to them at six to eight weeks old and its foster-owners are asked to give it the normal basic training, such as house-training and collar and lead drill. The latter is a little more difficult since the puppy has to be taught to walk on the left hand side of the handler and a little in front (the normal working position for guide dogs). The puppy is taught some basic obedience such as to 'come' when called, and to 'sit'. In addition, it is most important that, as soon as it is old enough, it should be introduced to crowded streets (see Chapter Three: Socialization), railway stations, traffic – in fact, it must become familiar with all the types of places in which it could possibly find itself in later life when it is a working guide. The puppy must also become

Right: Many dogs may become alarmed by the sound of approaching trains, but guides must sit quite calmly until it is safe for their owners to move.

Far right: No matter how many obstacles are in the way, the owner can be quite sure that his dog will find a safe path round them.

Above: Guide dogs must become used to the feel of a harness rather than the normal collar and lead used for family pets.

Above right: Cars would be a dangerous menace to blind people if their dogs were not trained to allow cars to pass before crossing the road.

accustomed to children, to strangers, and to other dogs and animals. This part of the puppy walker's work is particularly harrowing since nobody likes to subject a young puppy to something which it might at first find frightening. Nevertheless, a good guide must be a brave guide.

The breeding manager and his staff provide an excellent 'back-up' system. At no stage should either a brood bitch owner or a puppy walker be left with a problem they cannot solve. The Breeding Centre staff visit brood bitches and young puppies regularly to see how they are and they are also always available for telephone advice if required. At roughly thirteen months old, the young dog will return to the Centre, having first been tested for training suitability. This test will involve being taken through a busy, noisy area to check the dog's reactions. The dog which remains unflustered will progress to the first stage of training at the Training Centre. The breeding manager is not looking solely for 'Guides', however. He has both the long and short term future to consider and he is also looking for potential brood bitches and stud dogs. A dog which comes into none of these categories will be sold as a pet – and the Association has a considerable waiting list for these dogs.

Training as a guide

The training of a guide dog can be divided into three main stages, before he is ready to work with a blind or partially blind handler.

When the dog arrives at the Training Centre, the basic training carried out by the puppy walker is assessed and perfected. One very simple point, which the average sighted person might easily overlook, is that the dog, when walking on

the lead and later on the harness, must walk quite straight, except of course, when avoiding obstacles. This initial basic training is most important and a thorough job on the part of the puppy walker helps to reduce the overall time spent in training.

The second stage includes the basic guiding training. 'Kerb drill' forms part of this – i.e. to stop and sit at all kerbs before crossing. There is also more basic obedience training and eventually the introduction to the working 'harness'. The dog must get used to this and learn to associate the harness with work. Once the dog is fully competent up to the 'harness standard' he will then be passed to the senior instructors who complete the 'guide dog' training. They will teach it to be aware of height and width. A dog, naturally, will not walk into something which is lower than its height but it has to be taught not to walk below something which is shorter than the average person. Similar thinking applies to width. The dog must learn to allow enough room for himself and his handler when avoiding obstacles. He must also be taught how to act in traffic – never to cross a road, for example, when there are moving vehicles about. The secret of successful training is repetition. The dog is taken through each procedure so many times that the responses become automatic. An intelligent dog, anxious to please, soon learns what his handler wants and when all three stages of the training are complete the dog is ready to act as a 'guide'.

At all times the trainers will be assessing the temperament of the dog, constantly aware that the dog will one day be leading a person who cannot see that there are roadworks ahead or that they have not reached the edge of the kerb. A good and reliable guide dog must have no temperamental defects and must always react correctly, since a blind person's safety will depend on this. All this may seem to be a policy of perfection: and indeed, what is ultimately achieved is something very near to perfection.

Not every visually handicapped person is suited to having a guide dog, perhaps because of a personal dislike of dogs or a physical incapacity. An applicant's needs are carefully considered and a suitable dog is selected for them. The applicant will then attend the three to four weeks training course and, in this short time, the instructors have to introduce the guide to the student and teach them to work together.

Some of the students may have had a guide before; others may be accustomed to dogs and others may know nothing about dogs at all. Some may be even a little afraid of them. But, no matter what a blind person's previous experience may be, there are tremendous problems to overcome and great courage is required. After a few days of introduction to the training course, an explanation of the dog's training and preliminary training with a dummy harness to familiarize the student with the correct way to hold it, he is then introduced to the guide dog. From then on the two are partners and the student will look after the dog in every way. He will groom him, exercise him and feed him. Whenever possible the dog will sleep in the blind person's room. This intensive training process is intended to help the student to get to know the dog as quickly as possible and to develop the dog's affection and loyalty towards the student.

The initial joint training of dog and student usually takes place in the Training Centre grounds, over a specially constructed course. As the two become more confident and proficient they will be taken out into a quiet residential area where they encounter some realistic experiences such as moving traffic, parked vehicles, road-works and road junctions. The student will be given a route and will have to give the dog the necessary commands, such as when to make a left turn or a right turn.

The final stage of the joint training is the introduction to a town centre where jostling crowds, busy roads and all the attendant problems have to be coped with.

The Training Course is an extremely taxing time for the student who has to put all his trust in a dog. It is also a difficult time for the dog, which – until the time of the Training Course – has always been handled by firm, confident, trainers

Below: Towards the end of its training the guide dog meets the new owner. This dog is performing kerb drill and stopping at the road side.

Above: A guide dog is not always 'on-duty'. There is plenty of time for relaxation with its owner.

and is suddenly expected to walk for what may well be a hesitant, unsure, person who lacks the command and confidence to which it is accustomed. However, by the end of the course there is a transformation, since the student will have learned to trust the 'Guide' and to appreciate the dog's capabilities.

The instructors have a two-sided job. On the one hand, they are teaching students how to handle a trained dog and to overcome their fears and, on the other hand, they have to teach the trained dog to work with the initially apprehensive student.

When the training course is over and the student and his guide return home, the handler is encouraged constantly to revise and repeat all aspects of the training, even those which are not in regular use.

A guide dog's working life can last as long as its good health remains. Should it have to retire for any reason, then, if its handler wishes, he may keep it as a pet. If not it will be looked after by one of the many people who help the Association.

'Hearing ear' dogs

Rather less dramatic than guide dogs for the blind, and certainly more recent, are the schemes for training dogs to help people with hearing handicaps. Deaf people face constant problems, such as an inability to hear alarm-clocks, telephones, door-bells, or a baby's cries. There are also serious risks such as fire or home intrusion. With adequate training, dogs can alert their handlers to such sounds by running to them, performing an alerting act, such as tugging at a trouser leg, and then leading them to the source of the sound.

Although only in its infancy, schemes are well under way for the large-scale training of 'hearing ear' dogs. At present, most of the work is being undertaken in the United States by humane societies. Many breeds have been trained, including German Shepherd Dogs and Dobermanns. The main requirement is that training should begin at an early age. Major obstacles in the deaf person's everyday life, such as an inability to hear an alarm-clock, can now be overcome when a lick or gentle paw tap from a dog can start the day.

Dogs in research

Whether one agrees or disagrees with the morality of experimentation on live animals, a substantial number of dogs are used for research purposes. The whole subject is an emotive one, charged with high feelings, but it is reasonable for us to look at some of the factors involved and at

Above: RAF dogs are trained to such a degree that they will go through fire hoops unflinchingly.

Left: The German police used German Shepherd Dogs as a deterrent against terrorist attacks during the 1974 World Cup.

Below: The British Army trains dogs to sniff out guns and ammunition.

the logic behind the issue. Numerical facts are difficult to obtain and easy to distort.

Dogs are chosen as animals for research for several reasons. First, they are manageable and highly domesticated mammals which generally adapt well to the experimental situations in which they are placed. Imagine trying to do any sort of research, even a feeding trial, on a wild animal such as a fox or an antelope.

A most popular research dog is the Beagle. Beagles are favoured because they are relatively small 'pack' dogs, usually very uniform in size, and they respond well to research situations. Most Beagles used in laboratories are reared in special disease-controlled colonies with a research purpose in mind. The dog is a 'much researched' animal. We know a lot about its structure, its blood and tissues. Whole books have been written about the biology of dog reproduction and the sort of diseases, such as cancer, which can appear quite spontaneously in any dog. Because of all this background knowledge, when an experiment does cause a change in a dog, the researchers can soon assess the importance and degree of that change. Ultimately, this means that fewer dogs are needed in a given experiment than would be so in the case of other animals. This makes the research better, quicker, easier and morally more acceptable since fewer animal experiment hours are needed.

Although more and more work is being done to try to find ways of biological research not dependent on higher animals, there are many situations where only an animal can be used. Some work performed on dogs is of special value; for example, research on dog diseases such as distemper, and other diseases important to dogs, such as rabies. The high proportion of dog experiments are ones involving nutrition and feeding trials, where dogs are not subjected to disease or to any physical interference. A large number of experimental dogs are 'controls' – that is, normal dogs which are in no way disturbed biologically, so that they can be compared with the animals 'on test' to see what effects the trial or experiment has had.

In most countries, there are very strict laws controlling tests on animals, with licensing systems and detailed inspections of premises and personnel and of the experiments themselves. We have laws which demand that new products, foods and drugs should be tested to avoid danger, damage and pollution, and many of the dogs used in research are involved in this sort of testing. Finally, there are many cases where research on dogs is performed as the only direct alternative to research on human beings. Whatever our opinion might be on the use of dogs in research, all of us owe a debt of gratitude to these animals.

Right: Airborne dog! Some police forces take dogs up in helicopters when searching for criminals and prisoners on the run. As soon as the escaper is sighted the helicopter lands, the dog is loosed and is quickly on the heels of its prey!

Below: These dogs are on their way to the Piccadilly Hotel in London to sniff out explosives planted by terrorists.

Bottom: Dogs play a vital role in today's fight against narcotic smuggling.

Dogs of the armed services and police dogs

It might be imagined that, with the increased complexity of military operations and civilian life, the value of dogs in these areas would be constantly decreasing. In fact, the reverse is true. Dogs still show many advantages over high technology and are expected to continue their important roles in our military and defence forces. This confidence in the dog's capabilities is shown by the continuing importance placed upon dog training and dog research in both the Forces and the Police.

In the Services, dogs are a relatively cheap method of carrying out certain functions. For instance, the extensive use of guard dogs at Air Force bases ensures the efficient patrolling of large areas of land. In a patrol situation, the dog may often be doing the work of at least two other men and the financial implications of this are obvious. Dogs can run faster than men, make an unarmed attack much more efficiently and effectively, and often command more respect from a criminal. They can get into places where a man cannot and they can smell and hear things beyond the human range, and which cannot easily be detected, even by sophisticated equipment. Dogs are not dependent on a power supply and do not need their batteries recharging. Moreover, they do not 'rust up' overnight in Malayan swamps like some equipment does. All these are important attributes and, when they are taken collectively, the dog's value becomes even more apparent. Technology has yet to produce a machine which can scent a person 45 metres (50 yards) away on a pitch-black night, track that person over wire fences, through water and vegetation and then either attack or corner him, holding him secure until help arrives.

Dogs are very predictable creatures and, with the correct training, they rarely act in uncertain ways. There are many situations where tracker dogs used in police and army work have taken a trail which, to the handler, initially seemed unlikely and yet which ultimately led to the correct goal. Dogs are also very adaptable and the police, especially, have made a great effort to ensure that all their dogs in regular use are trained and experienced in all their capacities. Thus we see police German Shepherd Dogs which can track, guard, attack and hold, besides responding to a wide variety of obedience commands.

Which dog?

Various breeds of dogs have been used by the Forces and there are still specialized contingents of breeds for highly individual tasks. However, bearing in mind that it is an advantage to have one type of animal – and, better still, one breed – a number of criteria must be satisfied. First, the dog must be sufficiently big to be robust enough to deal with all varieties of work, including man-hunting. This excludes most breeds. If sheer size were not a major consideration, then probably breeds such as the Border Collie would be used. In fact, these dogs are used for some specialized obedience tasks, but they are just not big enough for the general run of work. Secondly, the dog must be 'intelligent'. We have already discussed the difficulty of using this word in the world of dogs, but in this context we may substitute the words 'highly tractable and willing to please'. This excludes many other breeds, including the larger hounds. Thirdly, the dog must have a tough constitution, must be adaptable to extremes of weather conditions and must have a weather-resistant coat. This criterion excludes many short-haired breeds and also some breeds with an excess of heavy, dense, coat which renders them uncomfortable in hot or humid climates. The Husky is an obvious example.

Finally, the dog must be respected by the public – even feared – and must have a latent capacity to attack in a controlled manner. Put all these factors together and the choice is limited. The German Shepherd Dog comes to the fore. This breed has an almost complete dominance over others in work for the Services and will probably continue in its strong position. However, their dominance is not absolute. Belgian Sheepdogs, Rottweilers, Dobermann Pinschers, Airedales and Labrador Retrievers have all been used, in addition to a few other breeds. For scenting and tracking, Bloodhounds and Labrador Retrievers hold the field.

It is a mixed blessing for the German Shepherd Dog that it has been adopted so universally by the Forces, since there is both honour and stigma

Below: Service dogs undergo varied training which often involves spectacular feats.

Above: Rottweillers are versatile dogs, making excellent guards, and are extensively used by the Services the world over.

attached to the work. The dominance of the breed in Service work probably did much to boost its popularity in the 1920's, when it was among the most numerically popular of breeds. However, many factors, including excessive press coverage of a few unfortunate incidents of savaging, severely damaged its reputation and popularity. Although the name change to Alsatian took away some of the stigma, in general the next twenty years were numerically slim for the breed. The big boom came again in the 1950's and 1960's and today it is again a top breed dog. Public education has done much to make people realize that a remarkable animal which has so many fine capacities is, in a curious way, a rather delicate creature which needs careful and steady training and control, so that one of its capacities does not become so heightened that it dominates all others. The Forces' training methods ensure this care.

General forces training

There is a general theme running through the training for all Service dogs, whether they be in the Army, Air Force or Police – and of dogs used for other guard and security purposes. The dog must be trained to perform a task because it likes to please its handler. This is quite basic. If ever force or fear have a place in the communication between the dog and his handler, then the relationship becomes unsound and the result a little unpredictable. So the training is done on a principle of 'task and reward' – the reward being either food or the congratulatory tone of the handler.

It is an almost universal practice that pups for training are 'walked' by handlers in much the same way that guide dogs for the blind or Foxhounds and Beagles are puppy-walked. This gives them a chance for human socialization and time to learn the usual basic commands. When

Left: A Service dog
brought to the
scene by helicopter,
takes off in pursuit
of a suspected
terrorist.

they are about a year old, dogs are given an intensive course by trainers to ensure that they learn the basic commands of 'sit', 'down', 'heel', 'come', 'leave' and 'stay'. These are fundamental commands for all obedient dogs. From then on, the training varies according to the function to be demanded of the dog.

Selection of stock
Nowadays many dogs are bred by the Services themselves. For instance, the R.A.F. have a breeding pool now, although the origin of their dogs was a nucleus of household pet Alsatians. The Metropolitan Police also breed most of their own dogs from a nucleus derived from German stock, although they sometimes buy promising German Shepherds. The advantage of breeding one's own stock is obvious – one roughly knows what one is getting!

Police patrol work
The work performed by police dogs includes three major functions: (1) *patrolling*, which includes search, arrest and control of suspect; (2) *tracking* of suspects or members of the public and (3) *recovery* of property. All police dogs have a training which will enable them to perform all these tasks adequately. The commands for patrolling are 'hand' (the dog comes close to the trainer); 'sit'; 'speak' (the dog barks and the importance of this in security is obvious); 'heel' (the dog goes to the left heel); 'right' (to the right heel); 'down' (crouching down with hind legs under); 'stay'; 'dead' (the dog lies flat out on his right side); 'stand'; 'fetch'; 'drop'; 'up' (to encourage the dog to jump over an obstacle); 'no' (to stop whatever he is doing); 'kennel'; 'quiet' and 'stop him' (the dog chases, stops and holds the suspect).

All these commands are very obvious and basic but they are vital to a good patrol dog. It is

beyond the scope of this book to describe the training methods for all commands, but 'stop him' is of great importance. The handler holds the dog on a lead and a person well known to the dog flicks a sack at the dog. The dog is encouraged by the handler to bite at the sack which is annoying the dog. Once it does bite, it is rewarded by encouraging words. By degrees the dog is taught to bite the sack wound round the man's arm and eventually to run at the man and seize his arm, the dog's travel being limited by a long cord. Any tendency to savage the man is discouraged by recall words like 'no' and 'hand'. Soon, the dog will be reliable enough to grab just the sleeve of the man and swing him round to control him. At no stage is the dog allowed an all-out savage attack which is not required or demanded of a police dog. The dog must always respond to the command 'leave'. Later on, the dog is taught with the word 'seek' to track down a person by entering a building, mass of undergrowth or other similar hiding-place, to discover a suspect and hold him.

At all times, police dogs are trained to the element of 'controlled aggression'. The police are very aware that the suspect *may* not be a criminal – an innocent tramp in a deserted building who was mauled by a police dog would certainly not be a good advertisement for the Force, or endear police dogs to the public. Dogs are taught only to bark at a pursued suspect who stands still but to attack one who resists – again, an example of very fine control.

This general training procedure is one now copied by many other organizations, including commercial security companies, who also have an important duty not to harm innocent people.

The use of dogs in the British Police Force is comparatively recent and they only reached respectable numbers after the Second World War. Britain was very late in their use. The Belgian and French police have used them regularly for nearly a century. Most forces have

Right: Dobermanns
are another breed in
regular use by the
Services. Cropped
ears are often seen
on the Continent
and in the USA.

Right: Weimaraners
originated as a
sporting breed in
the nineteenth
century at the court
of Weimar in
Germany. They are
now used for Police
and Service work.

experimented with breeds other than German Shepherd Dogs and the German breed – the Dobermann Pinscher – which is a comparatively new breed, with Rottweiler and German Short-Haired Pinscher origins, has proved of particular value. It is somewhat quicker and keener to attack man and has a special use in very tough areas.

Tracking dogs

Tracking is an important function of all Service dogs. The behaviour is a basic one and is easily taught. The Army use a six-stage procedure always starting with the tracking of a beret dropped by the trainer. The dog is put into a breast harness when working and is then instructed to 'seek' by a long, drawled-out tone. The training then progresses to tracking a stranger, finding him on 'track' with turns, then 'back doubles', and eventually selecting the scent from a group of several people's tracks. This training can be quite a lengthy process and can take a year or two to perfect.

Dogs can also be taught to follow 'drag line' tracks with some object at the end and a meat reward. Army dogs, by repeated and patient training, have been taught selectively to scent out explosives and firearms. This has given them a real value in modern guerrilla warfare and civil disruption. Recovery dogs are specifically trained to scent buried objects, such as ammunition. They seem able to detect freshly buried objects which would defy discovery.

Although Alsatians are quite suitable for tracking work, the Army favour Labradors and there are some Labradors used by the police for very delicate scenting, such as the detection of illicit drugs.

Red Cross dogs and search dogs have been trained specifically to scent wounded people – both soldiers and civilians. Their scenting capacities are particularly acute and, when they have located a casualty, they return to their handler and sit in front of him until he follows them to the injured person.

In Britain, Army dogs are tattooed on the left ear for identification purposes and are trained by the Royal Army Veterinary Corps.

Police trackers perform work which is very similar to that of Army dogs and they are trained in much the same fashion.

The dog in the Army

We have already described the essentials of the Army dog's work but there are additional duties, such as messenger work. This was first regularly performed by French dogs in the First World War, although it took some time to perfect their

129

training. Training depends on teaching the dog to go between the handler and an accomplice. One disadvantage of the method is that either man may have to change his position. A modification in training was to get the dog adapted to following a particular scent, which would be laid down by 'drag' if either handler moved position. Radio-control and other methods of communication have largely supplanted the need for messenger dogs but occasionally, often in desperate circumstances, their work is needed.

Unlike Police dogs, when Army dogs are asked to attack they do so in a full-blooded way and they are not expected or trained to attack in a controlled fashion. The reason is obvious. Army dogs are also never trained to retrieve. The retrieval of a grenade, for example, could be a disaster.

The general training of Army dogs is accomplished in a very short time – often after only a few weeks. When any dogs are seen to have a particular aptitude for one of the selective forms of work, such as tracking or guarding, they are given further specialized training. The basic commands for Army dogs are few and simple – 'heel', 'sit', 'stay', 'come', 'leave', 'down' and, for guarding and scenting dogs, 'attack'.

Army dogs are kept well up to complement and specialized uses for their skills are constantly being developed. Their presence has a great morale effect on the rest of the Force.

Below: Service dogs are handled by one person throughout their working lives.

Above: A team of Huskies hard at work in a modified Eskimo fan trace. One dog is the leader and the pack behaviour is well fixed within the team.

Obedience and working trials

Trials are so close to the work expected of Forces' dogs and sheepdogs that they may be considered here.

In Britain, the Kennel Club sets the rules for obedience trials. These trials involve simple command work, scenting and retrieval. There are five classes: Beginners, Novices, A, B and C.

In working trials, the classes are Police Dogs (P.D.), Companion Dogs (C.D.), Utility Dogs (U.D.), Working Dogs (W.D.) and Tracking Dogs (T.D.). The tests are very practical and involve basic obedience. Specialized tasks, such as tracking and gun-steadiness, are included in the Utility Stakes and 'Man Work' tests in the Police Stakes.

Many breeds compete in these sensible competitions. In Great Britain, both registered and unregistered dogs are eligible but only registered pure-breeds may compete in the United States.

Obedience and working trials are becoming increasingly popular and have a great future.

The Arctic and Antarctic

Nowhere is the link between man and dog as strong as it is in the Arctic. For centuries, nomadic Eskimos have depended on Husky dogs for their survival. The dogs provide transport

and, in turn, the Eskimos provide the dogs with food. This is an intriguing example of symbiosis – one creature living by grace of another – and is reflected in the deep attachment which exists between man and his dog team.

The Arctic also provides us with a fascinating opportunity to observe how the dog can adapt to his environment. The Eskimo survives by clothing himself in furs and by building igloos but the dog has adapted much more efficiently. He has a dense coat with thick underhairs, and a complex blood circulation system which can divert blood to deeper layers. This minimizes heat loss.

'Husky' is the name given to all sledge dogs. It does not refer to a well-defined single breed of dog but is a corruption of 'Esky' – a slang word for Eskimo, which was used by early white travellers. All Husky dogs are Spitz-type. They have a wolf-like appearance, with slit eyes set obliquely in the head. They howl rather than bark and some evidence suggests that the Husky was developed by selective breeding of the timber wolf.

There are four distinct types of Husky dogs – the Eskimo Husky, Samoyed, Malamute and Siberian Husky. They are all named after the tribe or race which use them. Eskimo Huskies are the dogs of the Arctic Canadian and Greenland Eskimos. They were probably used as sledge dogs as long ago as A.D. 1000. Samoyeds are named after the Siberian tribe of the same name. The

131

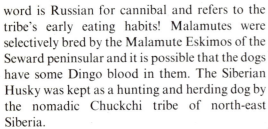

word is Russian for cannibal and refers to the tribe's early eating habits! Malamutes were selectively bred by the Malamute Eskimos of the Seward peninsular and it is possible that the dogs have some Dingo blood in them. The Siberian Husky was kept as a hunting and herding dog by the nomadic Chuckchi tribe of north-east Siberia.

Although all four types are distinctly recognizable, inter-breeding and the introduction of new blood are common practices.

Essentially the Husky dog is recognized for its tremendous powers of endurance and its capacity to withstand temperatures of 60–70°C below zero. The heaviest Huskies weigh up to 45 kilogrammes (100lbs) and dogs of about this weight are most popular for sledge teams.

Despite its toughness, the Husky is not naturally vicious towards man. Even in a pack situation, it shows respect and affection if it is well treated. It will, however, become sullen and ill-tempered if it is badly treated.

The respect with which most polar travellers speak of dogs is displayed by Hanssen, who accompanied Amundsen on his South Pole journey:

'They are supporters and friends. There is no such thing as making a pet out of a sledge dog; these animals are worth much more than that. I looked upon that little bitch as a trusted companion; more loyal and dependable than a human being'.

As well as using Huskies to pull sledges, Eskimos use them as a pack for hunting polar bear or musk ox. They may be used in summer for pack carriage and can carry up to about 20 kilos (44 lbs) in pack saddles with pouches hanging on either side.

Motor driven canoes and toboggans are replacing the Husky but the Eskimos' initial 'love affair' with motorized transport has now cooled a little. The Eskimos are quite aware of the contribution that the Husky makes to their civilization.

The Antarctic

Dogs are not indigenous to South Polar regions. They were introduced there by explorers. Until very recently, exploration in the Antarctic relied heavily on the dog for transport; the success of Amundsen's journey to the South Pole in 1911 was due, largely, to well organized dog sledging. Much of the scientific investigation conducted by the British Antarctic Survey (formerly the Falkland Islands Dependency Survey) was, until recently, heavily dependent on dog teams for sledging. As recently as 1966, there were 152 dogs at the five bases. BAS used a Husky of Greenland and Labrador stock. It has a short thick coat and longish legs for coping with deep snow. Other countries have introduced other types of dog – the Argentinians at Esperanja tried to use Husky/St. Bernard crosses, and the Japanese Antarctic Research Expedition used Saghalien dogs. It must be remembered that all these dogs were kept in bases and have not been liberated. Their survival without man would be impossible and their impact on wild life might be catastrophic.

Huskies, sledges and exploration

Even today, Nomadic Eskimos use Huskies as sledge dogs. Much of the early explorers' knowledge of sledging comes from them, right down to the pattern of trace used to couple the

Above left: During one Transarctic Expedition the climate became too severe, even for the Huskies. Members of the expedition dug a tunnel under the icecap to protect the dogs.

Above right: At Halley Bay the temperatures are *always* too severe for the dogs to be kept out at night. When their day's work is done they are housed in a permanent dog tunnel.

dogs to the sledges. Northern Eskimos used a fan trace where individual dogs were linked to the sledge directly by a seal skin rope. The spread of the traces suggested a fan. This very simple system works well when dogs are pulling on even surfaces but, on uneven or soft snow, the centre trace is better and is most used nowadays by surveyors or explorers. With this system, each dog is coupled by a short trace to a single central sledge trace. Dogs are attached to their traces by a harness which crosses over the shoulders to a single lead which runs along the back. Individual harnesses are tailor-made from soft, tubular lampwick material so that freezing and chafing are unusual. Leather boots may be used to prevent damage to the dogs' feet if the snow tends to ball-up, or if they are pulling on bare ice or crunchy snow.

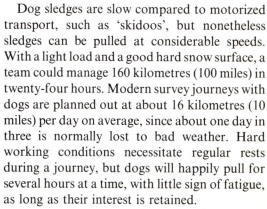

Dog sledges are slow compared to motorized transport, such as 'skidoos', but nonetheless sledges can be pulled at considerable speeds. With a light load and a good hard snow surface, a team could manage 160 kilometres (100 miles) in twenty-four hours. Modern survey journeys with dogs are planned out at about 16 kilometres (10 miles) per day on average, since about one day in three is normally lost to bad weather. Hard working conditions necessitate regular rests during a journey, but dogs will happily pull for several hours at a time, with little sign of fatigue, as long as their interest is retained.

Although Huskies are bred for their haulage prowess, they easily become bored on long, dull hauls over featureless polar terrain or sea ice. Sometimes a man ski-ing in front of the team will reduce this boredom. Changing the lead dog in the trace or singing, or even talking on the sledge, may also make the journey less tedious for them. Encouragement by whip is seldom effective. The whip is used mainly for training or to change direction of the dogs. On the rare occasions when punishment is necessary, a short rope is often used. Voice commands are highly effective and are simple and few. Dogs respond to 'OK, YUP', to start the sledge; 'RRR' for a left turn; 'AUK' for a right turn and a gentle 'AARRH' for stopping. The tone of voice used also has considerable effect.

As with most team or pack dogs, training is largely by example from older and more experienced members of the team. Huskies pull by instinct but rather erratically, so new dogs which are brought into sledge training between nine and twelve months are, at first, run close to the sledge to keep them in check. The modern principle is to train at least two dogs as leaders in a team. The leaders are experienced, usually

133

older, dogs; often bitches, which are very enthusiastic at their work.

Most teams have a ratio of about six dogs to one bitch. This ratio is maintained throughout the complete colony. The useful life of a sledge dog obviously varies considerably but is usually about seven years. During its useful life, a dog could easily cover 12,800 kilometres (8000 miles). Towards the end of their active life, Huskies become prone to osteoarthritis, but older and slower dogs are sometimes suitable for light pack work, or for training puppies.

Breeding from Huskies has generally been quite discriminate. Matings are planned to produce pups with the strong attributes required. Bitches or dogs are not mated until they have proved themselves and only the best pups are reared. Natural pup mortality is around forty per cent. Huskies have rather short heat periods compared with dogs in temperate regions. During heat, they are kept well away from the rest of the dogs. If they go on heat on a journey, the driver just has to cope. Whelping down is preferable at a base, as pups born in the field have to be carried on the sledge or put down. Bitches have been known to produce pups when actually in harness. When this happens the pups are cared for on the sledge by the driver and the bitch runs lightly alongside. Handling the pups at a very early age helps their relationship with man, and

so, too, does commencement of weaning at four weeks. By six weeks, pups are usually fully weaned on to artificial milk and minced seal meat. The mother then returns to life in harness.

A primary requirement of the sledge dog's diet is that it is high in calorific energy provided as protein and fat. Seal meat is an excellent source of energy, mainly because of the fat content of the blubber. High energy compounded artificial diets have been devised, such as modified Pemmican, which contains up to forty-six per cent fat. These diets are convenient and light when on journeys and are a substitute for seal hunting in the Antarctic, where a permit is now required. Provision of water is usually unnecessary, as dogs happily eat snow. Some dogs never learn to lap liquids properly during their whole lifetime.

Generally, dogs and people in the polar regions are very healthy. Distemper was unknown until transmitted to indigenous Arctic dogs by early explorers. Then, even adult dogs had no natural immunity and large numbers died. In recent years, however, a strict vaccination policy has stopped deaths. Amongst sledge dogs, abscesses, cuts and fight wounds will occur, but the only major reason for culling dogs from teams is osteoarthritis. This is more common in dogs introduced to heavy work at too early an age but occurs in many older dogs and

Above: Older Huskies are sometimes used for pack-carrying. This uncommon method of carriage is sometimes used during the Antarctic summer.

Above: These dogs are about to be harnessed to the sled in a fan formation rather than to a central leading rope.

Below: After a trek across the snow, the dogs are rested so that they are fresh enough for the second leg of the journey.

results in lameness and failing performance. It would appear that it is mechanically induced by the excessive stresses on joint surfaces.

Huskies may be penned at exploration bases but, out in the field, the dogs are invariably chained to a lightweight wire or 'span'. This prevents inveterate chewers from damaging harnesses or other equipment and also discourages fighting and obstreperous dogs. No shelter is needed as Huskies happily sleep on snow or ice. At the Halley Bay BAS base, snow kennels were made for the dogs during the exceptionally cold winter.

The part played by sledge dogs in the early exploration, charting and development of the polar regions is almost impossible to over-estimate. The records of Amundsen give an idea of the tough life of early polar exploration. His South Polar Expedition of five men, fifty-two dogs and four sledges left the Bay of Whales on October 19, 1911, with a total payload of over 1,500. Many dogs were killed on the outward journey. Some were fed to the remainder and some cooked as food for the return journey. A further six dogs were killed on the return journey and one was lost. The remaining eleven dogs returned on January 17, 1912 having travelled 2,576 kilometres (1,610 miles) in the round trip of ninety-nine days.

Such losses are seldom necessary today. Supply aeroplanes can drop food for dogs and men – and even spare dogs! Longer journeys, too, are now more often undertaken by motorized transport. Dog teams are reserved for shorter journeys around base camps, but they are still considered a very safe form of transport, even out of the range of light aircraft support. If a machine fails or fuel is exhausted, little can be done. If a dog dies or is killed, then he and his food supply can be eaten by his team mates and the journey can continue. Machines are inedible, and much more prone to unpredictable failure.

Similarly, machines are incapable of discerning such dangers as thin sea ice or crevasses. Sir

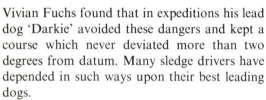

Vivian Fuchs found that in expeditions his lead dog 'Darkie' avoided these dangers and kept a course which never deviated more than two degrees from datum. Many sledge drivers have depended in such ways upon their best leading dogs.

Sledge dogs are declining in number but they still have their firm advocates. Small numbers of dogs are kept at isolated polar bases to help maintain the morale of the men during long periods when contact with main bases is often infrequent.

To complement the rather grisly records of Amundsen, let us hear the epitaph of Peary on the dogs which travelled with him to the North Pole on 6th April, 1909:

'And never were dogs or men
more faithful than those poor
brutes.
Day after day they struggled
back across that awful frozen
desert
Fighting for their lives and
ours; day after
day they worked
Till the last ounce of strength
was gone from them
And then fell dead in their tracks
without a sound.
Forty one of them, out of the
forty two, with which I left
the "last cache".'

Dogs at 'work' in our homes

So far, we have looked at dogs performing tasks for which they are specifically bred, selected and trained. This is the classical view of working dogs. But there is a much wider definition. With only a little licence, one could consider a working dog as 'a dog whose work makes life for a man a little better, a little easier, a little happier'. If we substitute 'existence' for 'work', this opens up another concept of the dog world – the idea that a dog can, by its very presence, make life happier and easier for a human being.

Psychotherapy

Some dogs have been specially introduced into people's lives to try to make them better people. One important example is the 'working' dog in mental hospitals. Over the last few years a lot of investigation has gone into the study of psychotherapy by the use of dogs. One such investigation studied a group of thirty mental patients who were introduced to dogs and their actions studied. Twenty-eight of them made some improvement, and, in five of these, the improvement was very marked. The two patients who did not improve refused to accept the particular pets and so no conclusion could be drawn. Most of the patients were almost hopelessly dependent on the staff of the ward and quite infantile in their attitudes, but, when the dogs were introduced, they began to lose some of

Above left: Not a cruel punishment! This Husky is being weighed, to check on its health and fitness.

Above: The dogs in this team are harnessed to a central lead. Some teams are harnessed individually to the sled and pull in a fan formation.

their dependence. They took on the responsibility of dealing with the dog – walking it, talking to it and feeding it. They gradually became less withdrawn and began to want to meet other people. They regained self-respect and came to experience a joy in taking exercise with the dog and sharing in its life.

An important point is that dogs will happily accept people who show behaviour abnormalities, a characteristic not shared by most normal people. Hence, a patient does not feel that the dog has 'rejected' him and will view it as an uninhibited and trustworthy companion. In one case, a nineteen-year-old psychotic boy, who spent most of his time immobile on his bed, was introduced to an 'aggressively friendly' Wirehaired Fox Terrier. The boy took an obvious interest in the dog, to the point of getting out of bed and following it. Within days he was working on the ward and was prepared to accept treatment. His interest in things *other than the dog* soon increased and he was eventually discharged. His psychiatrist considered that his introduction to the dog was the turning point in his road to recovery.

The theory behind much of the beneficial results with dog-facilitated psychotherapy is that, by being dependent on man, the dog gives the patient a responsibility that he or she cannot reject. This leads to self-esteem and gives the patient a reason for living. This, in itself, improves the sense of mental well-being; in psychotherapy, one tentative step forward can lead to ten firm ones.

Dogs and young people

Dogs have also been used in prisons and remand homes for young people. Their function is very similar to that in hospitals. Once again, it hinges around the dog's demand for attention and dependence. Criminals and socially deprived people often lack any self-esteem or responsibility to others. Dogs can help them regain a sense of responsibility, which they then apply to society at large.

In schools, dogs have a dual use. To reach maturity, children need the opportunity to accept responsibility. Giving them a dog to walk, comb and feed makes them take care of the animal and they immediately feel responsible towards it. The responsibility that they have thrust upon them is so pleasant that they neither fully realize it or mind it! The second function is concerned with the natural expression of sexuality which dogs show. This is very well accepted by children – matings, pregnancy and whelping a bitch are simple and unembarrassing ways of introducing sexual matters to children, both at school and in the home, who will normally accept them in a matter-of-fact way.

Left: Dogs are many things to many people. This Labrador gives companionship to his elderly master.

Below: The bond between dog and mistress is so strong that the dog sits patiently while its mistress knits.

Dogs at home

The advantages and importance of dog-keeping may not always be obvious. Dogs can keep single or widowed people company. Doctors often hear widowed and sick old people say to them, 'I mustn't be ill, doctor, I've got the dog to look after – I must keep him fed and happy'.

Dogs can be substitutes for children or lost partners, and here they can be important in bringing happiness to empty lives. There is, however, the problem that responsibility may become overwhelming. This can result in a reversal of roles, so that the person becomes dependent on the dog.

Nowadays, with a decrease in the size of the family unit, the family dog can swell the numbers of the family group. An interesting extension of this is the 'proxy-pet' of children's television programmes. Many children live in homes where keeping a pet is not desirable or possible and the children's programme dog is a recent innovation which has fulfilled the need for a pet. Television programmes' mail is full of children's letters to the dogs.

Children derive other benefits from dogs. A child sees the pet being taught self-control. He sees the results of this control in a well-mannered pet. If this is explained to him, he can see a reason for control – whether it be self-control or control

coming from others. Ultimately he sees the dog grow old and eventually die – an important lesson in social destiny.

Some psychiatrists see an advantage in dog-owning for pregnant women. They maintain that young women with dogs have learnt how to care for a dependent individual; so, when the baby is born, they are better prepared for the care-giving procedures.

Over the last few thousand years, man has developed a livestock-keeping behaviour. Modern society has robbed him of the opportunity to express this behaviour but keeping a pet dog may fulfil the need. Man loves to be close to animals, to tend them and watch them grow.

As we have already mentioned, the affection displayed by a dog can be overwhelming and there are quite tragic cases on record where this affection has raised guilt complexes. Rare, but documented, circumstances have occurred when a frustrated and unhappy person has lost his temper with a dog and caused it pain. Dogs are forgiving animals and soon return to their owners to lick them and make amends. Some owners have been so disgusted with themselves at hurting the dogs and have felt so guilty that they have committed suicide as an expression of their own worthlessness.

Above: A lively Dandie Dinmont is judged during a dog show. The breed is named after a character in Sir Walter Scott's *Guy Mannering*.

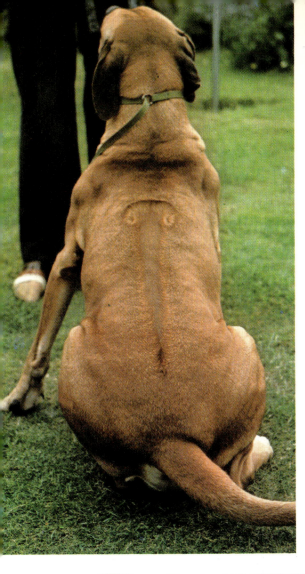

Above left: The markings on this dog's back clearly show why the breed is called Rhodesian Ridgeback.

Above: Papillons derived their name from their large, heavy fringes and upstart ears which resemble a butterfly.

Left: Despite their undoubted eagerness to pounce, the dogs are well enough trained not to.

Showing and Breeding

There are obviously plenty of reasons for keeping a pet or a working dog, or even a pack of hunting dogs, but a different psychology is attached to keeping dogs purely for showing and breeding purposes.

Showing a dog is not quite a sport; it is too extensive to be called a hobby, and it is more serious and involved than just another pastime. It is almost a way of life and, once bitten by the bug, few people can resist the temptation to continue showing.

It is not easy to define the reasons and attractions for dog showing, but they must be related to a basic desire that man has to be closely associated with something living, to enjoy its beauty, whilst realizing its value and, in some way, shaping its destiny. People who show and breed dogs often do so as a form of escape from the pressure of today's world. Not uncommonly they are rather carefree, even eccentric, people who see nothing abnormal about taking half a dozen Pyrenean Mountain dogs for a stroll, driving long distances to a Championship dog show or having a Yorkshire Terrier bitch produce her litter under their bed!

Besides fulfilling the natural competitive spirit which people extend from themselves to their animals, showing also fulfills the need for a system of evaluation or judgement among the dog population. Obviously there is no need to show a dog, however good its potential, if you have no desire to, but to many people the show provides a shop window for their kennels and their particular line of breeding. To others, it is an enjoyable occupation in which they take part as often as possible or something they do perhaps only once a year to support their local show. Dog showing is an activity which crosses all barriers; an interest in dogs is the uniting factor which draws together a great variety of people.

In essence, showing a dog is an exhibition of its aesthetic qualities; mainly its conformation, colour and proportions, but also its movement and its whole ambience – in other words, all the points which can be visually appraised. Many of the toy breeds are shown standing on a table, so

Below: This champion Pembrokeshire Welsh Corgi is the perfect result of centuries of breeding. The breed was referred to as long ago as A.D. 920 in the old laws of Wales.

movement is virtually discounted. In contrast, however, the action of the bigger breeds is a vital factor and the fluidity of gait will be assessed at all paces.

The newcomer to the world of dog shows must be prepared to take the rough with the smooth – to win at one show and be way down the line at the next. You are, after all, asking the judge for his (or her) opinion of your dog on a particular day. That opinion is a personal one, although, of course, it is guided by a knowledge of breed standards and fashions. On a different day, under a different judge, the result may be entirely different. With experience, usually gathered over many years, the competitor gets to know exactly the points demanded of a particular breed, together with those favoured by a particular judge.

The showing system

The object of showing a dog is to compete against others in order to win the highest possible awards within the breed and thus accumulate 'points' for the various awards offered by the canine governing bodies (such as the Kennel Club). As in most rather specialized activities, there is quite a complex jargon associated with dog showing. It will help you to understand the system if the jargon is explained.

The classes within which dogs are classified and judged, are as follows:

Puppy – Dogs between six and twelve months. (Pups under six months are not shown.)

Maiden – Dogs which have not won either a Kennel Club Challenge Certificate, or a First Prize, at an Open or Championship show.

Novice – Dogs which have not won a Challenge Certificate, nor three or more first prizes, at Open or Championship shows.

Limit – Dogs which have not qualified as a Champion, or have not won seven or more first prizes in Limit or Open classes at Championship shows.

Open – All dogs which are classified in the schedule of that show.

Veteran – Dogs of seven years old or over.

Apart from any dog shows which are held independently, shows are held under the jurisdiction of the Kennel Clubs (which obviously vary from country to country). These shows are classified according to their degree of importance. In order of increasing importance, those in Britain, for example, are:

1. Exemption Shows: local events permitted by the Committee of the Kennel Club and often held in conjunction with local fêtes, agricultural shows, etc. The atmosphere is very relaxed and the programme may include such novelty classes as 'the dog with the waggiest tail'. Only four pedigree classes are permitted. These shows are useful for introducing inexperienced dogs to the rest of the world.

2. Matches: held between pedigree dogs, often between breeds. Again, they are social affairs which provide good experience for dog and owner.

3. Sanctions Shows: these are licenced by the Kennel Club and are subject to more rules and regulations, for example, a schedule (layout of breeds, classes, judges, etc.) must be published, and there is a limit on the number of classes.

4. Limited Shows: these are slightly more advanced with regard to the standard of classes and their limitations, and they have tighter restrictions still (for example, there must be a

minimum of thirteen classes if only one breed is scheduled, or twenty-one classes if there is more than one breed). No dog who has won a Challenge Certificate is eligible.

5. Open Shows: these important shows are open to all dogs – champions or otherwise.

6. Championship Shows: these are the most prestigious of all and are held for one or more breeds. The best known are 'Crufts' and 'The Three Counties', but there are many others, some of which may be held at the same time as major agricultural shows. It is at these shows that 'Challenge Certificates' are awarded, which go towards a dog becoming a Champion.

All these shows are organized by show societies, the committee members of which are required to act as 'Guarantors to the Kennel Club'. This means they have to guarantee payment of prize money should the society default but the guarantee is rarely high.

First, second, third, and fourth or reserve, prizes are generally awarded in each class. At the end of the show, the winners are assembled before the judges, who assess them for the Best of Breed and Reserve Best of Breed prizes. The Best of Breed winners, if still unbeaten after any Variety Classes in which they have been exhibited, are then eligible to compete in the Best in Show Award. This final accolade is sometimes arrived at by judging breed winners in groups, such as the Hound Group or the Toy Group. The dog that wins will have beaten all the Best of Breeds classified within that group. Best in Show is obviously the most coveted award, although its importance clearly depends on the standing of the show itself.

The ultimate award, for which every exhibitor aims, is The Challenge Certificate. A dog which has received three Challenge Certificates, under three different judges, at least one of which was received after the dog was twelve months old, is granted the title of *Champion*. This is a most coveted position in the dog showing world.

Preparations for showing

Before deciding to show a dog, you should become familiar with the Rules and Regulations of the Kennel Club, who is the governing body of the dog showing world. It is also sensible to seek the advice of an experienced dog exhibitor, both on the suitability of your dog for showing, and on

142

Left: Long-haired Chihuahuas wait patiently for the judges' inspection.

which shows and classes would be most suitable for it.

The Kennel Club lays down various standards for each individual breed and, to be successful, a dog must conform to these standards. For example, if a Dalmatian is 'patched' – that is, has a large area of black or liver coat colouration unbroken by white – there would be little point in showing it, even if it is pure bred and has a pedigree. The breed standard for Dalmatians decrees well-defined spots about 3 cm ($1\frac{1}{4}$ ins) in diameter and dogs with small spots or large patches will be heavily penalized in any show ring. Similarly, a White Boxer or Alsatian would not conform to the breed standards, as their colour is not allowed.

Show training should be started very early in a pup's life. General socialization and manners are a good start, and this sort of training is described elsewhere in this book. A nervous or aggressive

Below: One of these English Setters has become so bored waiting that he has gone off on his own tour of inspection.

dog will be unsuitable for showing, as it has to remain unperturbed while its mouth is examined, its tail lifted and its body felt. In addition it has to be unruffled when meeting lots of other dogs and people in strange circumstances. Ring-craft classes and exemption shows can be invaluable as part of a dog's training for showing.

Having decided to exhibit your dog, it is important to ensure it is in good health and correctly groomed on the day of the show. It is not a good idea to show a bitch 'in season'. Although there is no rule against this, it can be extremely annoying to the exhibitors of male dogs, particularly if such dogs are in regular use as studs. A bitch in an advanced stage of pregnancy should not be shown either.

Always allow plenty of time to get to the show. Classes are seldom delayed for more than a few minutes, even if all the exhibitors are not present, and, if you miss a class, it may render you ineligible for further classes.

The specific points demanded of a particular breed (as opposed to the specified standards) can only be learned by studying that breed. However, there are a number of general factors common to all breeds which the judge will consider. He will be looking for correctly co-ordinated movement, with an overall 'balanced appearance', and may well decide to penalize a very fat or excessively thin dog.

A dog which has been taught to 'show' properly and exhibits itself well so that it looks its best in the ring, is more likely to take the eye of the judge than a dog which is either unruly or disinterested in its surroundings. It is therefore a good idea for both dog and owner to learn the 'ring procedures', and to have practised them beforehand, so that when they go to their first show, all is not totally strange. The summer months are the busiest time for shows – the dogs are generally benched in marquees while the judging takes place in rings outside. Indoor shows are held almost exclusively in the winter, late autumn or early spring.

Shows are great social occasions for dog people. They bring opportunities to discuss dogs and breeding and to renew old acquaintances. The atmosphere is frenzied; the noise of human talking is far in excess of any canine sounds. Dogs are usually amazingly well-behaved at shows, which says no end for the control and training by their owners.

Transport to and from a show can be a problem to non-car drivers although, quite recently, groups of people have begun to hire coaches to take them and their dogs, at least to the bigger shows. It is well worth while to see if such an arrangement has been made in your area, whether or not you drive a car. A busy dog show will be a more pleasant experience if you do not have to rush for buses or trains, contend with

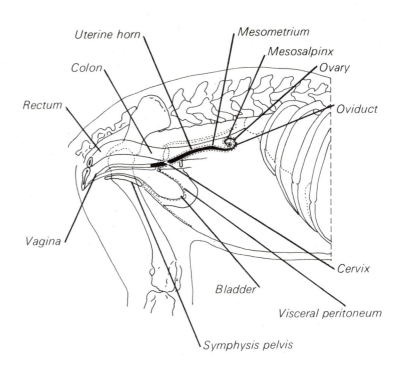

busy roads in an unfamiliar area, or drive home at the end of an exhausting day. For those who do drive themselves, most dog shows have reasonably good car parking facilities.

Above: The reproductive tract of the bitch.

A dog's pedigree, registration and recognition

Dog owners often say, 'He's got a good pedigree *and* he is registered.' What does this mean and can we tell anything from a pedigree, which is actually the canine form of a birth certificate? In theory, all dogs have a pedigree but, in today's dog parlance, a pedigree dog is a 'pure bred' dog with a known parentage.

A registered dog is a pedigree dog which has been registered with the Kennel Club; i.e., it has been given a name which the Kennel Club has accepted and recorded and it has also been given a number. Even cross-bred dogs can be registered but, to obtain Class I registration, dogs must be pure-bred and of known parents and the parents themselves must be registered.

An exception is the Obedience Record, where the dogs registered are allowed to compete in obedience tests and working trials, but this registration does not make the progeny of the dog eligible for recognition by the Kennel Club.

The registration of dogs is undertaken by the canine governing bodies in each country – the Kennel Club in Britain, the American Kennel Club in the United States, the Canadian Kennel

Below: The Schipperke was once used for guarding barges and river boats in Belgium. They normally have their tails docked but this one still has its spitz-type tail.

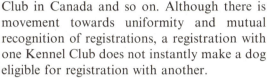

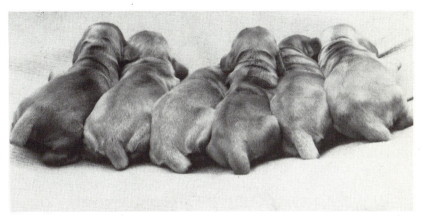

Club in Canada and so on. Although there is movement towards uniformity and mutual recognition of registrations, a registration with one Kennel Club does not instantly make a dog eligible for registration with another.

The registration of a dog is no longer the simple procedure it used to be. The registration declaration must be signed by both the owners of the sire and of the dam. This litter registration form can be handed to the dam's owner after the mating. After whelping, it is completed, to give details of the number of live puppies and their sex. It is then sent to the Kennel Club. The breeder of the puppies is then sent a 'litter pack', which includes an application form for registration on the *Basic Register* for each member of the litter. This can be completed at any time subsequently. A dog is advanced to the *Active Register* when shown, bred from or sold abroad.

A newcomer to the canine world should make a careful study of the registration requirements, since these are fairly complex. Once a dog has been registered, the owner is sent a card which shows the name and number, date of birth, parentage, breeder and owner.

A pedigree and registration card are *no guarantee* that a dog is a good specimen of its breed. Some breeders automatically register an entire litter and sell them with the pedigree and registration card, although some of the pups may not have show potential. A good pedigree does not make a good dog. Even a full complement of champions on both sides will not *necessarily* mean that the pup will be any good for showing purposes, although of course, a good pedigree gives it a better chance. Unfortunately, some unscrupulous breeding establishments have been known to supply inaccurate pedigrees, hence the importance of finding a reputable breeder from whom to purchase a puppy.

Subject to suitability, the Kennel Club will grant, on application, a name to a breeder for his/her/their exclusive use. That is to say, this name can be used in addition to the personal name chosen for the registration of the dog. There are certain limitations on the type of words granted for this use but, once granted, no other breeder will be allowed to use the same name, nor will any one be allowed to use one very similar to it. Breeders often have more than one 'affix', as this personal name is known in the dog world.

The breeder

The breeder of a puppy (litter/dog) is the registered owner of the dam at the time of the birth. If a puppy is then sold it can be transferred to its new owner. The Kennel Club supplies transfer forms. In the case of a bitch, which is eventually used for breeding, the owner to whom it has been transferred is the breeder of the subsequent litter. If not transferred, the original owner is the official breeder of the puppies.

The owner

In the eyes of the Kennel Club, the owner of the dog is the person who is the registered owner of the dam at the time of its birth. Should it then be sold or given away, ownership can be transferred to the new owner.

Transferring a dog

Unless you intend to breed from, show, or in any way exhibit your newly acquired puppy,

Above left: This cut down peanut box makes an ideal temporary home for small dogs such as this Pomeranian.

Top: These undocked Cocker Spaniel pups are just three days old. The following day they 'lost' their tails.

Above: The same family group – tails gone!

transferring the ownership to yourself is a formality. If you do intend to breed or show, then you *should* transfer the puppy, or it will be shown as 'officially' owned by the person from whom you bought it. This can produce considerable complications – for example, entry forms require the signature of the 'owner'. There are nominal fees for the various bits of documentation.

Registration of breeds

Not all breeds are recognized by a country's Kennel Club and each national canine body varies in this respect. The Kennel Clubs are constantly reviewing the situation and debating whether they should recognize new or rare breeds. Some breeds, such as the Staffordshire Bull Terrier, have been recognized for many years while others, such as the Siberian Husky, have only just gained Kennel Club recognition in Britain.

Recognition of a breed means that the Kennel Club considers that the breed has reached a stage in its existence where the dogs are of a relatively uniform type. In fact, recognition usually occurs when a breed standard can be agreed upon and set. This explains why a breed such as the Jack Russell Terrier is not recognized. The variation between individuals of the breed is so extreme that it is not possible to say that any one dog is typical and can therefore set the standard.

Breed standards are only a guide. They are not a die into which every dog of the breed is cast. No living creature can ever be perfect in the strict sense of the word and no group of dogs or puppies of any one litter can be identical. Indeed, it is this inevitable slight variation which allows the dog breeder scope for improvement and gives to the breeding of dogs a tantalizing uncertainty and interest.

Dog breeding

It is impossible to divorce dog breeding from dog showing, if only because so often one is the very reason for the other. It is rare to find someone who shows dogs, enters them in obedience trials or even uses a dog for a work or recreational purpose, who does not have an interest or commitment to dog breeding, however detached.

No dog is perfect, but his – or her – progeny might be! This is the stimulus which excites people to breed dogs, and the aim is almost always to produce better dogs – more beautiful, faster, stronger, more agile, more intelligent, or more equable in temperament. Whether for a seasoned breeder of a fine line of prizewinning show dogs, or the owner of a pet bitch, this aim is the same. The means to it lie in dog selection and the science of genetics (briefly discussed in

Left: Breeding takes a lot out of a bitch. This Great Dane may take several months to regain top condition for showing.

Chapter Two). The methods employed today are essentially the same as those used by the Egyptians or Chinese thousands of years ago, coupled with the invaluable practical experience gained over those years and the advantages offered by the modern breed societies, which provide a reliable genetic pool of material.

There are many questions that should be asked before a decision is taken to breed puppies. Has

Below: The Standard Poodle – when properly clipped and groomed – is a magnificent-looking dog.

the bitch or dog a good temperament? Do they both have good show points (if pedigree specimens) and are they both fit and free from inheritable abnormalities? Is the bitch old enough? Can you cope with the puppies in nine weeks time and are you prepared to be tied to them for at least eight weeks after that? Are you sure you can sell them or find good homes for them? If the answer to any of these questions is no, or uncertain, then you should seriously reconsider the proposition. Advice from a reputable breeder, officer of a Canine Society, or veterinary surgeon, will also be helpful in making the decision.

If you are also committed to showing dogs as an integral part of your life, then take extra care over breeding plans. Have you got the space to house and exercise the bitches, and their litters, and will you be able to keep some pups well into their adolescence, to assess whether they have show prospects? Remember that the basis of successful breeding lies with using your own bitches and good show stud dogs.

Some words of warning: don't expect to make a fortune from dog breeding – few people do,

indeed most hardly break even. Don't breed from bitches every season. Be very selective in the dogs you keep or buy, and be prepared to be ruthless in culling out and selling any dog which is less than superb. Finally, you must expect and accept disappointments.

There are few specific medical reasons for breeding from a bitch but many people feel that bitches mature when they have a litter. There are virtually no good reasons for allowing a male dog to mate, unless he happens to be a really good pedigree dog, or possesses a very good working record. Male dogs do not become better pets after having been used at stud and they can become bitch-orientated and generally 'sexy' which is usually a great nuisance.

Mating

Having taken the decision to breed from your bitch, take her to the very best stud you can find to complement her conformation, colouring and temperament. If you are breeding from a mongrel, choose a dog with a strong constitution and equable temperament, and one that is a

Above: The Pug's tail curls over its hip.

Below: The Wire (left) and Smooth (right) Fox Terriers have black and tan markings.

suitable size for your bitch. Again, the advice of a helpful breed society official will be invaluable.

Make enquiries well in advance about the dog you intend to use. It is advisable to contact the stud owner as soon as your bitch comes in season, for good studs have a busy calendar.

The best time for mating is generally ten to fourteen days after the onset of bleeding. As a rule the bitch goes to the dog, and most stud owners are very experienced in the procedure. After an adequate introduction (necessary to make sure the bitch is not totally averse to the dog and vice versa), the bitch will stand, often with her tail held slightly to one side – a good sign of readiness for mating – and allow the male to mount. He pushes his penis into the bitch's vagina and the bulbus glandis (an enlarged area at the base of the penis) swells inside the vulva. This results in the 'tie' which is the mechanical joining of the bitch and dog. Either of their own accord, or with the help of the handlers, the male then puts one hind leg over the bitch's back and turns round so that the two are facing in opposite directions. Neither the 'tie' or the 'turn' are vital for a fertile mating, but they are considered desirable. Mating may take anything from ten to thirty minutes, after which the bitch becomes restless and will probably move. It is desirable for at least one owner to be present at a mating, to assist if necessary, or to prevent a possible fight.

If the bitch will not accept the male, it is usual to re-introduce her to him a couple of days later.

Pregnancy

Soon after mating, the eggs, which have been fertilized, become attached to the wall of the uterus. There they develop into foetuses and grow for the next sixty-three days.

For the first thirty-five days, little difference can be seen in the bitch, although a veterinary surgeon may be able to feel the swellings in her uterus at about twenty-four to thirty days after mating. At about five weeks, the bitch becomes noticeably fatter in the abdomen, her mammary

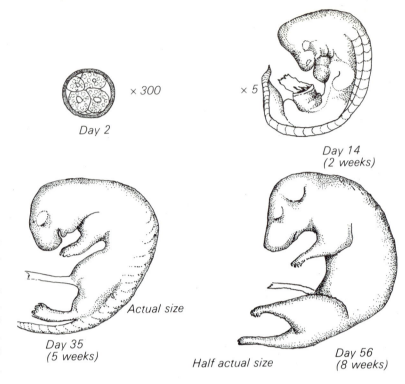

Day 2 × 300

Day 14 (2 weeks) × 5

Day 35 (5 weeks) Actual size

Day 56 (8 weeks) Half actual size

glands enlarge and, by the end of pregnancy, there may even be a little watery fluid or milk in the teats. Pregnant bitches often become rather quiet; for the second half of the pregnancy, they must be allowed to go at their own time and pace when being exercised. Often, bitches show discomfort at about forty-two days, when the uterus folds on itself, and also a few days before they have their puppies, or 'whelp'. In the twenty-four hours immediately before whelping, the bitch may be very uncomfortable and may even become hysterical. Her vulva will become quite swollen, her temperature will drop a degree or so (which is a good sign of imminent whelping) and she will start 'bed-making', often in inconvenient corners. Bitches often lose all appetite and may even vomit just before whelping.

Commonly, bitches have a sticky vulval

Above: The development of pups in the womb. The gestation period is nine weeks from mating.

Below left: The dog, having been introduced to the bitch, sniffs around her as part of the 'courtship'.

Below: With the owner holding the bitch steady, the male 'ties' with the bitch.

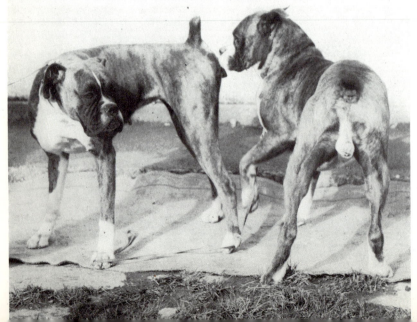

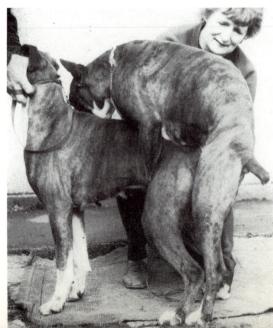

discharge throughout pregnancy but, if any pus or greenish-black fluid is passed, a veterinary surgeon should be consulted at once. Abortion is quite a rare event with dogs. It is a good idea for pregnant bitches to have a 'check-up' at some time during pregnancy. Twenty-four to thirty days after mating is a good time, as the veterinary surgeon may be able to feel the puppies and thus confirm the pregnancy.

Whelping

Not much equipment is needed for whelping, except a box for the bitch, some old towels – and start saving all the old newspaper you can get! This is invaluable for the puppies' beds. A good whelping box can be made by cutting down the sides of a large cardboard box, which has to be big enough for the bitch to stretch out easily. Get her used to sleeping in this a week or so before she is due to whelp. Do not let her whelp in her normal bed – whelping is a messy process and a box used specially for the purpose can be burnt when the puppies have all gone. Put the box in a quiet place away from other dogs, cats and household thoroughfares. Bitches need to be warm for whelping – but not too hot! Provide plenty of newspapers or towels, but remember that more harm than good is done by raising the heat to tropical levels with heaters or thermo-electric lamps.

Bed-making begins when the bitch starts to tear up the newspaper and turn round and round in the box. She may squeak as if in discomfort, or groan and pant, until eventually she starts to strain with her tail raised, her body hunched up and her sides 'blown out'. A little mucus may appear at the vulva and the straining becomes more intense. The bitch then licks her vulva and eventually the foetal membranes, or 'water bag', are pushed out. These stages of labour may continue over a period of twelve hours from the initial bed-making stage.

Once the water bag has appeared, the bitch licks it vigorously and usually bursts it. With considerable effort, she forces out the pup and licks and breaks any membrane round its head, whereupon the pup gasps its first breath. Very soon after that, it begins crawling around and soon starts to suckle. Often, the green/black placenta is born with the puppy and the bitch usually bites the cord and eats the placenta. After a rest, while the pup sucks, the bitch will start straining again and the next pup is born – and so it continues. The intervals between the births of the pups can vary greatly. Sometimes it is only minutes – other times it can be two to three hours. Breeds such as the Chihuahua are very rapid whelpers and often expel all their pups in an hour. The arrival of the placentas also varies greatly from breed to breed. Sometimes they are presented with the pups, and sometimes three or four come together after the pups have been born. It is advisable to keep a count of these afterbirths to see if any are retained within the bitch, in which case the vet should be consulted.

Although there are great variations among bitches in normal whelping, there are surprisingly few problems. *Never panic* if things do not seem quite right, for there is rarely an emergency. Veterinary attention is necessary if a bitch strains with no result and then gives up straining. If, however, she is just 'slow', and nothing has happened for a while, yet you suspect there are more pups to come, try taking her for a short walk. This may help to get things moving.

It is not a good idea for novice breeders to probe around a bitch's vagina during whelping but if a puppy is partly born, so that half of its body is clear of the vagina it is permissible to pull it very gently. In fact, this is a rare problem and, once the head and shoulders have passed through the vagina, the rest of the body usually follows quickly. Pups are quite often born backwards, which usually results in a normal, if rather protracted, birth. If a reverse born pup appears 'stuck' when it is only half born, then do gently help the bitch by easing out the puppy. If the head is not brought clear of the vagina quite quickly, it may suffocate.

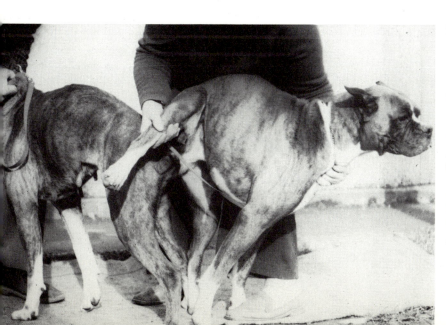

Below left: The dog 'turns' by putting one hind leg over the bitch's back and turning round.

Below right: Having turned, the couple continue the mating process. The whole procedure often lasts half an hour or more.

Sometimes bitches are very slow to lick the membranes away from the pup's head and this is especially true of inexperienced bitches, who may ignore the pups once they are born. If so, wipe the pup's mouth with a clean towel. This will usually be sufficient stimulus to get the pup breathing.

Never take any of the pups away from the bitch during the whelping period. The stimulus of suckling lets down her milk and also causes the uterus to contract and expel more pups. Do not fuss round her, or bring in strangers and *never* allow another dog or animal near her. It could cause her to kill and eat the pups.

When the bitch has finished whelping, all straining will stop. She should then be left in peace with her pups. Offer her a drink but no food, as her stomach will be full of afterbirth.

After whelping

Bitches often have transient diarrhoea after whelping, from the afterbirths they have consumed. This soon passes. Keep strangers and other dogs away from the bitch and her litter, for at least the first four to five days. You should, however, get her used to you handling the puppies. The bitch will hardly leave her litter at all for the first few days and will attend to them constantly.

Considerable controversy surrounds the docking of puppies' tails, and, to a lesser extent, the removal of dew claws. Dew claws are the vestigial toes found on the inside of the front legs, just above the pads. They are also sometimes seen in the same position on the hind limbs. The front dew claws rarely cause much problem but the hind ones can be large, in which case they tend to flap around, often becoming caught and damaged in undergrowth or on furniture. They

are also generally unsightly. Dew claws are best removed when the pup is newly born, at least before it is four days old. This is a simple job, requiring no more than a clean cut with a pair of sterilized scissors. It is probably best, however, to get the veterinary surgeon to do it or, at least, to demonstrate the technique. Any bleeding (which is usually very minor) can be arrested by pressing some cotton wool, sprinkled with potassium permanganate crystals, against the area. Providing this operation is done before a puppy is four days old, it will cause him no pain. If it is done later, an anaesthetic would be necessary. Incidentally, a few breeds, such as Pyrenean mountain dogs, require dew claws to be left on for show purposes.

Some people regard docking (together with ear cropping, which is illegal in Britain) as a barbaric mutilation. They claim that not only is it unnatural to remove the tail from a dog, but it causes a puppy unnecessary suffering and causes an adult dog unnecessary indignity. Protagonists of the practice argue that docking is virtually painless, and that in docked working breeds, such as a Cocker Spaniel, the presence of a tail would be an encumbrance, and possibly a hazard, to the dog.

Whatever one's views happen to be, breed standards lay down which breeds should be docked, and at what length. Any deviation from these standards either results in show penalization, or it renders the dog totally unshowable. If docking is to be done, it should be carried out within four days of birth by a competent operator, and preferably by a veterinary surgeon. Breed standards should be consulted before the job is done, as docking length varies greatly. In Old English Sheepdogs, the tail is almost totally removed; in Boxers a short stub is left; in

Right: Dogs are judged for appearance and fluidity of movement. These German Shepherd Dogs are being paraded for the judges who will scrutinize them in motion.

Right: This Airedale waits expectantly for his owner to return.

Cavalier King Charles Spaniels, only a few tail vertebrae from the tip are removed.

Ear cropping in dogs is performed in some parts of Europe and the United States. As it is done purely for aesthetic reasons and is performed after the puppy age, criticisms of it as a mutilation are valid.

A problem that can beset bitches around whelping is that of milk fever or *Eclampsia*. This disease is caused by the lowering of the calcium level in the blood, when this mineral is moved into the milk. It occurs most commonly during the lactation period, although it is also known to attack before, or during, whelping. It can even occur in severe cases of false pregnancy. When afflicted, the bitch becomes very restless and

Far left; left and right: All sorts of techniques are applied, from artificial curling to delicate brushing, to make show dogs appear to be at their best for the final judging.

excited, and often has a wild look in her eyes. She may become staggery and have convulsions, with very rapid breathing. This constitutes a real emergency, and a veterinary surgeon must be contacted very quickly to administer a calcium preparation.

A word should be said about infertility. This term covers the whole spectrum of reproductive incompetence, from the individual male with temporary sterility, through to diseases which cause total infertility in both dogs and bitches. In no other area of dog disease is so much rubbish spoken or inappropriate action taken. Each case has to be individually assessed and hasty decisions should always be avoided. It is advisable to seek the advice of a veterinary surgeon in all suspected cases of infertility.

Assessing the litter

It is no easy task to assess the merits of a litter – all puppies are beautiful! But appraisement is necessary and, indeed, should continue throughout a dog's life. Breeding from any line is a continual process of change in temperament and form. The successful breeder notes these changes and acts on them when considering his breeding policy.

Many experienced breeders are able to make very precise assessment of adult development by looking at a newly-born puppy. Most people can see the relative ear length, mouth conformation, head shape, and body, limb and tail proportion, when a puppy is four to five weeks old, but they cannot judge the eventual coat length and colour, except to make general comments on the depth of pigment and the coat quality. These physical characteristics change continually until a dog reaches puberty. The animal's character also changes.

By four to five months old, body proportions and general shape will be fairly well fixed, but coat colour and length may still change. These characteristics, together with movement and general demeanour, may take another two years to develop to their full potential.

It is, of course, just as important to take note of the faults as of the good points in a puppy. Faults may be inherited from either parent or from a combination of both. Sometimes it is quite obvious that a puppy has inherited a conformation fault – such as an overshot jaw – from its parents if one or other parent has the same fault. At other times, the fault may not appear in the parents, but still shows in their offspring. In this case, the fault is recessive. Or, again, the fault may be attributable to some more complex method of inheritance. In any event, that particular mating should be avoided in the future to prevent imperfect pups being born.

Choosing and Training a Dog

What kind of dog should you have? Such a decision should not be made lightly, in a hurry or without plenty of frank family discussion. Your dog will be part of your family life for the next ten or twelve years, so your choice of such a companion is all important.

All too often the decision is forced upon you quickly at a time when you are quite unprepared for it. The children discover that a neighbour's bitch has pups and ask if they can have one; a visitor tells of a young dog about to be put to sleep because it is homeless or unwanted, or a stray simply arrives on the doorstep. These are temptations to avoid, unless you are really in a position to have the dog. Generally, sacrifices have to be made even in the most ideal circumstances – and, if the situation is not ideal, the sacrifices will be much greater, possibly so great as to become a burden. In such cases, the dog will almost certainly get less than its share of attention or else it will have to leave. Either way, it is the dog who suffers most.

The first and most important consideration is – can you have a dog at all? If you live on the top floor of a high-rise block of city centre flats and are away from home for ten hours every weekday, not only would it be ludicrous to have a Great Dane as a pet but you should consider whether it is right for you to own a dog at all.

Modern housing conditions, financial stringencies, working wives and a current fashion for big breeds have resulted in many cases of unhappy dogs with frustrated owners. So do think really carefully before you make this big decision of dog ownership.

Choosing a breed

A number of factors combine to dictate a sensible choice of breed. Although these must be considered in relation to each other, they can be discussed individually at this stage.

No single point is necessarily more important than any other, but the amount of time you can, and are prepared to spend with your dog is a major consideration. In general, the bigger breeds demand more exercise, more care and more attention. A young, lively Labrador dog, for example, will probably need at least three kilometres (two miles) walk per day or an hour's play with a ball in a large garden. In addition, he will want company of some sort for a fair proportion of the day. If you deprive him of these activities, you run the risk of him becoming bored and exhibiting the destructive tendencies discussed in Chapter Three.

The time and attention demanded by a dog is not only dictated by its size. Many terriers and members of the Hound Group need lots of attention. In addition to exercise and activity, there are such things as grooming to be considered. Dense-coated breeds, such as Shih Tzus and Pekinese, have to be regularly and thoroughly groomed and adequate time must be allowed for this.

The space in the house and garden must be taken into account, too. The bigger breeds are often clumsy in the house. Tails sway just at the right height to remove bone china ornaments from low shelves. When a Mastiff decides to bury his bone in the garden, he produces a crater of prestigious dimensions. The big breeds also produce a lot of faeces and urine, which can be quite a problem if you have a tiny garden and no open ground nearby.

Although many potential dog owners are reluctant to admit that finance can limit their choice of dog, it is stupid to overlook this aspect, both from the point of view of initial purchase and the upkeep thereafter. Well-bred dogs with a good pedigree are not cheap – after all, they have

Above: Both the Sealyham and the Pyrenean Mountain Dog may appeal to you, but would they be suitable for your way of living?

Opposite: The German Mastiff (Great Dane) grows to a height of two-and-a-half-feet and a weight of 120 pounds. Standing on its hind legs it dwarfs its owner.

been an expense for the breeder to rear. Buying the best pedigree dog may theoretically give the best chance of a future show specimen, but it is virtually unknown actually to recoup the purchase price in show prizes, stud fees or puppies. The price of a puppy, therefore, must be regarded as a lost figure. Prices of puppies vary greatly with the breed popularity, the pedigree of sire and dam and the conformation of the puppy, as well as many other geographical and local factors. The puppies of bigger breeds are always more expensive – feeding the sire and pregnant dam, and rearing the puppies, cost more than it does with small breeds. If you want to be the owner of a rare or newly-introduced breed of dog, you must be prepared to pay a premium for the 'privilege'.

The financial implications of a dog certainly do not stop at the initial purchase and, although licensing or vaccination charges are the same whether you have a Cairn or a St. Bernard, many other recurring costs are not. A dog of quite modest size will consume about 150 kilos (330 lbs) of canned dog food a year and half that weight again of dry biscuits. This can be doubled for a big breed or halved for, say a small terrier. Other costs, such as kennelling, purchase of leads, collars and so on, tend to be greater for the bigger breeds. Veterinary attention, apart from vaccination, also costs more; big dogs need a higher drug dosage than smaller dogs and they are certainly more accident prone.

A final consideration when choosing a dog is what you want it to do and to be for you and your family. If you are an active person who regularly enjoys longs walks, then, assuming all other aspects are catered for, a lively, exuberant dog like an English Setter, Retriever or Boxer would be ideal. If you are retired, with plenty of time and a penchant for the aesthetic or exotic – why not a Pekinese or Dandie Dinmont Terrier?

Much of the description of the characteristics of dogs discussed in Chapter Three will have helped you in the choice of a breed but, if you are still uncertain, then try discussing the relative merits of breeds with people who own them. A breed club official could put you in touch with an owner who is prepared to help in this way, and you should be able, then, to make a final choice from a short list of breeds.

The final choice – dog or bitch
Whatever type of dog you finally decide upon, be it a pedigree puppy or a rescued cross-bred adult, you are still faced with the major decision of which sex to have. Although you have recourse to neutering and various heat control methods, there are fundamental character differences between the sexes. In general, male dogs are more exuberant, tougher and inclined to be slightly

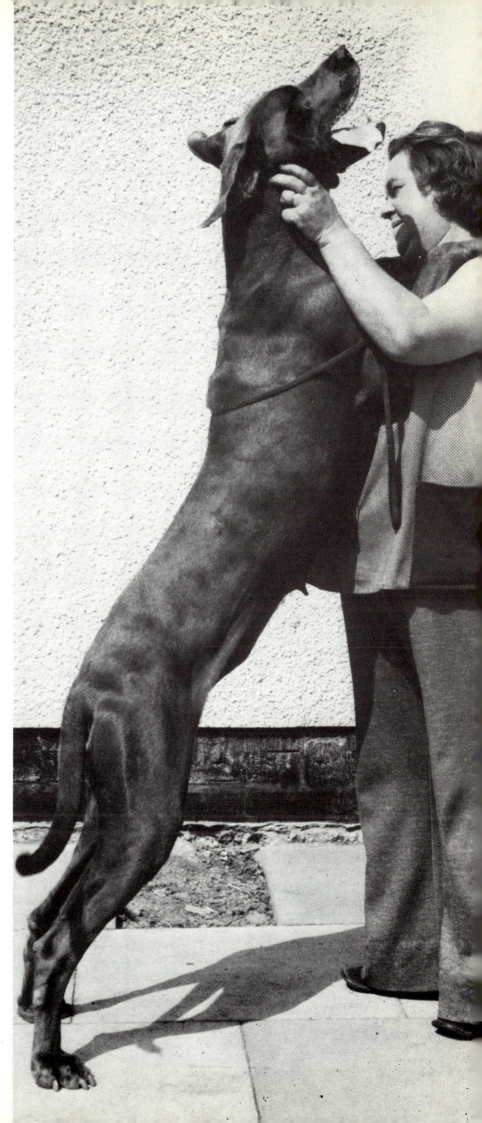

more independent and difficult to train than bitches. They have an undeniable tendency to wander, particularly when bitches nearby are in season, and it is often difficult to keep them confined to bounds. Bitches tend to be quieter, more affectionate and easier to confine and train.

Unspayed bitches usually come on heat twice a year and, for a period of a week or so during each heat, are attractive to males. People will often say, 'I wouldn't want a bitch, with all that trouble of her being on heat twice a year', but the true counter argument to this is that dogs are on heat all the year round! Certainly some bitch owners find the heat periods – with the vaginal bleeding and male attraction – a severe problem, particularly if they have a plethora of amorous males in the area, together with bad garden fences and young children who cannot be relied upon to close gates and doors. Most people, however, find little worry in coping with these inconveniences and, instead, benefit from the bitch's temperament. There is also the added advantage of being able to breed from the bitch, if she is suitable. (Further aspects of sexual behaviour, reproduction and neutering will be discussed in Chapter Eight.)

The choice of dog or bitch may not be vital for the first family dog, but it becomes more critical if there is already an un-neutered dog or bitch in the house. It is certainly unwise to bring together un-neutered dogs of different sexes in the same household, for then the heat periods can be extremely trying. Not only is it cruel to keep a male dog in close proximity to a bitch on heat, without letting them mate, but it will actually be difficult to avoid them doing so. This then brings problems of trying to prevent future over-sexuality of the male, while a litter at every season is undesirable for many reasons.

The only way the issue can be avoided is by

Top left: Cairns do not need excessive exercise but enjoy short romps.

Bottom left: It is unfortunate that Schnauzers are not more popular as they are sensibly sized dogs with equable temperaments.

Top right: An Afghan is a dog which should not be closely confined. It needs extended runs.

Bottom right: Irish Setters are ideal pets for a young family as they enjoy plenty of exercise.

sending one or other dog away to kennels (or friends or relations) during the heat, although this can bring expense and inconvenience. Professional breeders have the same problem, but they overcome it by keeping on-heat bitches kennelled well away from the others. Male dogs at stud are anyway more used to the stimulus of bitches on heat, are generally better disciplined than domestic pet dogs and, of course, usually have a number of bitches to mate in a year.

The possibility of an adult dog

When the possibility of acquiring an adult dog occurs, it should be approached with the greatest care. A well-balanced, happy, adult dog will usually settle down well in a household, but it will nevertheless have already established its character, which the new owner will have to discover over a period of time.

There are many genuine reasons why an adult dog is offered for sale or 'free to good home'; the previous owners may be emigrating or changing their home or work to a situation where it is impossible to keep a dog, or a breeder may be selling a dog which is not suitable for further showing or breeding. In these cases the dog's previous history should be known and you should ask for it. Remember, though, that although you can *see* just what you are getting, you don't *know* just what you are getting. Not having reared the dog from a pup, you will be unfamiliar with any faults, bad habits and quirks of character, so you must be prepared for some shocks.

Adult strays are an even bigger risk. Strays are often strays for a very good reason. The practice of abandoning a dog is obviously to be deprecated, but it is also true that strays are extremely independent dogs which have little desire for human contact, so the previous owner may genuinely have had his dog simply disappear. Many stray males are prone to over-sexuality and have a constant desire to search for bitches on heat.

Stray bitches will often be in whelp, as irresponsible people will often abandon bitches when they find they are pregnant.

The previous medical history of stray dogs is obviously quite unknown, and is usually vague for any adult dog. It must always be assumed that stray dogs are unvaccinated unless you can acquire a signed vaccination certificate for them.

If you do decide to give a home to a stray dog, always take it to a veterinary surgeon for full examination and a course of vaccinations. Give it all the care and attention you can but be prepared for the worst possible behaviour. And take great care with introducing a stray dog to children, other pets – and your furniture. Many strays are practised home wreckers!

Above: Boxers make good guard dogs and affectionate, but damp nosed pets.

Below: Large dogs need lots of exercise. To walk them on the road like this requires absolute control and the knowledge that they will always come to heel when called.

Choosing your puppy

Having decided on the breed and the sex of your future dog, all you have to do now is find the right puppy. Again this is often easier said than done. Beware of advertisements in papers which advertize puppies of all breeds. These usually refer to 'puppy farms', where bitches are bred from every season with the sole objective of rearing as many marketable pups as possible to sell at an inflated price. You may be lucky and get a good pup but the chances are low. Similarly, if you decide against a pedigree dog but feel that a mongrel would suit you well, it is best not to be tempted by the 'puppy in the window' at pet shops. Rarely can you even obtain an inspired guess at the parentage of such pups and their age may be equally uncertain. Far better to try to find a local dog owner with a whelping mongrel bitch where, at the very least, you know one side of the parentage and some breeding history is available. Alternatively, officials of the R.S.P.C.A., or other canine societies will be able to put you in contact with private owners who are desperate to find good homes for well-reared pups.

If you want a pedigree puppy, you may need to spend quite a lot of effort, and time, in looking and waiting for the right pup. Also be prepared to travel a distance for it. Most serious breeders of pedigree dogs are trustworthy and caring people who are unlikely to 'sell you a (proverbial) pup'; bad news travels fast and they value their reputation. A good way to find a breeder is to contact a breed club official through one of the dog enthusiast magazines or papers, a dog show or local veterinary surgeon or canine society. Having located the breeder, you can visit his or her home to see the adult dog and thus get some idea of the 'type' and temperament of the dogs. For example, one breeder may have a predominance of one coat colour or type of markings.

Assuming the breeder has a litter at the time of your visit, he will show you the pedigrees of the parents and explain their temperament and character. He will also explain what characteristics seen in a pup may develop in the adult. Some tiny abnormalities, such as slight dental malocclusion, may rectify; slight tail kinks may straighten and, often, slight umbilical hernias may disappear. Equally, sometimes they don't – but breeders can usually advise as to what will happen. Do not be too influenced by a puppy's coat colour, as this often changes dramatically, just as size variations may also even out later. The smallest pup in a seven-week-old litter could eventually grow to be the biggest adult dog.

The price of a pedigree puppy depends to a large extent on the potential of the pedigree; parents or close relations who were champions will augur well for the potential of the pups, and make them relatively more expensive. Nothing is ever certain in dog breeding, however. There is no guarantee that pups from a champion dam and sire will even be suitable for showing although, statistically, the chances are better than for pups from parents of poor show capability. Prices can also vary within one litter, depending on the qualities of the pups. If you have no intention of showing, then slightly poor markings, or less than perfect conformation, will be of no importance to you, and the price of such a pup may be less than that for its brothers and sisters.

Never be afraid to go away and think over the matter before returning for another look. Genuine breeders never mind such concern.

Many potential dog owners ask, 'What should I look for in a puppy; what characteristics will help me to make the right choice?' This is virtually impossible to answer, not least because puppies vary so much in their activities, attitudes and moods from one minute to the next. Examining the litter at one time may show a puppy who is particularly lively – perhaps playing with his mother and trying to wake up his brothers and sisters in an attempt to get them to play. Within half an hour, he can be the only dozy one of the litter, waddling along half-drunk

Above left to right: Introduction to the lead may be met with complete refusal to co-operate, but with a little gentle persuasion, the puppy soon realizes that he may as well become used to it and is soon walking quite happily on his lead.

with tiredness, showing no inclination to play and giving his brothers and sisters a disgruntled snarl if they invite him to do so.

Coupled with this are the tremendous changes which occur in pups from weaning through to adulthood, although much of this is in the hands of the owner and will be discussed further in the next chapter. Puppies which were the aggressive pack leaders of an eight-week-old litter often end up as docile pets with submissive natures.

The only sensible advice which can be given on choosing a puppy is to select the one which you like and which captivates your attention. It is this puppy that is most likely to claim your affection and respect. In turn, it is your affection and respect which will most influence your puppy's character development.

Above all, do not press the breeder to let you have the puppy before it is ready to leave its mother. No one will benefit, least of all the puppy. In general, puppies are rarely ready to leave the rest of the litter until they are eight weeks old. Although there may be slight variations either side of this age, a puppy leaving the litter too early will receive an extra shock to its system and will also have had insufficient time to socialize with its litter-mates. It will therefore be set back in its development. Much better to use the time between choosing the pup and collecting it, to prepare your house, your family and yourself to accept the new arrival.

Training your dog

Training a dog is a slow and often tedious process, throughout which you must display great patience, interest and affection for the dog. Well-trained dogs not only trust their masters, but will actually repay that patience, interest and affection.

Training starts at a very early age; in fact the mother has already begun it by the time the pup comes to you and you continue, partly, in her role. Much of early puppy training goes hand-in-hand with the health care of the puppy and it is almost impossible to divorce the two (see Chapter Eight). Furthermore you need to understand quite a lot of dog psychology.

Early puppy training and care
Remember that in his early days with you, your puppy will sadly miss his mother and litter-mates. In one harsh break, he has lost his source of food, warmth, comfort, nice smells, play and companionship. You must replace all of these, or at least try to – simulating the smell of his mother's nipples and litter-mates' breath is a bit difficult! Do not imagine that training a puppy consists only of buckling new collars round its neck, smacking it on the nose with a rolled-up newspaper and yanking it along with a lead. Such things come later and, in any event, should be gradually introduced.

The puppy must be allowed to get used to one place and one set of homely smells. Much damage is done by carting him around different homes (or even different parts of one home) for the first few days. Arrange to get him when you have plenty of time and opportunity to be with him in one place, such as over a long weekend or a short holiday at home. He needs his own bed, always placed in the same warm, draught-free place, where he can find his own bedding and toys. As puppies often chew their beds, it is sensible not to buy an expensive basket at this stage, but instead make do with a strong low-fronted cardboard box for a few months. This can be changed later for something more suitable and probably larger. A safe, chewable plaything is vital – the cheapest and most expendable being an old sock stuffed with rags. This is better than an old slipper, for a puppy will soon associate play with all footwear – new or old!

Full details of diet and nutrition are given in Chapter Eight but, obviously, a puppy must be fed regularly. When he first arrives, it is

Below left to right: Occasionally he may tug and look sorry for himself and, what is more, get tied up in the lead; but he soon consents to good behaviour. Sometimes though, enough is enough.

Right: The Miniature Bull Terrier should weigh no more than 18 lbs. The breed is not particularly popular despite its physical attractiveness.

Below: This puppy will need not only plenty of fun and games but also lots of sleep.

important to continue the feeding regime of his litter with the same quality and quantity of food. Nothing upsets a puppy quicker, or is more certain to give him diarrhoea, than irregular meals of strange food. When you first collect him, ask what and when he was eating before he left his litter and then follow this pattern.

House training

Training a puppy to be clean demands a little knowledge and lots of perseverance. Eight-week-old puppies will urinate up to about twelve times a day and pass motions probably four to five times. Much of this is linked to behaviour; once you have 'cracked the code', house training becomes simple. A puppy nearly always urinates when it first wakes, so make a habit of whisking it outside the moment it does so. It will then quite quickly associate waking up with urinating outside. Once this is learnt, the puppy will seek the garden for urination, especially if you give praise and encouragement each time.

Some people train puppies to urinate on newspaper. This is convenient when they are small, but should not be continued exclusively for too long or it may be difficult to break the habit at a later stage. Some newspaper 'sense' can be useful, even in adulthood, however, when, for example, a dog is suffering from diarrhoea.

The behavioural 'code-link' for puppies passing faeces is eating. Most puppies wander around for a short time after feeding and then, having found a place they like, defecate. Simply putting a puppy out after feeding will soon result in defecation. Thus, if a routine is adopted of putting the puppy out every time it wakes and after every meal, the majority of occasions for defecation and urination will be covered. Accidents are still bound to happen but very soon the puppy will be disinclined to pass motions or urine indoors. Obviously, this means great vigilance by the owner, but that is a small price to pay for rapid house-training.

It can also help to give a command each time. Using a phrase such as 'be quick', or 'hurry up', said in the same tone of voice every time before excretion, will soon have the pup virtually excreting to command. This will be useful in adult life to encourage a slow or shy dog who is reluctant to excrete in strange places. Of course the word or phrase itself does not actually

Right: With a comfortable and sensible collar and lead, this Welsh Springer Spaniel is quite happy.

Far right: A badly fitting and unsuitable collar and lead will make the job of training your puppy all the more difficult. The studs on the collar are quite unnecessary.

Below: The two sandy-coloured pups are the happy result of an 'accidental' mating between the Norfolk Terrier and the grey-coated Miniature Schnauzer.

matter; just remember that it must be the same each time and should be socially acceptable, so that you can use it in all circumstances!

The average pup should be reasonably clean by three to four months and quite reliable at six months.

Play and exercise

The physiological and developmental importance of play, activity and regular exercise has already been mentioned in Chapter Three, but it is so important that it needs further discussion.

Play is vital to the correctly balanced development of a puppy's brain and body. Without it, he becomes introverted, slow moving and possibly also aggressive. Play gives a reason for athletic movements and body skills, thus teaching a puppy how to move to avoid objects and how to 'thrust' and 'parry'. Behaviourally, play teaches a puppy how to react with contacts, how to be aggressive in a *controlled* way and how to accept a beating. Play denial, and thus boredom, spells great problems for a puppy's later development, but he must be taught just how far to go in his mock fights. His litter-mates will have done that up to the time of weaning and it is now up to the owner to take over. This means allowing him gently to bite your hand. When the 'nip' gets too painful, you should show a counter-attack, by gently squeezing his lower jaw in the way a litter-mate may do, or gently shaking him by the loose skin on the neck or shoulder. Simply withdrawing your hand is *not* right, for not only has he then won the battle, but he has shown his dominance over you and will continue to push his luck, both then and in future.

Puppies also soon learn to play with their own toys and the stuffed sock previously mentioned is particularly good. He will 'kill' it by shaking it; he will launch at it and 'bowl it over' and he may make sexual pelvic thrusts at it. This latter behaviour is all part of normal development but it must not be allowed to become excessive, particularly in older pups, and should be prevented by a sharp tap.

Provided with its own toys and given plenty of play time, a puppy should do little damage to furnishings. A small amount of damage has to be expected, particularly when a puppy is left for a long period without company or confined in a strange place such as a car. Providing him with his own toys should help to minimize this, however. If he does do damage, then it is your fault for not keeping him occupied, and remember it is virtually useless to reprimand him afterwards for damage he has done.

Although play is so vital, be careful not to over-extend or over-tire a puppy. Puppies of ten weeks old will need in the region of eighteen to twenty hours sleep a day. Pack lots of activity into the waking hours but allow him peace to sleep when he is tired. Children are especially liable to over-tire puppies and it is then that puppies are most inclined to become wayward, maybe snarling and snapping.

Enforced exercise has little place in a young

Above: This Bearded Collie is tethered to an easily portable dog hook.

Above right: This Miniature Schnauzer is under control in its harness.

Above: Dogs travel happily on the back seat.

Below: Estate cars are ideal for transporting dogs.

puppy's life. Lead training is especially difficult and nearly all new owners are sadly at fault in trying to train puppies to a collar and lead at far too early an age. The street or park are not places for a young puppy for many reasons; they harbour risks of disease, and frights from traffic noise, other dogs, people and strange objects. In any event, a puppy should be allowed to become used to a light collar well before being taken for a walk. The collar should fit securely, but allow room for expansion. Do not compromise by buying a collar which will fit him as an adult.

Lead control is a difficult lesson for puppies. Initially, they will tug backwards violently, shake their heads and sit down. Walking periods should be short and gentle; puppies can soon tire when forced to walk in a fixed direction and may need carrying. Above all, be patient.

The simple commands

Many owners confuse puppies by using too many and too lengthy commands. Puppies don't speak English and to tell them 'not to be naughty' or to 'run after Johnny to find your supper' is plainly stupid.

A dog must learn to know its name and to respond to it. All commands should initially be prefixed by the puppy's name so it knows that you are addressing it. Calling its name and rewarding its arrival by an occasional tit-bit is a very quick way of obtaining a response. Better still is to say 'come' or 'here' after its name, so

that it does not associate its name with food.

In every case a positive response to command should be rewarded by an encouraging tone of voice or a friendly pat. A negative response should never be ignored. This is tantamount to saying, 'Well, it isn't really very important so don't bother in future'. Always make sure the puppy does what you want, even if it means showing him how to do it – for example, pushing him down on his rump to make him sit. Always try to use the same tone of voice which is appropriate to the command; 'come' in an encouraging exciting tone, or 'no' in a firm, deep tone.

'No' is a really important command. It should mean stop whatever you are doing, whether it is chewing the chair legs, making sexual thrusts at a maiden aunt's leg or growling at the cat. Early on, it can be associated with a smack on the nose with that rolled-up newspaper, but later the word and tone of voice should be all that is needed.

The commands 'wait' or 'stop' are very useful and should be taught as soon as possible. 'In your bed!' is a convenient command, for however much affection you have for your dog there are times when you do not want him around.

'Down' is often needed for exuberant dogs who invariably jump up at visitors and children. It is an annoying habit in small dogs and a painful and dangerous one in big dogs.

The other important commands are those associated with walking, defecation and urination (already mentioned) and those for car training.

Car training and travel

Cars have become part of our lives and part of the lives of our dogs too. Sadly, a frightening number of dogs' lives are lost through car accidents, mainly because dogs have been allowed to wander loose in the streets. Cars are responsible, too, for the vast majority of bone fractures and serious bodily damage suffered by dogs.

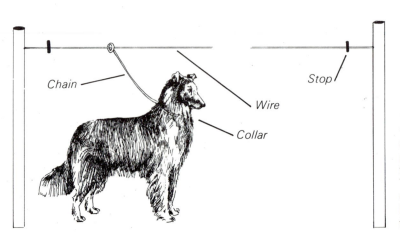

Chain   Wire   Collar   Stop

Left: Large dogs which are to be left alone for long periods adapt well to running chains. These allow the dogs a reasonably large area in which to roam.

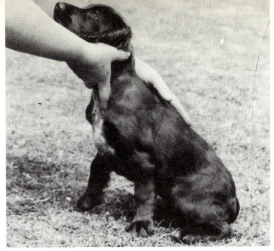

A small proportion of dog/car accidents result from dogs chasing cars and bikes, which in itself is an aberration of the natural tendency to chase prey. Curbing this can be very difficult but, if verbal commands fail, the lesson must be taught by keeping the dog on a choke chain and tugging sharply on it every time the dog runs off.

A dog should be taught that it is part of the home; that it is welcome there, that it should do no damage, and that it has places in it where it may – and may not – go. Equally, it must be taught how to behave in a car. If a dog is allowed to leap all over the inside, not only is this messy and inconvenient, it is also very dangerous. The most appropriate place for a dog is on the back seat of a saloon or in the rear luggage compartment of a shooting brake. If a command such as 'in the back' is always used, a dog will soon learn that this is its place. It must never be permitted to travel with its head leaning out (or even its nose poking out) of the window. This, again, is very dangerous for you and the dog.

Leaving a dog in a car can be a problem. A small gap must always be left at the top of one or more windows for adequate air exchange. This is absolutely *vital*, particularly in warm weather. As a species, dogs can stand amazingly low temperatures, but the build-up of warmth and carbon dioxide in a closed car on a hot day can be lethal. Shading the car by laying a white sheet over the sunny side helps, but if in doubt, don't let your dog risk a dreadful death. In hot, sunny weather try to find a shady parking spot, preferably in an underground or multi-storey car park, and leave some water in a bowl on the floor.

Many dogs will sleep when left in cars but young or exuberant ones can wreak frightful damage, which can be both expensive and dangerous. Remember to put map books, sunglasses etc. in the glove box or boot and leave some chewable toys to help allay the boredom. If the problem persists, try leaving the dog for very short periods, which are gradually increased.

Never let a dog get used indiscriminately to jumping out of car doors the moment they are opened. Make him wait for the command 'come-on'. Dogs do not have traffic sense and could jump straight in front of an oncoming car.

Walking training

The only major problem in this area is the dog who persistently pulls. This is an exhausting fault which many people seem to accept, particularly owners of the bigger, tough dogs, and yet the cure is relatively simple. Firstly, try a tug on the lead, accompanied by the command 'heel', pulling the dog gently back to the level of your left leg. If this fails, then use a light, thin choke chain; give a sharp tug on it and repeat the command. Once the lesson has been learnt, the choke can be discarded. The idea of the choke chain is *not* to allow the dog to continue pulling, so that it is persistently half-throttling itself and emitting a gurgling wheeze. In fact, violent use of choke chains can damage the neck area.

A nice finesse when walking a dog is kerb drill. This is routine for Guide Dogs for the Blind, but it can be rather frustrating for a sighted owner to have his dog stop every time it steps down a kerb. However, it is a safety point and prevents dogs bounding into the traffic stream.

A few golden rules about walking dogs:

1. *Always keep your dog on a collar and lead when anywhere near traffic or on public roads.*

It is unrealistic to think that the risk of problems is minimal on quiet roads which carry little traffic. This is just the time when the sudden appearance of a fast car panics the dog, maybe causing him to run on to the road.

2. *Walk between dog and the traffic.*
3. *Make certain collars and leads are strong and are properly fastened.*

We have discussed commands in this chapter and much about dog mentality and approach to humans in Chapter Three, but the practical end result is that the dog must always know who is the boss. Undisciplined dogs who have the upper hand are like undisciplined children – unpleasant and embarrassing to be with, and eventually dangerous. If your dog wins a battle once, it will try the same trick again and again. It can grumble and groan when you tell it, 'in the bed', but it must go. It can growl when you take its bone away, but it *must* relinquish it. Show your dog every affection and respect, but never be afraid of it. There should be a mutual affection and respect, between you, the boss, and your dog.

Above left: Sensible dog beds are both comfortable beds and places to which the dog can retreat if it does not want to socialize.

Above centre: the command –'sit' – is given at the same time as gently pushing down the hind quarters of this young pup.

Above right: 'Sitting is a bore'.

Below: Driving with your dog hanging out of the car window is both distracting to other drivers and dangerous to the dog.

The Dog in Health and Illness

To deal practically with a dog who is ill, it is essential to have an understanding of its normal functioning. A dog owner must be able to recognize all the signs of health in his dog, so that he is able to notice any variations. This will not only help him to keep his dog healthy, but will also alert him when things are going wrong so that he can seek expert veterinary advice at an early stage. Regular and careful grooming plays an important role in the prevention and detection of disease and injury.

Grooming

The primary aim of grooming is to keep the coat, skin, feet, ears and eyes – in fact, all the 'outside' of the dog – in a first class and healthy condition. The pleasant side effect of grooming is that the dog looks good, but this aesthetic reward is secondary to good skin health. Good grooming does not end with coat care alone, although this is obviously a major feature.

There are very few hard and fast rules for dog grooming. We must disregard some 'old wives' tales' such as 'Alsatians must never be bathed' or 'Old English Sheepdogs must never be clipped since clipping stops the coat from growing'. There are, however, many quite important criteria to be maintained for show dogs and if you intend to exhibit a dog it is vital to get authoritative advice on show preparation from an expert, such as a breed club official.

In general, long-haired dogs need more attention than the short-coated breeds and many terriers may need 'stripping'. This means that excess, and often 'dead', hair must be removed. In most cases, however, brushing, combing, an occasional bath and a regular inspection of feet, ears, eyes and anal areas will be all that is needed.

In dog grooming five minutes daily care with a brush is always better than long periods of neglect followed by a thorough grooming. Neglect can result in a tangled mess which can take hours to correct and causes pain to the dog and irritation to the owner. Moreover, a two-hour fight with tangles, matts, last season's briars, burs and grass seeds will put the dog off being groomed. This means he will be unco-operative next time.

Most dogs, provided they are not hurt in the process, will be quite co-operative during grooming and puppies should become accustomed to the procedure as soon as possible. Making the whole affair a game, with possibly a reward at the end, will make for easy grooming in the future. Special care must be taken not to hurt puppies with combs that are too stiff or with too vigorous use of brushes.

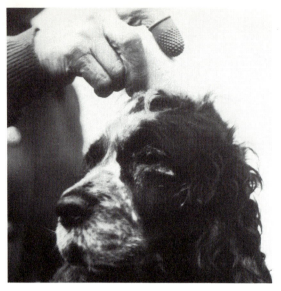

So that you can be sure that parts of the grooming procedure are not forgotten, we suggest a strict routine of grooming in which all procedures are followed in turn. Perhaps one part of the routine may be resented by the dog. It is important for you to respect this, but never let the dog get the better of you. Be firm.

Equipment

Except for specialized equipment, such as electric clippers, which may be an advantage for some breeds, the equipment needed is quite simple and cheap. However, all of it should be of the best quality, with well-plated metal parts. It should be capable of being washed and disinfected.

The first requirement is for a brush which is not too stiff. Long bristles are best for long-haired dogs and short bristles for short-coats.

You will need a comb – a fine-toothed, for short-coated dogs and one with more widely spaced teeth for long-haired dogs or those with thick coats. A pair of very sharp scissors is essential (more harm is done with blunt scissors than sharp ones) and they should have quite fine points. Nail clippers are also needed – the guillotine type is ideal except for dogs with very thick nails. Then large, scissor-type, bevelled clippers may be needed.

A few old towels that can be used as dog towels are useful for wiping wet feet and drying off after bathing. Use them dry as a 'rubber' to put a final shine on short-coated dogs.

Brushing and combing

Brushing and combing are the essentials of coat care and will vary from the little more than two-minute brushing for a short-haired breed, up to a

Above left: When grooming a Spaniel, rub some chalk over any tufts to be removed and pull them off with finger and thumb.

Above: Brush downwards with a strong, firm action to remove any matting and dirt from your dog's coat.

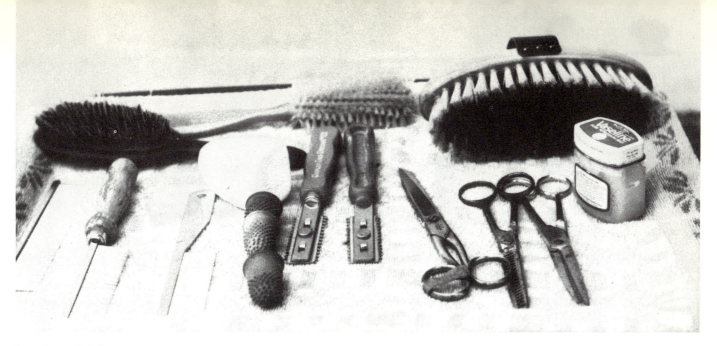

lengthy and daily routine in a long-haired breed such as a Maltese Terrier.

The aims are to remove any foreign bodies such as grass seeds, to lay the individual hairs into parallel formation, to ensure a distribution of natural skin oils and, incidentally, to show the owner if any parasites are present.

Combing is chiefly for long and wire-haired dogs to remove matts and tangles. The combing must reach the full depth of the coat, but great care must be taken, especially with fine tooth combs, not to damage the skin.

Although the comb can often be dispensed with in short-haired dogs, the brush is vital in all coat types. Brushing should always be with the lie of the hair except in very dense coated, long-haired dogs such as Collies, where it is impossible to brush through the whole depth of the coat. In these cases the coat is dealt with in 'sections' and the brush is used against the lay to fluff out the hair.

When either the comb or the brush, or both, are used, the whole of the coat must be groomed and not just the easily accessible areas such as the back. Special attention should be paid to areas prone to knotting, such as the hair behind the ears, the tail, the lower areas and the dense coat or 'feather' on the rear of the hind legs.

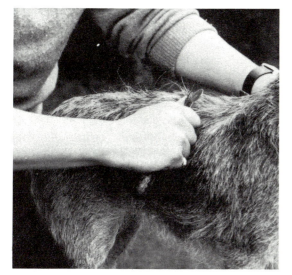

Stripping, plucking and clipping

All these are methods of coat removal for some of the longer-haired or dense-coated breeds. If the dog is to be exhibited, the greatest care should

Above: A selection of essential grooming equipment.

Opposite left: Trimming knives are useful for stripping harsh-coated dogs.

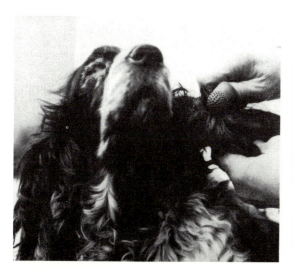

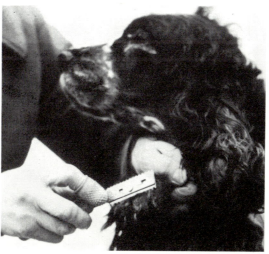

Far left: Spaniels need special grooming attention, particularly around the ears.

Left: Even the paws have to be groomed and cleaned to keep the dog in perfect condition.

163

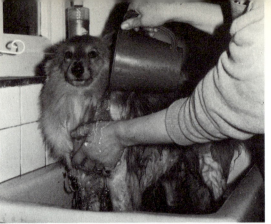

be taken over coat removal and, if in any doubt, a reputable breeder or breed club official should be consulted. Once removed, the coat can only be replaced by time.

Plucking and stripping are methods for removing either an excessive depth of coat, or a dead undercoat. In the former, the hair is plucked by hand alone and, in the latter, a stripping knife or stripping comb is used. Both techniques take a little mastering to produce a good result without hurting the dog.

Clipping is reserved for shortening a long coat. It is an essential part of grooming for the woolly-coated dogs such as Poodles and Bedlingtons, and an occasional necessity for others, either to comply with show standards or just to make the dog look comfortable and good-looking. Most trimming can be done with scissors, but electric clippers do a quicker and generally better job. Here again, consult an expert. An amateur's results can be disastrous.

Although regular coat care should never allow the build-up of dense matts and tangles, there are occasions where ignorance or neglect produces a coat which defies all routine care. In these cases the only answer is a complete clip-out. Here electric clippers are virtually a 'must' and there may be a need for this operation to be done under an anaesthetic by a veterinary surgeon – particularly if the dog objects violently. Never be afraid to admit that a dog's coat has got beyond you and needs professional care. The dog will only suffer more by delay.

Bathing

Disregard comments that dogs never need bathing or, regardless of breed, that they should be bathed twice a year. There are no hard and fast rules and frequency of bathing depends on many variables, such as how much dirt is present in the coat, the grease accumulation, whether the dog is prone to rolling in 'choice' substances, and problems of skin parasites or skin diseases.

If regular grooming seems to keep a dog's coat in good condition, then baths are not necessary. Most dogs hate being bathed although they may cheerfully swim of their own volition in the filthiest of water. Violent shivering when being bathed, is not necessarily a sign that the dog is cold. However, warm (not hot) water will help to avoid the unlikely possibility of chills and it is wise to bath the dog indoors or to choose a warm day if it has to be done outside. All that is needed is a sensibly sized receptacle, water, the shampoo, towels and some protective clothing.

Many dog shampoos are available and all of them are much the same. Human shampoos will be just as effective and may be cheaper. If the dog has fleas or other parasites, an insecticidal shampoo will be an advantage and a veterinary surgeon will be able to advise on this. Household detergents should not be used for bathing dogs, nor should disinfectants.

There is no need to plug the dog's ears before bathing, with cotton wool, or to use eye ointments. The only preparations for the dog will be combing for long-haired breeds. The coat should be thoroughly wetted, the shampoo applied, lathered and then thoroughly rinsed off with plenty of clean, warm, water. With parasiticidal or antiseptic shampoos it may be necessary to leave the lather for a prescribed time before rinsing.

Pay special attention to the anal and genital areas during lathering and make certain that hidden areas, such as the abdomen, are well washed. Avoid getting soap and water into the ears and eyes although, if gently poured over the head, water does not usually enter the ears, even

Above (left to right): When washing a dog, place it gently in a sink or bath. Rinse it with warm water and shampoo with a firm, but not rough action. Pay particular attention to its paws as dirt can collect here. Rinse it down gently.

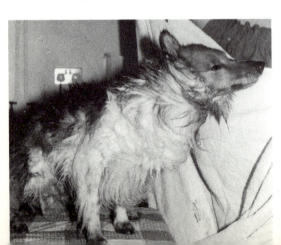
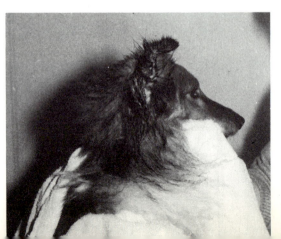

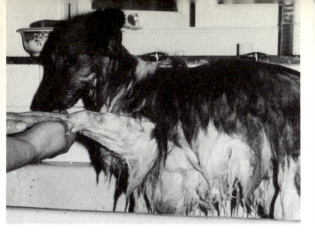
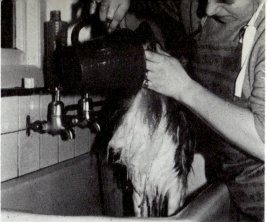
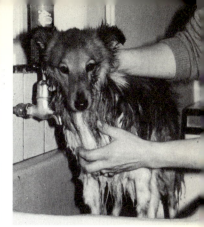

on prick-eared breeds. After a thorough rinsing, the coat should be squeezed by hand, the dog allowed to shake itself, and then vigorously rubbed in towels.

Very often the coat can be left alone for its final drying but in dense coated dogs, a hair dryer may be helpful.

It is quite normal for many dogs to 'scoot' along the ground after a bath with their head on the ground and this is not usually a sign that they have water in their ears. A word of warning: dogs often like to roll after a bath – presumably to replace the nice 'ripe' smell which has just been removed!

Care of feet

Many dogs have quite excessive hair growth on their feet. It grows between the pads, up between the toes on the upper surface of the feet and backwards above the top pad. If left untrimmed, the hair becomes matted and caked with muck. Besides looking unkempt it attracts such objects as grass seeds and can prevent wear of the nails. In addition, the feet retain dirt, which will be deposited all over carpets, cars, etc.

In some breeds this 'feather' is a breed standard, as in the case of the Cavalier King Charles. In such cases, if the dog is to be shown, it should be retained. However, in other cases, much the best course is to trim off the hair to pad level underneath and level with the toes above.

The pads usually need no attention but they should be checked after country walks for cuts and penetrations by stones or thorns. Many dogs who are unaccustomed to hard walks may have slightly soft feet and may get 'nettled feet' after a country walk. Nettles may sting the sensitive pads or thistles may prick them and the dog may violently scratch the ground or chew his feet. No

treatment is needed and the discomfort disappears after an hour or so.

Dogs that do regular strenuous work usually wear their nails down to a normal, short length. However, the majority of pet dogs and many working dogs, too, will need their nails trimmed, and the frequency of this trimming depends on the dog's activity. Long nails can cause great problems. They can get caught and be pulled off. They can grow so long that they curve round and press into the toes, causing local infection and lameness.

Trimming nails is a simple process, but, if you have any doubt about how to do it, ask an experienced dog owner or veterinary surgeon to demonstrate the method. This is another procedure which should be started young in puppies and care should be taken not to hurt the

Above: The ideal method of trimming the bottom of a dog's paws.

Below (left to right): After it has been bathed, the dog will shake the water from its coat. Dry it with a large towel and comb and brush it to bring it to sparkling condition.

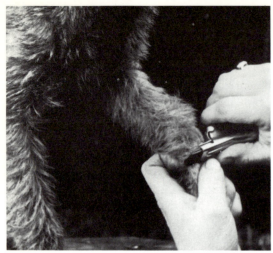

Left: If the nails are black and the quick cannot be seen, carefully cut off the thin slices of nail or the sensitive tissues of the nail base may be damaged and bleeding may occur.

Right: Cutting nails properly will cause the dog no pain or discomfort.

Right: Long-coated dogs need special care when trimming around the ears. Pulling the ears back and trimming gently is painless.

dog, in case it comes to resent the operation.

The nail should be trimmed at a slight angle, but to within about 0.5 cm ($\frac{1}{4}$ in) of the sensitive 'quick'. The quick can be seen easily in non-pigment nails as a pink area, but in dark nails it cannot be seen and the length of cut has to be finely judged. Firstly, a tiny amount of nail should be removed, working backwards until close to the quick. It is better to leave slightly too much nail than to risk causing bleeding. If the quick is cut, however, stop the bleeding by holding a small pad of cotton wool on to the nail.

Nails on the dew claws, if present, can also cause problems if left to grow and these, too, should be kept short.

Ears

The ears should be regularly inspected, but they usually need very little attention. If they look normal and the dog shows no evidence of ear problems, such as shaking the head or scratching the base of the ear, then *leave well alone*. Never probe or push anything down a dog's ear. The most that is regularly needed is wiping out any accumulated dirt or excess grease from the inside of the ear flap with a moist piece of cotton wool.

Some dogs, particularly Poodles and some terriers, have an excess of hair growing in the upper ear canal. Although this does not often cause problems, it can result in poor ear ventilation and wax accumulation, in which case it can be removed by careful hand plucking.

Ear disease, heralded by smell, scratching or head shaking, could be the start of severe problems and a veterinary surgeon should always be consulted as soon as possible.

The anal and genital areas

Although most dogs keep these areas remarkably clean, there are some dogs, particularly those with dense coats and lots of 'feather' in the rear regions, who soil themselves. Diarrhoea, urinary

Below: Some dogs may be prone to ear troubles. Regular inspection will disclose any problems at an early stage.

upsets or genital diseases will exaggerate this problem and so will old age and infirmity.

Under these circumstances it is vital that the owner helps the dog to keep clean. Dogs are basically clean animals and will not be happy when soiled by their own excreta. This unpleasant task needs to be regularly under-taken, often daily, and may involve quite extensive cleaning. Failure to do so will result in

Above: To clean the anus and genitalia, lift the tail and wipe gently with a cotton pad.

local skin disease and sometimes in maggots.

It may also be necessary to clip hair from around the anal or genital areas to avoid soiling and to facilitate cleaning. Soiled areas should be gently washed, rinsed and dried and, possibly, the area smeared with petroleum jelly to avoid 'scalding' and ulceration. In all cases, if the underlying cause of self-soiling is disease, then veterinary attention should be sought.

Mouth and teeth

Care of the teeth will be mentioned later, but the skin around the mouth may need attention in those breeds with deep skin folds such as some Spaniels, Old English Sheepdogs and Bloodhounds. Sometimes these skin folds become infected from constant wetting by saliva and they can smell very badly. Regular, gentle, washing, drying and possibly protection with a grease may be needed to avoid problems. In severe cases surgery can reduce the folding.

Eyes

The skin round the eyes should be inspected during the grooming procedure. This skin is remarkably resistant to disease but, in some dogs – probably owing to conformation of the eyeball and the bones around the eye – tears overflow and can stain the coat or even cause skin damage in the area. In these dogs, the area should be cleaned at least once a day and it may be an advantage to apply a small amount of petroleum jelly to the area where dried tears accumulate. Severe and long standing tear overflowing should be referred to a veterinary surgeon.

Signs of health

Experienced dog owners and breeders might find it quite difficult to give an exact definition of the signs of health in a dog but they rapidly recognize tiny changes in demeanour and behaviour which suggest a problem. The signs often quoted – 'bright eyed, glossy coat and cool, damp nose' – are rather overplayed and too facile to be a useful guide to the discerning owner.

Many signs of health in the dog are actually negative, in that it is the *absence* of the tell-tale signs of disease which tell us that a dog is well.

General appearance and behaviour

Healthy dogs shake themselves occasionally to rearrange their coats. This often accompanies yawning after waking up. On the subject of sleep, normal dogs may sleep up to sixteen hours a day. Puppies and older dogs will sleep more than young adults.

Taking into account the tremendous individual variations, dogs are generally lively animals, ready to play, to greet their friends and to ward off strangers. Sluggish movement, lack of desire to take exercise and general 'mopiness' are often the first indication of general system disease – that is, the dog being 'off-colour'.

Shivering *can* be normal in some dogs; for instance many individuals of the toy breeds and terriers have periods of shivering, known as 'terrier twitch'. It can also be a sign of general excitement (see Chapter Three) or fright. Dogs also shiver when cold, sometimes when running a temperature and as a sequel to nervous disease such as distemper.

All dogs scratch occasionally, just as humans do, but excessive scratching and nibbling at the skin is usually evidence of a skin disease or ear disorder.

Licking plays an important part in dog behaviour and in general exploration. Only excessive licking is abnormal.

Eating habits provide useful pointers to a dog's health, for dogs generally have very good appetites.

Loss of appetite is a good indication of illness in most dogs. Of course, some individuals are finicky eaters and a bitch having a false pregnancy or heavily in whelp may eat less than usual. On the pro-rata bodyweight comparison with humans, healthy dogs drink little water.

How frequently a dog urinates varies considerably with behaviour. In bitches it may be as infrequently as once or twice a day; in dogs it is usually three or four times daily. Most normal dogs will pass motions of putty-like consistency at least once a day. Again, there are variations between individuals but great frequency, constipation, and excessively hard and soft motions are obviously abnormal.

Breathing varies tremendously with the temperature, dog's exercise, the breed (small dogs tend to breathe faster) and general activity

Above: This Labrador has progressive retinal atrophy. The open pupil is trying to accept as much light as possible.

Below: A 'wall-eye' is caused by lack of pigment and does not affect sight.

Below: Calculus on the teeth is a common reason for gum disease and bad breath.

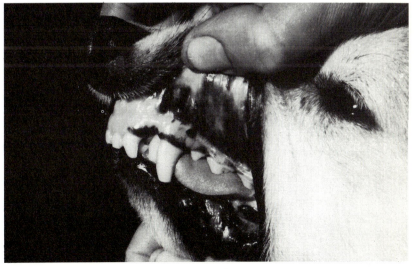

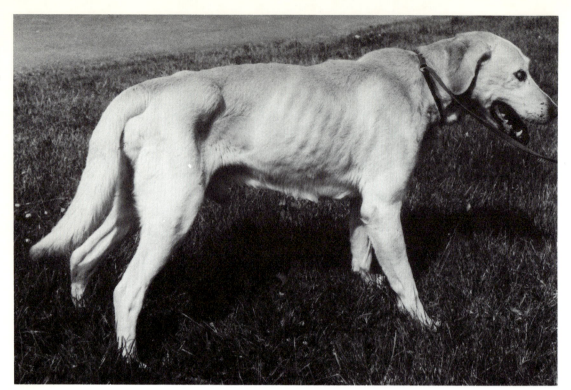

but, for a dog at rest, the rate is usually in the region of fifteen to twenty-five breaths per minute.

The temperature of excited, exercised dogs tends to be higher than those that are resting. Usually the normal temperature is in the region of 38°C/101°F. If it is higher it can be a sign of some disease. Incidentally, a dog's temperature should always be taken by rectum. The procedure is carefully to insert a clinical thermometer, which has been suitably lubricated, into the rectum with a gentle twisting motion, until about half its length is protruding.

If you are in doubt about how to do this, consult a veterinary surgeon. Although not needed for the everyday care of a dog, it is useful to know how to take a dog's temperature if you suspect a problem.

Healthy dogs have a non-odorous breath and clean white teeth. The surfaces of the gums, tongue etc., are pink, except for some breeds, such as the Chow Chow which has a black tongue. Although healthy dogs usually have moist, cool tips to their noses, these can equally be dry if, for example, the dog has been lying in the hot sun or by a fire. Some normal dogs have quite dry noses. Contrary to popular opinion, this is not necessarily a sign of ill-health.

Conformation and degree of fitness will vary according to breed and individuals, but healthy dogs should be athletic and have hard, well-defined muscles. The skin should be supple and freely moveable over the muscles. In all dogs, the coat should be glossy, although this may not be obvious in wire-haired breeds. Dry, harsh or excessively greasy coats may be associated with systemic or skin diseases.

Healthy dogs do not smell 'doggy'. There are many reasons for detectable odours on dogs, such as skin diseases, bad teeth, anal and genital diseases, or severe systemic disease. Owners of smelly dogs should consult veterinary surgeons about them. Regular grooming will eliminate problems of soiled coats and can do much to reduce this source of odour.

Structure and function

Whether the dog is a Chihuahua or a St. Bernard, the basic structure and function is the same. Any variations relate mainly to anatomical shape and size – St. Bernards have just the same number of vertebrae in their backs as Chihuahuas, but the individual bones are bigger. Miniature Dachshunds have very short leg-bones, but there are just as many of them as there are in a Greyhound.

Dogs possess the general characteristics of all animals, but they have various specific features that are important. Some of these have already been mentioned in Chapter Three when discussing the functioning of the dog's special senses and its behaviour.

Essentially the dog is a perfectly designed machine for hunting by sight and scent, and catching, killing and eating its prey. Anyone who has seen a Whippet hunt, catch and kill a rabbit will realize that the machine works well.

As the dog is digitigrade – that is, it walks up on its toes – it is able to use the whole potential length of the limb for running. In having this facility, dogs have lost the capacity for the fine detailed movement that humans display with

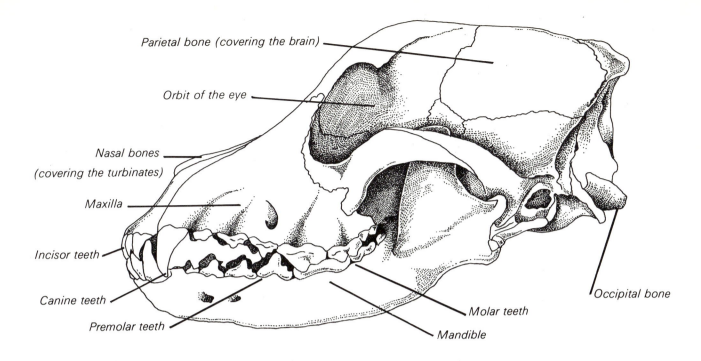

Parietal bone (covering the brain)

Orbit of the eye

Nasal bones
(covering the turbinates)

Maxilla

Incisor teeth

Canine teeth

Premolar teeth

Occipital bone

Molar teeth

Mandible

Above: The skull of a normal dog.

their hands. Much of what we do with our hands, therefore, dogs have to do with their mouths – breaking up food, digging, moving their young around and so on.

A dog's skull is highly developed as can be seen in the diagrams. The front incisor teeth are used for nibbling, the four canines behind for killing prey and tearing flesh, the pre-molars for chewing up lumps of food and bones, and the molars for completing the chewing and grinding, before swallowing.

Immensely strong muscles, which run from the skull to the lower jaw, are used to close the jaws. Unlike such animals as sheep or cows, dogs have little side-to-side movement of their jaws but, as they do not need to chew their food finely, they have little need for such a facility.

Digestive system

A dog's digestive system is that of a typical carnivore. The stomach is quite large and distensible, so that it can accept and contain a large quantity of food in a short time. The food is mixed in the stomach, where the chemical breakdown begins. It then passes gradually into the small intestine where the major part of the digestion occurs. The intestines are quite short – about four times the length of the dog – and have thick walls so they are not damaged by segments of bone. (It takes less time to digest meat than it does herbage, which is why a dog's intestine is shorter than that of grass-eating animals.) Water is absorbed from the digested food in the large intestine.

The length of time taken for food to be digested varies, but it can be as short as thirty-six hours.

Diet and nutrition

Although dogs are carnivores, this does not mean that they should have a diet composed solely of meat. Studies on wild dogs and their close developmental cousins have shown that they eat all the carcase of their prey and a lot else besides. Complete ingestion of prey means not

only the flesh and muscle, but also the skin, fur, bones, and all the intestines together with the vegetable matter these usually contain. Dogs will voluntarily eat grass and other vegetable matter and sometimes will even 'graze' on fruit such as berries and apples. So, to feed a domestic dog solely on meat would not only be wasteful and expensive but also nutritionally incorrect.

Generally, adult dogs need only one meal a day, although some very small breeds may welcome two small meals. Puppies and old or ill dogs need more frequent meals. In some situations, such as in Foxhound kennels, dogs are commonly fed only five or six times a week and this is perfectly acceptable practice.

It is quite impossible to say how much food any particular breed of dog needs. Not only does the requirement vary with the size of the dog, but also with the exercise it takes, its environmental temperature, whether it is pregnant or lactating, growing and fit, old and infirm and, most important – its individual 'nutritional character'. Just as with humans, some dogs have a tendency to put on fat, while others naturally stay slim however great their dietary intake. Owners must make adjustments to the diet of their dogs to account for these individualities.

Even if we were to know exactly what quantity of food a particular dog needed, this could vary the moment the quality of the food was altered. This is because of variations in energy, protein, fat, vitamin and mineral content, as well as the enormous variations in water content. The fact is there are just no hard and fast rules about feeding dogs.

However, there has to be a basis on which to start. Primarily the diet provides energy to run the body functions. This is referred to as 'maintenance energy'. If the dog is growing,

laying down fat, or using a lot of energy in muscular activity, then the diet needs to include food which will release more energy. Dietary energy comes mainly from carbohydrates (e.g. sugars, starches, etc., in biscuits and bread type foods) and fats. Energy can come from proteins (the 'building block' components found in meat and nutritious plant foods) but carbohydrates and fats are 'burnt' by the body to provide energy in preference to proteins. If the diet is providing more energy than the dog is demanding, then fat is laid down in reserves. If, on the other hand, the dog's energy demand outstrips dietary supply, then the reverse occurs and the dog uses up its carbohydrates supplies first (in the liver), then the fat deposits and, finally, in dire circumstances, the protein (muscle mass).

Food also supplies the components that build up the body. Even a fully-grown adult dog is constantly losing some of its body chemicals during the basic functions of life. A little protein, fat and carbohydrate is needed regularly, therefore, to replace the unavoidable losses. These amounts are generally very small but when a dog is growing rapidly or working hard, or a bitch is pregnant or feeding puppies, then these amounts increase. All food chemicals are needed, but in these circumstances, the proteins are the most important.

Besides these three basic food components, the dog also needs some vitamins and minerals.

Right: The Yorkshire Terrier is ideal for people who require a dog which is affectionate yet does not demand much exercise.

Below: This Dachshund/Beagle cross has a longish muzzle and pale beagle markings. Having inherited the characteristics of both parents, he will be a happy, energetic dog with a mind of his own.

Below: With a West-Highland White Terrier sire and a Pekinese dam, this puppy seems to have the physical appearance of both parents.

Again, the requirements of these 'trace nutrients' increase when a dog is working, growing, pregnant or lactating.

A diet, therefore, must contain carbohydrates, fats, proteins, vitamins and minerals.

Basic diet

Although, as previously stated, the quantity fed in a diet comprising, say, equal quantities of raw meat and biscuit meal will vary greatly, the following is a rough guide:

Dog	Approximate Body Weight	Daily Intake
Pekinese	4.5 kg (10 lbs)	0.25 kg (8 oz)
Corgi	11 kg (25 lbs)	0.5 kg (1 lb)
Basset	18 kg (40 lbs)	0.75 kg (1 lb 8 oz)
Labrador	27 kg (60 lbs)	0.8 kg (1 lb 10 oz)
Rottweiler	45 kg (100 lbs)	1.1 kg (2 lb 6 oz)

Providing the meat was only slightly fatty, the nutritional composition of such a diet would be in the region of:

Water	60 per cent
Carbohydrate	19 per cent
Protein	12 per cent
Fat	6 per cent
Ash	3 per cent

These would be quite adequate proportions for most adult dogs under stable conditions, although, in fact, such a diet is quite high in protein content. Most dog nutritionists agree that, unless a dog has a high protein demand for any particular reason, it would remain quite healthy on protein levels of 6 per cent (provided by wet food).

Increasing the cereal content of the food by adding a higher proportion of biscuit will not, unless added to excess, drop the protein to dangerously low levels. This is because there is quite a high percentage of protein in cereal. Besides being expensive, feeding a diet with a very high protein level (e.g. all raw meat) is wasteful. The dog's energy will have to come from the protein and, as protein rich foods are comparatively low in energy value, a lot more weight of meat will have to be fed.

The most concentrated form of dietary energy is fat and the carbohydrate content of a diet can be reduced markedly, if more fat is added. Dogs can tolerate tremendously high levels of fat in the diet – as much as thirty per cent. The fat can be provided as lard, maize oil, mutton fat or suet but, whatever the source, it must *not be rancid*, for this can lead to problems of vitamin A and E deficiency. As fatty diets are highly calorific, dogs tend to eat less of them. To keep the protein up to a reasonable percentage, therefore, it is necessary to increase protein levels. The overall quantity of food should be reduced, however, as fats are energy-rich and, if constantly fed fatty diets, dogs will soon become obese.

Dogs do not specifically need a high roughage percentage in their food but, in certain dogs, who either have a tendency to constipation or diarrhoea, increasing the roughage 'normalizes' the flow of food through the tract and a more stable motion is produced. This is an important point to remember with dogs of the giant breeds (i.e. Great Dane, Old English Sheepdog), who commonly have loose motions. Giving them two or three tablespoonfuls of bran, or bran-based, breakfast cereal in their food each day will 'bulk-up' the food and help this problem. Curiously enough, the same trick often works with small breeds, such as Poodles or Pekinese, who commonly have very hard motions (although obviously the amount of bran fed is reduced in such dogs).

Minerals

The formidable list of minerals needed for dogs can sometimes confuse and worry dog owners. Although the requirements are numerically large, however, the actual quantities of minerals needed are very small and, in fact, are usually fully provided by the average diet. Some trace elements (minerals needed in minute quantities) are present in tap water.

The adult dog only needs enough minerals to keep its body 'ticking-over'. A bitch providing milk to puppies and a very active adult dog, or one recovering from a disease, will need extra. Young dogs also need plenty of minerals to assist the building process of 'laying down' new tissue (bones, muscles, skin).

Even in times of increased mineral requirement, it is rare for a diet to be deficient in minerals. Those which can be in short supply are calcium, magnesium and phosphorus. These are

171

all 'bone and milk minerals' and are thus important in rapidly growing young dogs (particularly of the bigger breeds), as well as lactating and pregnant bitches. These minerals can all be provided in extra amounts by feeding a simple mineral supplement in the diet. Probably the best is sterilized bone flour, in which calcium and phosphorus are present in the right ratios (two calcium: one phosphorus). Sterilized bone flour is generally well absorbed from the gut, providing there is adequate vitamin D in the diet. It is relatively cheap and completely safe, and is usually well accepted by dogs of all ages, as long as it is mixed in well with the rest of the food.

The occasions when a diet is deficient in other minerals are very rare. Most of the problems caused by mineral deficiencies are reversible and will be noticed by a veterinary surgeon at a routine health check.

Vitamins

As with minerals, vitamins have an aura of mystery about them but, again, the vast majority of diets are quite adequate in vitamins and deficiencies are rare. In fact, probably more harm is done by overdosing with potent vitamin supplements than has ever occurred through true vitamin deficiencies in diets.

Vitamins are complex, naturally occurring chemicals, found in a variety of foodstuffs. They are classified by the letters A to K, with some sub-classifications. The basic diet already suggested of meat, some fat and biscuit meal, will be vitamin sufficient, although the addition of some fresh vegetables, liver, a little corn oil and yeast tablets occasionally will make certain that all is well.

Feeding excessive amounts of some vitamins, such as Vitamins C and B, does not cause much harm, but care must be taken not to feed too much Vitamin D and Vitamin A. Whilst it is reasonable to give the odd yeast tablet or dribble of cod-liver oil to most dogs, it is worth discussing vitamin (and mineral) supplementation with a veterinary surgeon to make sure that you are not doing harm to your dog or wasting your money.

Mineral and vitamin deficiencies

The requirement for individual minerals and vitamins for dogs varies with the age, work, growth rate and breed. It is impossible to give a table of requirements that would hold true for all dogs and all occasions. Beware of glossy advertisements for food supplements which claim that the product they are promoting is 'All-Correct'.

Although specific deficiencies can result in the corresponding (rare) deficiency diseases, a much

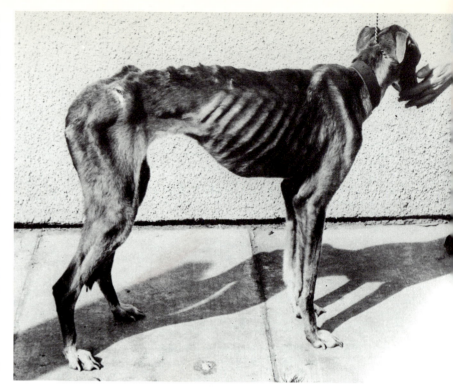

Above: Emaciation is not only due to inadequate feeding, but can also be seen in senile and sick dogs.

more common deficiency is when dogs are fed on very poor diets that are deficient in nearly all minerals and vitamins. These are often near-starvation diets and may occur, for example, when puppies are weaned very early and not given enough food. Then low mineral and vitamin levels, as well as insufficient energy foods and protein, will be responsible for their poor growth and emaciation. Remember that growing dogs need good quality food, in good quantities.

There is, however, one fairly common deficiency state which is seen in otherwise well-fed dogs – that is *rickets*. This term can be used to describe a range of bone problems usually seen in young animals. The bones become distorted, and pups fail to grow well. The legs are often very bent, causing lameness and even fractures.

A common cause of rickets is when a pup has had insufficient calcium and phosphorus in its diet, either as an embryo, or in its mother's milk, or (more commonly) since weaning. Bone also needs Vitamin D to be formed properly and this is found in large quantities in animal oils, such as cod liver oil. Care needs to be taken when feeding this, as too much can cause other problems.

Because of their great bone formation, the giant and bigger breeds are more prone to rickets, and it can be quite hard to provide enough bone-forming elements for such dogs.

Bone formation should be discussed with your veterinary surgeon at a puppy health check. A good start, however, is to feed the bitch bone flour and a few drops of cod liver oil from mid-pregnancy until she finishes feeding the pups.

If a pup becomes lame, walks bow-legged or has swollen joints, then rickets must be suspected and veterinary advice sought immediately.

Appetite variations

Just like humans, dogs vary tremendously in their appetite. Some breeds, like Dachshunds, are naturally greedy and will easily become overweight. Others, such as Irish Setters, are just the reverse and it is really difficult to put weight on them, particularly when they are young and active.

There are also great variations between individuals within a breed. This is particularly true of Miniature Poodles which can equally be quite rotund or very thin. The fact that a dog is thin does not necessarily make it abnormal, nor does it suggest that you are not giving it enough food.

The quantities of food given earlier provide a rough guide to the food intakes in adult dogs. These will have to be increased for growing youngsters, breeding bitches and working dogs, or decreased for old, inactive dogs. Try to differentiate between muscle and 'flab' when assessing the body condition of your dog. It is possible only to give rough guides for body condition in breeds – Bull Terriers for example are stocky, muscular and appear 'barrel-like', with excess fat seen as unsightly 'slabbing' behind the ribs and above the root of the tail. A direct contrast is provided by the English Setter, whose coat does not allow the fine back and ribs to be seen; yet it is quite normal to be able to feel all the ribs and many other bones of the body.

If you are concerned that your dog is too fat or too thin, then either consult a breeder or veterinary surgeon, or visit a dog show so that you can compare your dog with those in the ring. Breeders make great efforts to be sure that their dogs are correctly 'bodied-up'. (Remember, incidentally, that non-exhibit dogs should not be taken to shows.)

Apart from some metabolic diseases, internal parasites and other medical problems, leanness is rarely a great problem in dogs. In general, it is better to have a dog thin than fat, as thin dogs are generally much happier, more playful and healthier.

The great nutritional scourge of humans – and their dogs – in the Western world is obesity. This one disease probably accounts for more early deaths, illness, lameness and unhappiness than any other.

Dogs do not naturally adjust their appetites according to their waistlines; it is up to the owner to do this for them. In general, obese dogs are better fed on diets which are lower in carbohydrate and fat, whilst still retaining the protein content. The protein requirement remains the same in slimming dogs or may even rise if extra exercise is given.

Cutting out a proportion of biscuit in the food and replacing this by a low energy bulking material such as bran, helps to satisfy the dog's appetite. Obviously, increasing the amount of exercise burns off more fat, but this is hard work for both owner and dog. *Suddenly* taking up long healthy walks each day is probably not the best way to attack obesity. Interestingly, nutritional statistics show that obese owners are more likely to have obese dogs.

There is a very small proportion of dogs who really are poor eaters and become painfully thin unless coaxed to eat. However, the vast majority of dogs who 'only eat fillet steak and chocolates' and turn their noses up at dog's meat and biscuits are clever canine psychologists, who have learnt that their doting owners can be made to feel embarrassed by uneaten food and will substitute delicacies.

A cure can usually be effected by twenty-four hours starvation, a brisk exercise session and a change of food. Competition also helps, which may explain why finicky eaters hardly ever occur in breeders' kennels or Foxhound packs.

The last fifteen years has seen tremendous exploration in the market of canned and dried convenience food for dogs. It has been accompanied by much debate on their nutritional quality and the advisability of feeding such food exclusively. Despite being relatively expensive, cans are a quick, clean and simple source of food. They have also stood the test of time – there have been very few proven examples of nutritional upsets associated with them. Most

Below: When the accumulation of calculus on teeth is this severe, it must be removed by a veterinary surgeon. Chewing bones can prevent the problem.

Bottom: Milk teeth are usually lost quite easily by adolescent dogs, but this West-Highland Terrier still has the hook-shaped puppy tooth behind its adult canine.

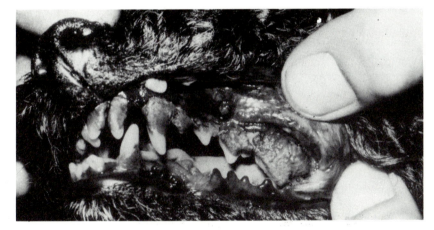

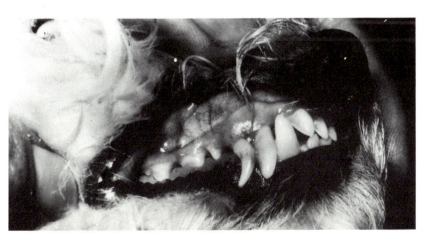

Above: Separate feeding dishes can be an advantage with young pups before they are accustomed to the competition of a large bowl.

Below: The size of the abdomen and mammary glands of pregnant bitches can be enormous and yet give no cause for alarm.

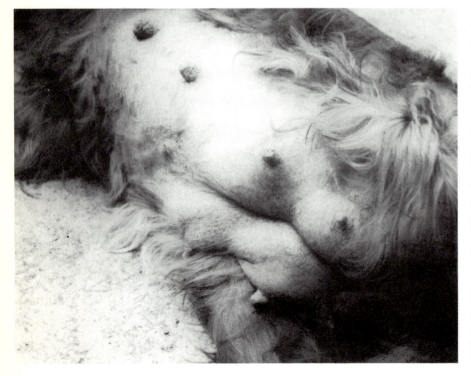

necessary (or even desirable).

Remember to allow your dog free access to fresh water at all times with all foods. This is important if you are feeding dried foods.

Bones

In the natural and wild state, there is little doubt that dogs devoured the entire carcases of their prey – bones and all. This enabled them to keep their calcium and phosphorus intake high, to obtain fat and iron from the bone marrow and to keep their teeth clean. Most dogs thoroughly enjoy chewing bones as well as burying them and playing with them; bones seem to play a part in behaviour generally, especially in puppies. However, in some individuals, they can cause an inexplicable diarrhoea. They can also become caught across the top of the hard palate between the teeth, and spicules of bones can cause obstructions in the gut, especially in the rectum. Brittle bones, such as chicken bones and roast lamb bones, are particularly liable to cause problems. Pressure-cooked bones still provide the bone minerals but, being soft, are quite safe. The best bones for dogs are the big limb 'knuckle-ended' bones.

On balance, the advantages outweigh the disadvantages. If a dog is particularly prone to problems with bones, then it is obviously best to avoid them and to substitute other playthings, such as sterilized hide bones. It is usually the smaller and toy breeds that get 'bone problems'.

Pregnant bitches

There is little need to give a pregnant bitch anything but her normal diet in the first month of her pregnancy. Indeed, it is not usually possible to tell that a bitch is pregnant until twenty-eight days after mating. From then on, her appetite will increase and she should be given extra food (one-and-a-quarter to one-and-a-half times her usual intake during the fifth, sixth and seventh weeks). This should be of good quality and high protein content, such as eggs and milk. If the bitch becomes quite distended with pups, then it is an advantage to divide her food into two or three meals per day. During the last four weeks of pregnancy, some bone flour and a little proprietary vitamin supplement (as suggested by your veterinary surgeon) should be added. Many bitches lose their appetite in the last few days of pregnancy – this is quite normal.

Lactating bitches

Although the bitch's appetite may temporarily slacken around whelping, she will soon become ravenous as her milk production rises. It is best to feed her virtually as she demands it, probably five

of the companies marketing canned pet foods have conducted extensive long-term feeding trials and have raised many successive generations of dogs on their products – sometimes with no additional foods, except small amounts of milk for young pups. Freedom from nutritional disorders and good fertility is proof that the products are entirely satisfactory. Most of the foods (and all, in the case of canned foods) are sterilized in production, which is an additional safety factor both for the dog and owner. Slaughterhouse offal or knacker meat always carries possibilities of health hazard.

The reputation and longevity of a pet food company usually speaks for the products, but beware of unprocessed raw meat composites unless you know a little of their history. Many composite foods and complete diets do have higher total protein content than is strictly

Right: This nine-week-old Spaniel puppy is fast approaching the danger age for distemper and will soon need vaccinating.

egg and glucose until, when the puppies are four to five weeks old, a mixture of egg and finely-scraped lean meat can be fed. (At this stage the bitch will still be providing lots of milk but this is gradually reduced to almost nothing at about eight weeks.) At five to six weeks old, the pups will be eating about five to six meals a day, consisting of minced meat, puppy meal, milk, bone flour, egg and cereals. Their intake will be virtually *ad lib* for all meals. By eight to ten weeks, they can be fed two milky meals and two meat meals a day; by sixteen weeks, this can be reduced to two meat meals and one milk-based meal. Water should be provided after eight weeks, but puppies drink very little water until they are about four months old.

Convalescent and senility diets

Although a veterinary surgeon may give special instructions, diets for convalescent and senile dogs should consist of low bulk, highly nutritious and easily digested food. Milk, eggs, good quality meat and fine biscuits are a basic requirement and the total feed can be divided into two, or even three, meals a day to aid digestion.

Digestion and digestive problems

The golden rule about feeding dogs with regard to their digestion, is to leave well alone. Once a dog is settled on a standard diet, there is no need to vary the food, merely for the sake of variation. Unlike humans, dogs do not become bored with a standard diet or need constant variations to keep them happy. Sudden changes of diet can themselves cause problems and a new food should be introduced gradually, preferably by mixing it with the original diet at first.

A certain amount of vomiting can be regarded as virtually normal in dogs. Some dogs habitually vomit back food, especially when they have 'bolted' a large meal and gulped down big chunks of food. The vomiting of bitches to feed pups has already been discussed and is also quite normal.

However, vomiting can also be associated with some generalized infectious disease, poisoning and, much more commonly, local inflammation in the alimentary tract.

Persistent vomiting, vomiting associated with other signs (such as coughing, general malaise or severe diarrhoea) or vomiting with blood, must be regarded as a serious sign and veterinary advice should be sought.

As a species, the dog is rather prone to gut problems, which may be due, in part, to its scavenging behaviour. Besides vomiting, diarrhoea is also quite common but it usually rights

or six times a day, and give plenty of milk, eggs, good meat of all types, brown bread and biscuit. She may easily be taking two-and-a-half to three times her normal quantity of food. This is not surprising, however, when you consider that, when the pups are three weeks old, their total weight can be over half that of the bitch and she is providing their sole source of food. Very often, despite tremendous food intake, the bitch still loses weight during lactation. However, once the puppies begin to be weaned, at around four weeks, she will start to put on weight again and she should be given sterilized bone flour.

Weaning pups

Most puppies can be introduced to lapping at about four weeks old, with human baby milk foods. Gradually this can be stiffened by adding

Below: These Old-English Sheepdog pups feed quite happily from the Boxer bitch.

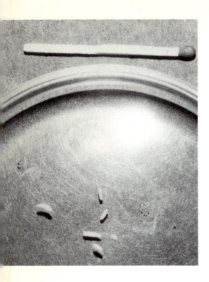

Above: Tapeworm segments look like grains of rice when they appear in the dog's faeces.

Below: It is unusual to find complete tapeworms such as these in a dog's motions.

itself with very simple treatment. Do not start dosing a vomiting or diarrhoeic dog with patent mixtures. The vast majority of gut upsets will rapidly cure themselves, if one simple practice is observed; that is, to starve the dog completely for at least twenty-four hours, or, better still, thirty-six hours! Allow free access to fresh water (not other liquids, such as milk, which is commonly not tolerated by dogs with gut problems) during this period, but no food of any description.

If the diarrhoea and vomiting have stopped in twenty-four hours (and they usually do) then food can *gradually* be introduced. Offer tiny quantities of soaked biscuit, egg or breakfast cereal at first. Over the next two or three days, food can be increased and return made to the normal diet, by feeding easily digested foods, such as chicken, fish, toast, and minced meat. Avoid all offal.

The astute and caring dog owner will soon pinpoint foods which his dog may not be able to tolerate. Obviously, these vary greatly but those which are known to cause gut upsets are liver, marrow bones, some brands of tinned meat for certain dogs and, perhaps surprisingly, cow's milk. Avoid giving these foods to your dog.

Whereas transient diarrhoea is no cause for alarm, obviously persistent loose motions, and very watery diarrhoea, or diarrhoea with blood, are all more serious, so consult your vet.

Sometimes particularly virulent forms of gastroenteritis (inflammation of the stomach and intestines) can sweep through a kennels. Specific bacteria have been isolated as causing the problem in some instances, but often the cause is obscure and the disease disappears almost as rapidly as it occurs.

Constipation is a much rarer problem than diarrhoea. It can be brought about by bones, which cause impactions in the dog's rectum, making the dog strain with little or no result. In male dogs, the prostate gland may enlarge and this causes straining. If your dog is badly constipated, seek veterinary advice.

Internal parasites

Most people have a real dread of parasites and will usually go to tremendous lengths to rid their animals of worms. However, their danger is often over-exaggerated. After all, most of us will have had human round-worm infestation as children, whilst knowing nothing about it.

At present, dog worms are an emotive subject in the socio-medical world. The anti-dog lobby use it as a major weapon of attack against the canine population (see page 186).

There are two main types of worms that may be found in dogs – roundworms and tapeworms. Roundworms are so-called because, in cross-section, the body is round. They are relatively small – the maximum length when uncoiled being about 15 cms (6 ins) – and white or grey/brown in colour. They are rarely seen in adult dogs, but may be passed in the motions of puppies. When they do occur in adult dogs, they do little harm, but they can make puppies rather thin, 'pot-bellied' and cause vomiting or coughing.

All pups are born with worms. During pregnancy the immature forms of worms leave the tissues of the bitch, enter the uterus and cross the placenta into the unborn puppies. These young worms grow in the pup and are adult themselves by the time the pups are about six weeks old. Once the worms are adult, they lay eggs which are passed out in the puppy's motions. These sticky eggs are of microscopic size and, if eaten by other puppies, develop into adult worms after migrating through the body. In adult bitches, they stay in a state of 'suspended animation' in different parts of the body, ready to infect developing pups in the uterus.

Worms in puppies can be controlled by routine dosing with a reliable wormer. The best advice on control, and the best wormer to give, can be obtained from veterinary surgeons. Modern worming compounds are both safe and effective and a good scheme is to worm pups at two, three and four weeks old and then again at three and

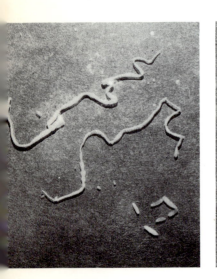

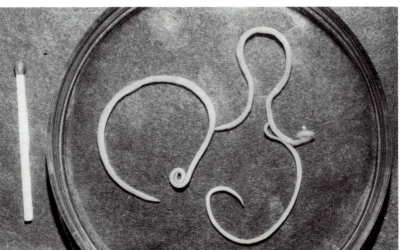

Left: This match gives some idea of the size of these toxocara dog roundworms.

Right: This mass of toxacara dog roundworms was vomited up by a young puppy.

six months. Whelping bitches should also be wormed.

Worms have some slight danger to humans in that, very occasionally, an egg eaten accidentally develops into a juvenile worm which migrates to nervous tissues, like the brain and the eyes. This is a slight but possible risk. General good hygiene, cleaning up and destroying dog (especially puppy) motions, keeping dog feeding dishes separate from those needed by the family, discouraging children from 'petting' puppies – all these precautions minimize the risks.

Tapeworms are flat in cross-section, segmented, and white or cream in colour. They also live in the intestine and rarely cause any problem in dogs, although occasionally they can cause intermittent diarrhoea and make dogs rather thin. The complete worm avoids being passed out in the motion by attaching itself to the gut wall by the suckers on its head. The usual sign of tapeworms is of segments passed in the motion. These look rather like rice grains.

The problem for man is that he can act as the intermediate host for some types of tapeworms. This is a rare risk most prevalent in young children whose habits obviously are not as particular as those of their parents.

Tapeworms in dogs are controlled by using worming compounds and prevented by boiling or otherwise cooking raw meat, especially sheep or rabbit offal. Flea and lice control is also important.

In many parts of the world there are other parasites, such as hookworms and flukes, which can cause problems. The occurrence of these parasites will be known by local veterinarians.

Other diseases and problems

The anal glands and sacs are modified grease glands which lie one on either side of the anus. Their possible function and significance has already been described in Chapter Three. The

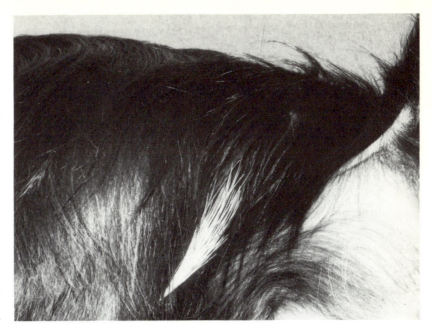

Above: Grass seeds can work their way through a dog's coat and into its skin.

solid cellular part of them produces a thick, pale cream-coloured secretion which accumulates in sacs. These open out at tiny orifices in the skin near the anus. In most dogs these structures empty themselves as the dog defecates and they cause no problem throughout the whole if its life. However, they can become inflamed, infected or blocked, at which time they will cause great pain. Dogs with anal gland problems can exhibit many tell-tale signs. Turning around sharply, biting at the tail base, suddenly sitting down, scooting along the ground on the back side, constipation and hind leg lameness are just some of these. Anal gland problems cause a dog considerable discomfort, so do not delay in seeking veterinary advice.

Unlike humans, dogs do not drink socially! In fact they drink a surprisingly small volume of water. For instance, a fully-grown Spaniel may drink less than 0.3 litre ($\frac{1}{2}$ pint) a day. Obviously this increases in hot weather, particularly when dogs are exercised. Individual dogs do vary in their water consumption and no hard and fast rules can be made. However, sudden increases in

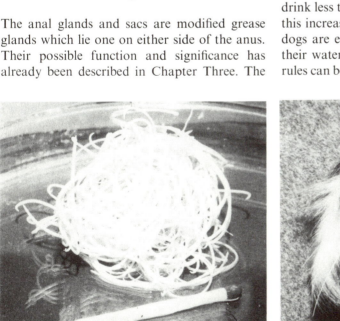

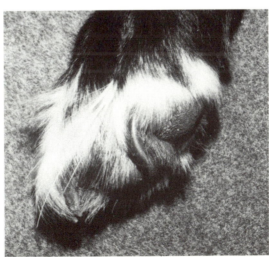

Left: Between the toes is a danger spot for grass seeds to enter into a dog's skin.

177

thirst can be a warning sign of illnesses such as *diabetes mellitus* ('sugar diabetes'), *diabetes insipidus* – which is much rarer – kidney or bladder diseases and, in bitches, pyometra. Always consult your veterinary surgeon immediately you notice an increase in thirst, but never withhold water from your dog at such a time.

All dogs, and especially older male dogs, are prone to kidney diseases. There is one very important, infectious kidney disease of which dog owners should be aware. This is called Leptospirosis, and it is caused by the bacterium *Leptospira canicola*. This disease can be protected against, and is included in the '4-in-1' vaccination. Regular boosting is necessary (see Vaccination).

Dogs are remarkable amongst other animals in having voluntary control of urination – a feature which obviously makes them socially acceptable. Bitches are generally able to 'last out longer' than dogs.

Increased frequency of urination may be a sign of bladder inflammation or bladder stones, both of which need veterinary attention.

The heart, circulatory system and lungs

The heart is proportionally a large organ in dogs, and comprises about one per cent of the total body weight. Athletic dogs, like Greyhounds and working Retrievers, have enormous hearts and lungs to pump and oxygenate the blood.

The heart beat of a dog can be felt directly by placing a hand around the bottom of the front area of the chest. The pulse can sometimes be felt in the femoral artery as it lies against the femur, the top bone of the hind leg. The heart rate (equal to the pulse rate) varies greatly between individual dogs. It can be as low as sixty in large, fit dogs at rest and sometimes as high as one hundred and twenty in small, excitable dogs.

Dogs are generally quite resistant to heart diseases. Although they eat high cholesterol diets, they do not suffer the social strains and stresses of humans and such diseases as *arterio sclerosis* of the coronary arteries (the vessels which supply the heart itself with blood) are virtually unknown. However, dogs can be affected by diseases of the heart valves. This condition is made much worse by obesity, especially in Toy Poodles and other small dogs.

Although dogs do not suffer from viral colds, they can get an infection appropriately called 'kennel-cough'. This is rarely a serious problem for individual owners and usually clears with veterinary attention, but it can be more of a problem in boarding kennels and other dog colonies. In older dogs a persistent cough can be caused by heart problems.

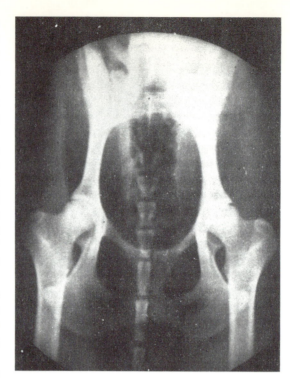

Left: An X-ray showing the hip formation of a normal, healthy dog.

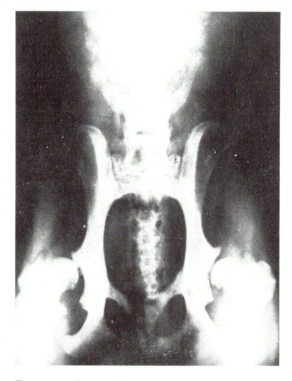

Left: Hip dysplasia causes severe changes in the hip joints.

Bones and muscles

The relatively short legs of dogs make them less prone to limb damage in exercise than horses for example, although lameness can be a problem in working Greyhounds and other racing and working dogs.

It would be impossible to deal in depth with all the causes of lameness, but there are some which are peculiar to dogs and particularly common in certain breeds. In general, lameness, or altered movement, can be caused by pain, nerve injury and/or structural deformity. Commonly encountered are sprains and muscular strains,

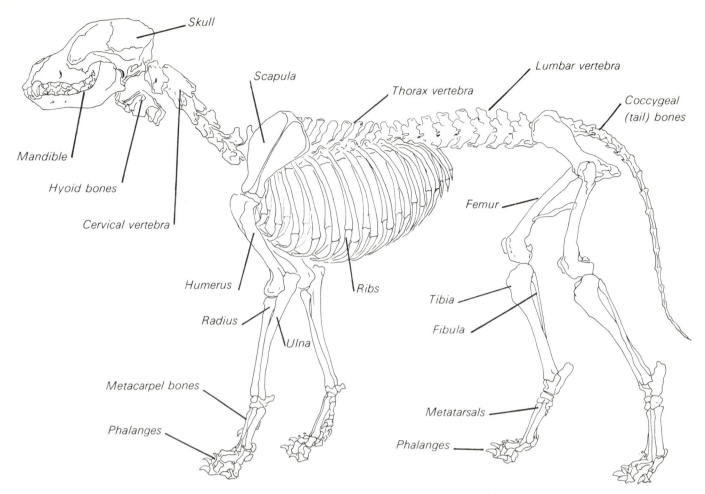

Skull

Scapula

Thorax vertebra

Lumbar vertebra

Coccygeal (tail) bones

Mandible

Hyoid bones

Cervical vertebra

Femur

Humerus

Ribs

Tibia

Radius

Fibula

Ulna

Metacarpel bones

Metatarsals

Phalanges

Phalanges

Above: The skeleton of a male dog.

gravel injury to feet or penetration and cuts in the pads and feet from sharp stones, wood or grass seeds. Lameness resulting from gross injuries such as dislocations and fractures is more serious. Never delay in seeking veterinary advice about dog lameness as early treatment can often prevent further damage.

Some lameness can be traced to spinal problems, particularly in older dogs. Between each spinal vertebra is an intervertebral disc. This is a fibrous pad or cushion which absorbs the shocks of movement and allows spinal flexibility. As dogs get older, the thicker walls of the discs can degenerate and gradually disintegrate. This process occurs earlier in certain breeds – particularly the chondrodystrophic breeds (i.e. breeds whose cartilage degenerates at an early age), such as Dachshunds, Pekinese, Sealyhams, Corgis and Boxers. Often a sharp movement can cause the walls of the disc suddenly to break, so that the centre part shoots upwards into the spinal canal. The correct term for this is disc protrusion or disc rupture; the disc *does not* slip. The pressure on the spinal cord usually causes great pain, together with hind leg lameness or even complete paralysis (in which case the dog drags its back quarters along).

With veterinary diagnoses and careful nursing, the condition will often improve in time.

Sometimes an operation can help. Prevention, however, is better than cure and there are certain precautions you can take. Firstly, take care that your dog, particularly if it is one of the chondrodystrophic breeds, keeps slim and active and is not subjected to sudden violent exercise as it gets older. If the problem occurs seek immediate veterinary advice, and, if possible, keep the dog quiet and immobile in the meantime.

Contrary to popular theory, this problem is not only pronounced in dogs with long backs. Breeders of the chondrodystrophic breeds are also making an attempt not to breed from strains which show a predisposition to bad backs.

Hind leg lameness may also be caused by hip dysplasia. In this condition, the hip joints degenerate. Any dog can have hip dysplasia at any age, although hip changes are most common in older dogs. In some breeds there is an inherited tendency to the disease, in which case the disease is known as congenital hip dysplasia.

The hip joint is a 'ball and socket' joint – the ball formed from the head of the femur and the socket being a corresponding cavity in the pelvis. The ball should fit the socket but, in dogs suffering from hip dysplasia, the femoral head may be slab-sided, pointed or facetted and there may be changes in the socket, such as lipping round the rim, shallowness or other irregularities. The end result is arthritis.

In general, it is the bigger breeds that are affected, such as Old English Sheepdogs, Alsatians, Great Danes and Retrievers, but there are notable exceptions such as Greyhounds, which remain unaffected. The degree of hip change does not always match the lameness seen – severe lameness and stiffness may be the result of only minor changes. Often the only sign shown by the affected dog is 'hind leg roll'.

Hip changes can be seen on X-ray examination and it is on the basis of this diagnosis that breeding schemes have been introduced. One such is the joint British Veterinary Association/Kennel Club Hip Dysplasia Scheme. The basis of this voluntary scheme is that dogs which are shown to be clear of the disease according to an X-ray examination are granted a certificate. Although the mode of inheritance is not fully understood, dogs showing no signs (or minimal signs) are more likely to breed 'clear' puppies. Of course, there is no way to prevent breeders from using affected dogs.

Heat control – skin and hair

The superb insulating properties of the dog's coat are mainly responsible for the animal's amazing tolerance to cold. Even in the short-coated breeds, the hair traps a layer of air between the skin and the outside and this acts as an insulator. The only areas relatively free of hair are the extremities, such as the feet, nose and genital region, and the dog will protect these in sleep by curling himself around and tucking his head under a hind leg or under his tail.

Body heat is also preserved by shutting-off blood vessels which serve the upper layers of the skin. As the flow of blood is reduced to the higher areas of the skin, less heat is lost to the cold atmosphere. Dogs can also 'fluff-up' their hair in the same way as birds ruffle their feathers and the trapped air then also increases the insulatory capacity of the coat.

Such efficiency of heat control means that the ability to lose heat is correspondingly inefficient. This can be a danger when dogs are kept in enclosed areas, such as cars, particularly of course in hot weather. Dogs lose little heat through sweating, since their only functional sweat glands are situated on the paws and on the tip of the nose. The main capacity a dog possesses to lose heat is that of panting. In such circumstances, the tongue, which hangs out of the mouth, acts as a 'radiator', in that the blood that is pumped through is cooled as the saliva vaporizes on the surface.

A dog's hair has phases of growth. Usually for two months a year, the old hairs are lost and

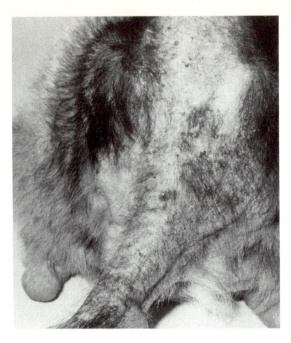

Left: Fleas can produce serious skin diseases. This unfortunate dog was allergic to these little, jumping insects.

replaced by young ones. Some dogs, especially Dalmatians and Labradors, have a continuous hair growth and moult pattern. Although dogs vary tremendously in the length, thickness and shape of their hairs, most breeds have long, thick, strong 'cover' hairs and an undercoat of finer hairs. The undercoat can become very thick in some breeds and requires stripping (see Grooming).

The sebaceous glands at the base of the hairs produce an oily secretion which protects the hair and skin from becoming sodden. It also gives the coat its shine. This greasy layer is so impervious to water, that the skin surface of some dogs can remain dry even after quite a long swim.

Contrary to general opinion, the food a dog gets has little effect on his hair and coat

Below: Because of its long hair and profuse feathering on its thighs, legs, tail and toes, the Pekinese needs careful grooming to maintain a pest-free coat.

condition, unless the level of nutrition is very poor or the fat content of the diet is very low.

Skin diseases in dogs can develop very quickly. They can be very serious if left untreated and can cause dogs much misery, so never delay in seeking veterinary attention. A few skin diseases can be transferred to other dogs, other animals and also to humans.

Many skin diseases are caused by external parasites, such as fleas, lice, ticks and so on. Of these, fleas are perhaps the commonest parasite of dogs, especially when a number of dogs and cats are kept together. Many animals have their own particular species of fleas – cats, hedgehogs, rabbits, rats, humans and birds – and all of these will also attack the dog. In fact, the flea most commonly found on dogs is the cat flea.

Fleas are tiny jumping insects which feed by sucking blood. This they obtain by piercing (in this case) the dog's skin and they are commonly found around the ears and near the base of the tail. Besides causing the dog (and you!) intense irritation, they can cause very acute skin disease and also carry tapeworm larvae.

You can reckon for every flea you find on the dog, there are a hundred more in his coat, in his kennel and in your home – so lose no time in de-fleaing him!

Fleas also lay their eggs copiously in the dog's immediate surroundings; that is, in his bed, your carpet, and so on. The cycle – hatching into a tiny maggot form, which changes to a pupa and then to the adult – may take only a few weeks, or as much as two years. Once an infestation gets established, therefore, it is a difficult and long job to clear.

Fleas can be killed on the dog by using appropriate shampoos, sprays or powders (see your veterinary surgeon for these) and by taking similar measures with his bedding and your home. If the infestation is heavy, it is best to burn the bedding and substitute newspaper, which you change daily. This control is also useful for other external parasites. Remember to treat other dogs and cats which may be in contact with the affected one.

There are two forms of dog lice – biting and sucking. The biting type move quite quickly, while the sucking type, which are often found as grey masses around the ears, are very slow. Both cause intense itching and can be controlled by shampoos, sprays and powders.

Ticks are blood-sucking parasites which attach themselves to the dog's skin. Gradually, over a few hours, they become grey and bloated, until they finally drop off. Most ticks come from cattle and sheep; dogs collect them by walking in long grass. They can be removed with tweezers (make sure you get out the head too, or else a septic area may result), by touching the tick's body with a lighted cigarette end (take care not to burn the dog), or by anaesthetizing the tick with a little cottonwool pad soaked in chloroform, ether or dry cleaning fluid. Alternatively, the dog could be treated with an insecticide shampoo.

Mange is caused by a variety of microscopic, spider-shaped mites which invade the skin. Most mange conditions are very itchy, the exception being 'demodectic mange', and should always be treated professionally, as should ringworm.

Nervous system

Much of the physiology of the brain and the rest of the nervous system of dogs has already been discussed; nervous problems themselves are not common. Distemper and rabies will be discussed under 'Infectious Diseases'. Fits sometimes occur in dogs. They may be caused by epilepsy or some other disease – for example, they can be the end result of distemper. Do not panic if your dog has a fit. You can do little to help, except keep him quiet and yourself calm. Your veterinary surgeon will be able to offer help and advice.

Eyes and ears

The eyes are well-protected in dogs by efficient eyelids and tear production. In many breeds, however, the head conformation leads to eye problems. Pekinese, for example, have pop-eyes which are prone to damage. The eyeball can even come out of the socket if the dog has an accident or is involved in a fight. Cavalier King Charles Spaniels, Papillons, Poodles and many toy breeds have an eyeball shape and tear duct conformation which can cause the eye to 'weep'

Below: Stray mongrels should be examined for fleas, ticks and other parasites before being introduced to a home.

181

constantly, thus staining the skin and hair. Some of the Collie type breeds can have a congenital abnormality that results in inefficient tear production for the eyes. This condition is known as 'dry-eye'.

One particular eye condition is worthy of special mention. This is progressive retinal atrophy – an hereditary disease in which a gradual blindness results from degeneration of the retina (the light sensitive area at the base of the eye). The condition is often seen in Toy and Miniature Poodles, Retrievers and Spaniels and is irreversible. As with hip dysplasia, there are certification schemes for freedom from the condition, so that breeders can be aware of 'affected' and 'clear' dogs.

The acuteness of a dog's hearing is remarkable and is not affected by the shape of the ear flap. Man, in fact, is greatly responsible for the varying shapes of ear flaps in dogs, for he has sometimes changed them through breeding for certain conformations.

Ear diseases can be a big problem in some dogs, particularly those with pendulous flaps, like Cocker Spaniels, or a predisposition to hairy ear canals, like Poodles. Apart from the routine grooming attention and removal of excess waxy secretion from the visible part of the canal, the owner should not interfere with a dog's ears. Any sign of discomfort or disease, such as head shaking or scratching, is a cause for early veterinary attention. Ear mites are often caught from cats, which seem to harbour them with few signs of problems.

A cause of acute ear pain to a dog is when a foreign body, such as spear grass seed, becomes lodged in the ear. These vicious seeds work down to the base of the ear and, because of their shape, resist simple removal. An anaesthetic is often needed before they can be retrieved. Avoid areas of this grass when it is at the seed stage.

The right-angle bend in the ear canal, which is so useful to the dog in preventing water and soil entering during swimming and digging, is the anatomical factor which makes removal of foreign bodies difficult.

Infectious diseases and their prevention

There are four relatively common infectious diseases of dogs, all of which are serious and can be prevented by vaccination. The most commonly known is probably *distemper* (hardpad). This virus disease has a variety of symptoms – coughing, vomiting, diarrhoea, running eyes and nose and high temperature, which lead eventually to fits, shivering, other nervous signs and sometimes thickening of the skin on the foot pads and nose. It can attack *all* dogs at *all* ages, but is most common in young dogs. It is a complete fallacy that pedigree dogs are more prone than mongrels. The only factor which makes any difference to the disease is whether the dog has any immunity. This disease, like the others mentioned below, commonly kills dogs. Little can be done to treat it and prevention is infinitely better than cure.

Infectious *hepatitis* is a killer virus disease which affects the liver and other organs. It causes vomiting and malaise, and eventually jaundice results.

The other killer disease is leptospirosis which is really two diseases caused by two similar bacteria. The first – *Leptospira canicola* – is a disease that primarily affects the kidneys and can be carried by rats. The second – *Leptospira ictohaemorrhagiae* – causes a liver disease. Both result in vomiting and malaise in the dog and

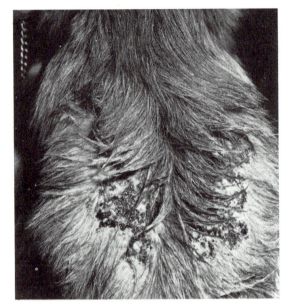

Left: Distemper causes damage to many tissues of the body, including the skin.

Below: Distemper causes a respiratory disease with a discharge from the nose. This dog also has skin problems and eye inflammation which are typical of the disease.

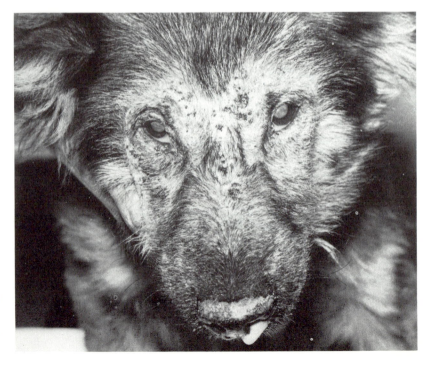

both are of public health importance, as they can affect humans.

All four diseases are caught from infected dogs, many of which carry the diseases, but show no signs of them. Highly effective, safe and relatively cheap vaccines are available, which protect against all four infectious diseases. They cannot be given at birth because the immunity transferred to the pup from the mother (both across the placenta and in the milk) would interfere with the 'take' of the vaccine. In most cases, they are given when a pup is about twelve weeks old, but this depends on a number of factors. The local veterinarian will be able to advise on the best time for the first inoculation. There is no sense in delaying or failing to get a dog vaccinated; the risk is too great.

Do not forget that dogs also need booster vaccinations as the primary vaccination does not protect for life. Again, take the veterinarian's advice on this.

Rabies

This inevitably fatal disease is caused by a virus which attacks the nervous system. It is nearly always transmitted by a bite from an infected animal. The virus then slowly travels up the nerves of the animal to the spinal cord and eventually reaches the brain. Descriptions of the signs of the disease are varied and frightening. Two forms are recognized – the 'dumb' and the 'furious'. The latter is more spectacular. Restlessness, nervousness, increasing viciousness and aimless wandering by the dog are early signs, followed shortly by snapping at anything and everybody, even at itself. The dog may even snap so violently that it breaks its own teeth. It is at this stage that there is the greatest danger for humans and other animals, as the virus will now almost certainly be present in the saliva. Bites are the usual means of infection, although it has been known for the virus to enter scratch wounds. It may even penetrate the intact skin, or the mucous membrane of the eye.

As the disease progresses, the affected dog may howl or scream and appear in pain. It may walk or run in an unco-ordinated fashion and swallow objects such as stones or bits of wood, indiscriminately. Eventually, the dog is overcome by seizures and dies, often in a series of convulsions. Unlike rabid humans, dogs seldom show hydrophobia (fear of water).

In the dumb form of the disease, the dog mainly shows signs of progressive paralysis, with its lower jaw hanging open and saliva hanging in strings. Infected dogs usually become rapidly paralyzed and die quickly.

The incubation period after infection varies greatly, but it is usually within three to six weeks, with very few cases developing after four months. It is this long and varied incubation period which necessitates a long quarantine period, either after a suspect bite or when dogs are imported into countries free of the disease.

If rabies is suspected in a dog, then human safety and speed of action are paramount. The dog should be carefully isolated in an area, such as a lockable room, or, preferably, a dog-proof cage or kennel, until veterinary attention is available. Never try heroics with suspect rabies cases; in countries where the disease is endemic, all stray dogs should be treated with the utmost caution.

There are now highly effective and safe vaccines available for dogs, other animals and humans. Their use is mandatory in many parts of the world where the disease is a problem, but they are not generally permitted in rabies-free countries, as they can interfere with diagnosis of the disease.

Countries, such as Great Britain, which are free of the disease, preserve their freedom jealously by strict quarantine. Heavy fines are imposed on those who import animals illicitly. A great problem with rabies is that it rapidly becomes endemic in the animal wildlife of a country. Foxes, wolves, racoons and vampire bats are just some of the animals that act as a constant reservoir of infection in which the disease is virtually impossible to eradicate.

The reproductive system

The study of dog reproduction and breeding is fascinating, for dogs show such a range of variations, as well as several features which are unique. Many of these variations have caused biologists to consider whether they point to a multiple ancestry of the dog. In fact, they are more likely to be an end result of man's 'unnatural selection'.

The bitch

The age at which bitches first come into heat is very variable. It may be as young as five months, or it may not be until nearly two years old.

The first sign of heat is often a slight quietening of behaviour, although often even the most discerning owner notices nothing until vaginal bleeding starts. This is a slight, watery, blood-coloured discharge from the vulva, which may sometimes be accompanied by a slight swelling of the vagina. Usually bitches are very clean and lick up any of the blood from themselves. Sometimes the bleeding is quite pronounced, especially in the larger breeds and at the first season. At this stage, the bitch is not generally attractive to male dogs, although they may show some interest in her.

Below: A rabid dog exhibiting the lack of co-ordination in its back legs and aggressive snarling which are common signs of the disease.

The bleeding continues at a steady degree for about ten to twelve days and then becomes much reduced. During this time, the bitch will become increasingly attractive to males. She then enters 'oestrus', which is the time when she allows herself to be mated and her eggs are released from her ovaries. This period of the heat lasts for about eight days and, by the end of it, bleeding has virtually stopped and the vulva has become less swollen. The vulvar bleeding of bitches is in no way analogous to menstrual bleeding in women. In bitches, it is associated with the preparation for mating and in women it is due to the degeneration of the lining of the uterus.

The whole heat period lasts for about three weeks, but it must be stressed that it is subject to tremendous variations in quite normal bitches. Some hardly bleed at all, some do so heavily for three weeks and some are attractive to dogs at the first day of the cycle and remain so throughout the cycle. All of these are 'normal' variations, associated with normal fertility and result in perfectly normal pups.

Most bitches come in heat twice a year – often in the spring and again in the autumn. However, some dogs, particularly big breeds, may have three seasons a year and others, notably the toy breeds, only one. Most bitches continue having seasons until they are quite old, but often there is reduced fertility in aged bitches.

Many owners find that this twice-yearly heat period, with its attraction to male dogs and the resulting accidental matings causes great problems. Others just do not want to breed from their bitch and feel that spaying (neutering) is vital.

The advisability or otherwise of spaying may be endlessly debated. Much will depend on the care you are prepared, and are able, to take in avoiding the attraction of males and possible accidental mating. Factors to consider are whether you have young children who leave gates open, the type of area in which you live and the density of stray males in the district. Spaying is advocated by many International Canine Bodies as the most desirable method of dog population control and in some countries and states there are subsidized spaying schemes.

If you are thinking of having your bitch spayed, discuss it first with your local breeders and veterinary surgeon. Remember that, once taken, it is an irrevocable step – there is no use in wishing to breed from your bitch at some time in the future. Spayed bitches cannot be shown at dog shows. In any event, bitches should always have one natural season before being spayed. This is an immutable law.

In spaying, both ovaries and the whole of the uterus are surgically removed. It is a major operation, necessitating a general anaesthetic. Once spayed, a bitch will not come into season, will not be attractive to male dogs, has no eggs to be fertilized and no uterus. One quite severe disadvantage of surgical spaying is that bitches often put on weight, partly because they are often quieter and less energetic. Great care must be taken to avoid obesity in spayed bitches, by careful food control and regular exercise.

There are alternatives to surgery; for example, several drugs are now available for delaying, or completely suppressing, a season. The advantage is that the bitch can be used for breeding at a later date. However, the problems of bitches in heat may be decreased in several ways. Old sheets make useful protection for furniture against staining, if your bitch is an 'arm-chair dog'. Exercising a bitch in the confines of a back garden or, better still, taking her some distance away in the car before walking, can help to prevent the attention of male dogs perpetually at your front gate. There are several anti-dog deodorants, which can be sprayed around the bitch's rear before exercising. These mask the scent and repulse dogs.

There are a variety of diseases which can affect the reproductive tract of the bitch. Most are quite uncommon and result in signs such as vaginal discharges, abnormal sexual behaviour, extended seasons or infertility. There are however, two more common problems which deserve special mention. The first is false pregnancy. Many bitches, often the smaller pet varieties, show signs of pregnancy even when they have never been near a male dog. This false, or pseudo, pregnancy is really a normal pattern of behaviour, but it can become very exaggerated – bitches seem quite ill, go off their food, become neurotic and often secrete milk. Much can be done to reduce this condition by keeping the bitch very occupied, but in severe cases it is wise to consult a veterinary surgeon. He will be able to give helpful advice and perhaps sedatives or other drugs to reduce the signs.

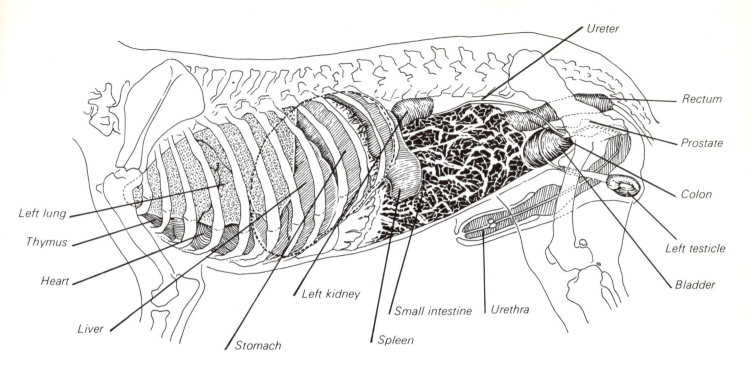

Ureter

Rectum

Prostate

Colon

Left testicle

Bladder

Left lung

Thymus

Heart

Liver

Stomach

Left kidney

Spleen

Small intestine

Urethra

Above: The internal anatomy of a male dog.

Another condition, pyometra, is more serious and is the result of an accumulation of pus-like fluid in the uterus. Symptoms are usually vomiting, extreme malaise, sudden increase in thirst and total loss of appetite. In some cases, there may be a bloody pus discharge from the vulva. The bitch generally becomes ill very quickly and urgent veterinary treatment is needed – usually an operation to remove the reproductive tract. The condition is more common in middle-aged or old bitches who have not had a litter and it often occurs about six weeks after a heat, and must be treated immediately.

The male dog
Like other mammals, male dogs do not have a reproductive cycle as such, but are only attracted to bitches on heat. The time of onset of sexual capacity and adult sexual behaviour in male dogs varies, but it usually occurs around five to seven months.

There is nothing particularly noteworthy about the reproductive organs in dogs. As with many young mammals, the testicles are not present in the scrotum at birth, but they usually descend from the abdomen within the first week of life. Male dogs with only one descended testicle are quite common and are usually fully fertile.

Reasons for castration in males are fewer than for spaying in bitches and it is not generally a routine measure. However, some over-sexed males can become quite neurotic, canine sex maniacs, in which case castration can be helpful. Some people (often men) find the idea of castration for dogs repugnant. This is quite illogical, as dogs do not have the mental capacity to recognize their loss of libido. In any event, castration does not remove all sexual drive or mating capacity. Obviously, removal of the testicles means that there are no sperms to fertilize bitches, but some castrated males will still mount bitches.

Old age and incurable disease

No reasonable comparison can be drawn between age in humans and dogs. Seven years of their life for one of ours is just not an accurate analogy; pregnancy at a year old is common!

Dogs usually die sometime between ten and twenty years old – the greater ages tend to occur in the smaller dogs.

Bigger breeds, in particular Boxers, die very young and a Pyrenean is really old at twelve.

As in humans, cancers can be either benign or malignant in dogs. Not all cancer is incurable and even some malignant ones can be treated successfully, as long as the dog is taken to the veterinary surgeon early enough. There is no sense in delay. Sometimes the most innocuous-looking lump can be highly malignant.

There are other infectious or degenerative diseases which really demand humane destruction. However, just because a dog is blind or deaf, it does not necessarily mean the end is nigh, for many such affected animals will live happily in the surroundings they know well. Usually, an owner knows when his dog is not able to cope with its situation and realizes that the time has come to have him humanely destroyed.

185

The Dog Today and Tomorrow

The dog undoubtedly has a well-established position in the world today, and yet there are factors which pose something of a threat to this position. A small, but very vocal and influential, 'anti-dog' lobby is making its presence felt virtually world-wide and could possibly have a profound influence on the numerical status of the dog in years to come.

At present, there is an enormous international dog population. In Britain there are about 5.6 million dogs, which means one to every ten people. In America, the ratio is one to six with a total of about 38 million dogs. In some instances, the size of the dog population appears to be directly related to the country's affluence. In other cases, this is not so; West Germany, for example, which can hardly be considered an economically depressed country, has only one dog per twenty-five people. It could be that other economic factors – perhaps the cost of a dog licence – together with social customs, exert some influence on the dog population.

It seems likely, however, that the country's wealth has an influence on the types of dog owned and the standard at which they are kept. In general, quantity and quality go together. The United States, for example, which has the biggest dog population in the Western world, also has the highest number of pedigree, pure-bred dogs.

Statistics can always be misleading and those appertaining to dogs are no exception. It is estimated that British dogs excrete 4.5 million litres (nearly one million gallons) of urine a day and 500 tonnes (490 tons) of faeces – equivalent to that produced by about four million people. The 'anti-dog' lobby will tell you, quite truthfully, that all pups are born with round-worms and that there are thousands of roundworm eggs in the faeces of a high percentage of even adult dogs. They will further tell you that there is considerable opportunity for human infestation with these eggs, which *can* (but only rarely *do*) cause blindness and brain damage in children. Try asking the 'anti-dog' lobbyist how many people he knows with toxocara-induced blindness – or even how many people in 10,000 have the disease. The answer will not be very alarming.

The statistics concerning stray dogs and, more particularly, the amounts of food eaten by dogs, do give more cause for concern. Arguments are advanced that if the food eaten by dogs were fed

Above: A bundle of fun and so appealing at this age, but he will still need love and attention as an adult.

Left: The Swiss Laufhund is the result of generations of breeding and inter-breeding. Many Swiss hounds were bred with Dachshunds to reduce height. Comparatively unknown outside its own country, it is slowly establishing itself as an affectionate pet.

to people with malnutrition, the world would be a better place. Such arguments, however, have flaws which are, perhaps, rather unpleasant to expose. An eminent environmentalist has made the valid observation that even in African villages with undernourished people, there are always a fair number of dogs. These dogs belong to the starving people, who want them and will always look after them.

The future of the dog as a pet and a worker is assured. Probably, in a thousand years from now, there will be species that we would not recognize – but they will still be man's best friend!

So, it seems that the dog is here to stay. What we have to do is to be rational about the position of the dog in our societies and do what we can to make our relationship with dogs as happy and comfortable as we can for both parties.

Running alongside the 'anti-dog' lobby is the 'pro-dog' lobby. This is just as sincere, just as outraged and just as well-informed. Both organizations have to realize that between the position of a total ban on dogs and total canine liberty, there is a sensible compromise, for which we must aim. An increase in licensing fees has been suggested as the only way to exert control, but a decrease in licences purchased does not, in itself, bring about a diminution of the dog population. Those who own badly-kept dogs are the people who do not buy dog-licences.

It seems likely that there will be some slight diminution in the pet population of socially-advanced countries in the future, if only because of government control and the ever-increasing weight of restrictive legislation. But this decline will not be steep. Increased social isolation, a growing desire for animal contact in a mechanized society and more leisure time are all factors that will do much to halt the decline. The dogs that remain, and there will be plenty, will mainly be pure-bred dogs, kept under superb conditions of hygiene and in a perfect nutritional state. The breeds will vary, for, as we have seen, no breed remains fixed forever, but the changes will come about mainly for aesthetic reasons and not for reasons of working ability or specialized behaviour. All we can hope is that the changes of temperament which are made will complement the increase in the beauty of the breeds.

The future of the dog must be bright. The dog has succeeded because he can adapt and live close to man, and he will continue to do so. The dog is no dinosaur, with a ponderous brain and body. Living close to man has meant that the dog goes wherever man goes. As long as there is man on earth, the dog will be there alongside him.

Below: Dogs, such as these Irish Wolfhounds, have befriended and served man for centuries.

Which Dog for You?

This information on the best type of dog to buy has been compiled by the publishers in collaboration with Leslie Scott-Ordish of the PRO-DOGS organization (President: Stanley Dangerfield)

It is virtually impossible to say that some breeds make better pets than others. Every dog owner knows that his dog is the best in the world!

But before you buy a dog, you must consider the sort of puppy that is most likely to suit you and your family.

A good way to select a breed you may want is to visit dog shows where you will see a wide range of adult dogs of different breeds. Having selected a breed you like, you can visit your nearest specialized breeder and see the parents of puppies for sale. This will give you an idea of the size and temperament you may expect the puppies to have when adult.

Directories of dog breeders are available at book shops, or Kennel Clubs will usually supply names if a particular breed is requested and a stamped addressed envelope is sent.

Here are a few tips for those about to make their choice. One of the best all-round family dogs is the Labrador Retriever. Temperamentally they are very sound; they are patient with children and easy to train. They are fairly large dogs and need proper exercise and a lot of food.

The really large dogs, Pyrenean Mountain Dogs, Great Danes, St. Bernards and so on, should not be kept in towns and cities. They need wide open spaces to get all the exercise they require and they cost a lot of money to feed.

German Shepherd Dogs (Alsatians) are among the most intelligent of breeds. However they require a lot of time and companionship and need to swear their allegiance to one person. If they are kept fully occupied, happy and understood they can be the finest and most rewarding companions in the world. If let down or in the wrong hands they become misfits and can cause trouble.

Gun dogs, such as Spaniels, have a gentle disposition and get on with almost anybody. They do not require as much room and exercise as their larger relatives. However, it is a good idea, if you live in a town, to take them into the country frequently for exercise.

Boxers are ideal pets for young people. They are bouncy, playful and good tempered.

Smaller terrier breeds tend to be bright, assertive, and occasionally, aggressive little dogs which demand firm handling. Settled in the home situation they are friendly, lively pets. Corgis are determined little characters, but properly controlled make good family dogs.

Some of the tiny Toy breeds – Yorkshire Terriers, Chihuahuas and others – are not the best of companions for families with boisterous children but they make good pets for people with limited house-room.

The Tibetan Spaniel is less well-known, but worth consideration especially where space is limited. They are intelligent little dogs, but aloof until they know you.

Because of space, we have only mentioned a few of the hundred or so breeds recognized by Kennel Clubs and we have not dealt with that most popular of dogs – the mongrel. The only snag about buying a mongrel puppy is that you're taking a gamble as you can have little idea how big he will grow or what sort of temperament he will have.

When choosing your breed BE SENSIBLE. If you live in a small flat it is not fair on the animal to buy a large dog. If you are living on a tight budget don't buy a dog that is going to cost a lot to feed.

If you make a wise, sensible decision, you will be rewarded with a lifelong friend and companion whose devotion to you will be second to none.

Below left: A Sealyham Terrier and two pups. They are attractive medium-sized dogs.

Below: A more expensive proposition to keep is this brindled Bull Mastiff.

Breeds recognized by the British Kennel Club

Hound Group
AFGHAN HOUNDS
BASENJIS
BASSET HOUNDS
BASSETS GRIFFON VENDEEN
BEAGLES
BLOODHOUNDS
BORZOIS
DACHSHUNDS (LONG-HAIRED)
DACHSHUNDS (MINIATURE LONG-HAIRED)
DACHSHUNDS (SMOOTH-HAIRED)
DACHSHUNDS (MINIATURE SMOOTH-HAIRED)
DACHSHUNDS (WIRE-HAIRED)
DACHSHUNDS (MINIATURE WIRE-HAIRED)
DEERHOUNDS
ELKHOUNDS
FINNISH SPITZ
GREYHOUNDS
IBIZAN HOUNDS
IRISH WOLFHOUNDS
PHARAOH HOUNDS
RHODESIAN RIDGEBACKS
SALUKIS
SLOUGHIS (ALGERIAN GREYHOUNDS)
SWISS LAUFHUNDS (JURA)
WHIPPETS

Gundog Group
BRITTANY SPANIELS
ENGLISH SETTERS
GERMAN SHORTHAIRED POINTERS
GERMAN WIREHAIRED POINTERS
GORDON SETTERS
HUNGARIAN VIZSLAS
IRISH SETTERS
LARGE MUNSTERLANDERS
POINTERS
RETRIEVERS (CHESAPEAKE BAY)
RETRIEVERS (CURLY-COATED)
RETRIEVERS (FLAT-COATED)
RETRIEVERS (GOLDEN)
RETRIEVERS (LABRADOR)
SPANIELS (AMERICAN COCKER)
SPANIELS (CLUMBER)
SPANIELS (COCKER)
SPANIELS (ENGLISH SPRINGER)
SPANIELS (FIELD)
SPANIELS (IRISH WATER)
SPANIELS (SUSSEX)
SPANIELS (WELSH SPRINGER)
WEIMARANERS

Terrier Group
AIREDALE TERRIERS
AUSTRALIAN TERRIERS
BEDLINGTON TERRIERS
BORDER TERRIERS
BULL TERRIERS
BULL TERRIERS (MINIATURE)
CAIRN TERRIERS
DANDIE DINMONT TERRIERS
FOX TERRIERS (SMOOTH)
FOX TERRIERS (WIRE)
GLEN OF IMAAL TERRIERS
IRISH TERRIERS
KERRY BLUE TERRIERS
LAKELAND TERRIERS
MANCHESTER TERRIERS
NORFOLK TERRIERS
NORWICH TERRIERS
SCOTTISH TERRIERS
SEALYHAM TERRIERS
SKYE TERRIERS
SOFT-COATED WHEATEN TERRIERS
STAFFORDSHIRE BULL TERRIERS
WELSH TERRIERS
WEST HIGHLAND WHITE TERRIERS

Utility Group
BOSTON TERRIERS
BULLDOGS
CHOW CHOWS
DALMATIANS
FRENCH BULLDOGS
GIANT SCHNAUZERS
KEESHONDS
LHASA APSOS
MINIATURE SCHNAUZERS
POODLES (MINIATURE)
POODLES (STANDARD)
POODLES (TOY)
SCHIPPERKES
SCHNAUZERS
SHIH TZUS
TIBETAN SPANIELS
TIBETAN TERRIERS

Working Group
ALASKAN MALAMUTES
ALSATIANS (GERMAN SHEPHERD DOGS)
ANATOLIAN DOGS
BEARDED COLLIES
BELGIAN SHEPHERD DOGS (GROENENDAEL)
BELGIAN SHEPHERD DOGS (MALINOIS)
BELGIAN SHEPHERD DOGS (TERVUEREN)
BERNESE MOUNTAIN DOGS
BOUVIER DES FLANDRES
BOXERS
BRIARDS
BULLMASTIFFS
COLLIES (ROUGH)
COLLIES (SMOOTH)
DOBERMANNS
ESKIMO DOGS (previously, HUSKIES)
ESTRELA MOUNTAIN DOGS
GREAT DANES
HUNGARIAN KUVASZ
HUNGARIAN PULIS
KOMONDORS
MAREMMA ITALIAN SHEEPDOGS
MASTIFFS
NEWFOUNDLANDS
NORWEGIAN BUHUNDS
OLD ENGLISH SHEEPDOGS
PYRENEAN MOUNTAIN DOGS
ROTTWEILERS
ST. BERNARDS
SAMOYEDS
SHETLAND SHEEPDOGS
SIBERIAN HUSKIES
SWEDISH VALLHUNDS
WELSH CORGIS (CARDIGAN)
WELSH CORGIS (PEMBROKE)

Toy Group
AFFENPINSCHERS
BICHONS FRISES
CAVALIER KING CHARLES SPANIELS
CHIHUAHUAS (LONG-COAT)
CHIHUAHUAS (SMOOTH-COAT)
CHINESE CRESTED
ENGLISH TOY TERRIERS (BLACK AND TAN)
GRIFFONS BRUXELLOIS
ITALIAN GREYHOUNDS
JAPANESE CHINS
KING CHARLES SPANIELS
LOWCHENS
MALTESE
MINIATURE PINSCHERS
PAPILLONS
PEKINGESE
POMERANIANS
PUGS
YORKSHIRE TERRIERS

Index

Figures in italics indicate illustrations

Photographic Acknowledgements

British Antarctic Survey (D. W. Matthews) 130, 131, 132, 133, 134, 135, 137. By courtesy of the Trustees of the British Museum 15. Camera Press 27, 41, 57, 129, 133, 187. Colour Library International 67, 114, 115, 119, 122, 126, 139, 154. Mary Evans Picture Library 21, 22, 23, 25. Sally Foy 93. Fitzwilliam Museum, Cambridge 16, 20, 23, 72. Michael Geary 50, 52, 54, 56, 57, 62, 63, 69, 70, 71, 74, 88, 89, 90, 91, 92, 93, 94, 95, 96, 97, 98, 99, 106, 107, 139, 142, 143, 150, 151, 162, 163, 164, 165, 166, 169, 170, 171, 173, 174, 175, 176, 177, 178, 182, 183, 184. Guide Dogs for the Blind Association 120, 121, 122, 123. Sonia Halliday 11. Michael Holford 6, 7, 15. Irish Tourist Board 137. Keystone 108, 124, 125, 128, 133. The Mansell Collection 9, 12, 13, 19. The National Gallery 14. Radio Times, Hulton 8, 17, 18, 19, 20, 22, 24. R.S.P.C.A. 166, 170, 172, 182. Servier Laboratories 183. Spectrum 4, 5, 29, 40, 50, 52, 56, 62, 71, 80, 91, 96, 111, 126, 129, 130, 139, 152, 171, 174, 184, 186, 188. The Tate Gallery 15. Sally Anne Thompson 17, 19, 23, 29, 32, 35, 50, 55, 56, 57, 58, 62, 63, 68, 75, 103, 115. Anne Roslin-Williams 20, 21, 24, 26, 27, 30, 31, 33, 34, 37, 38, 39, 40, 41, 42, 43, 44, 45, 46, 47, 48, 49, 50, 51, 53, 58, 59, 60, 61, 64, 65, 66, 67, 69, 71, 73, 74, 75, 76, 80, 81, 82, 83, 84, 85, 86, 87, 100, 101, 102, 103, 104, 105, 107, 109, 111, 112, 113, 115, 117, 118, 119, 122, 123, 127, 128, 129, 131, 138, 140, 141, 145, 146, 147, 148, 149, 152, 153, 155, 156, 158, 159, 160, 161. ZEFA 10, 11.
The diagrams on pages 8, 17, 18, 19, 20, 22, 24 were drawn by Fiona Almelah.